W9-AHR-237

the seeds™

BERGER
BOOKS
AN IMPRINT OF
DARK HORSE COMICS

Editor.................................. KAREN BERGER

Art Director................ RICHARD BRUNING

Assistant Editor......... RACHEL BOYADJIS

Digital Art Technician.... ADAM PRUETT

Logo/Letters/Book Design...... DAVID AJA

President & Publisher. MIKE RICHARDSON

the seeds™

by

ANN NOCENTI

and

DAVID AJA

a graphic tale in FOUR acts

[1. Before We Go.]

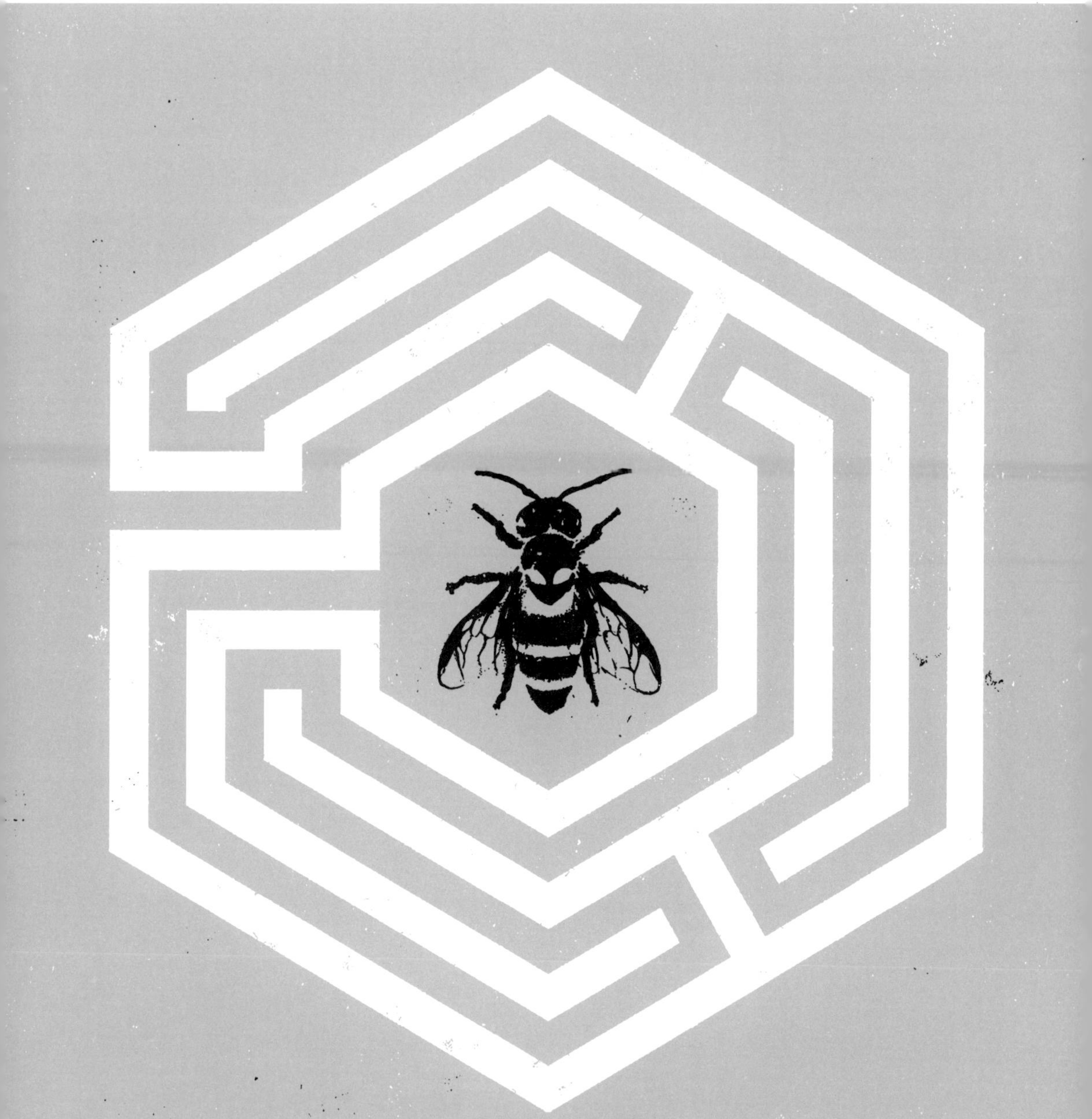

Fig.1

"They tried to bury
us. They didn't know
we were seeds."

- Mexican proverb

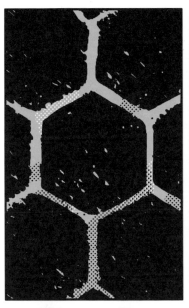

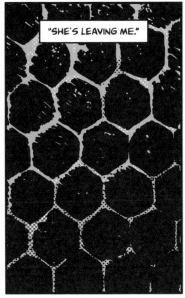

"SHE'S LEAVING ME."

"GET ANOTHER ONE."

"SHE WAS A GOOD GIRL. HARD WORKER."

"YOU NEED A WILD ONE."

"I CAN'T CONTROL THE WILD ONES, SUSAN--

WHY DID SHE LEAVE ME?"

"YOU WANTED TOO MUCH FROM HER, JACK."

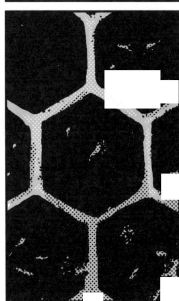

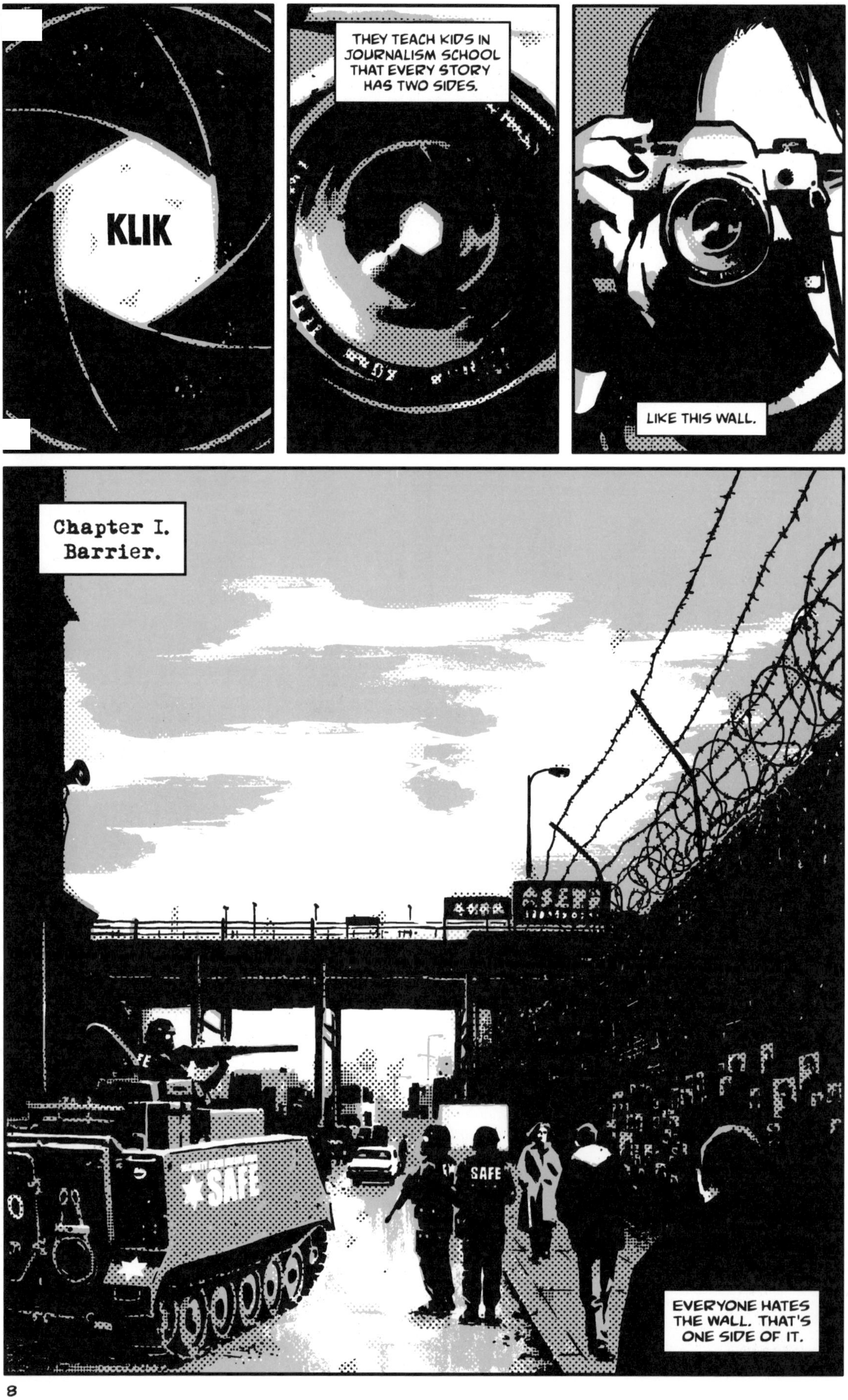
KLIK
THEY TEACH KIDS IN JOURNALISM SCHOOL THAT EVERY STORY HAS TWO SIDES.
LIKE THIS WALL.
Chapter I.
Barrier.
SAFE
SAFE
EVERYONE HATES THE WALL. THAT'S ONE SIDE OF IT.

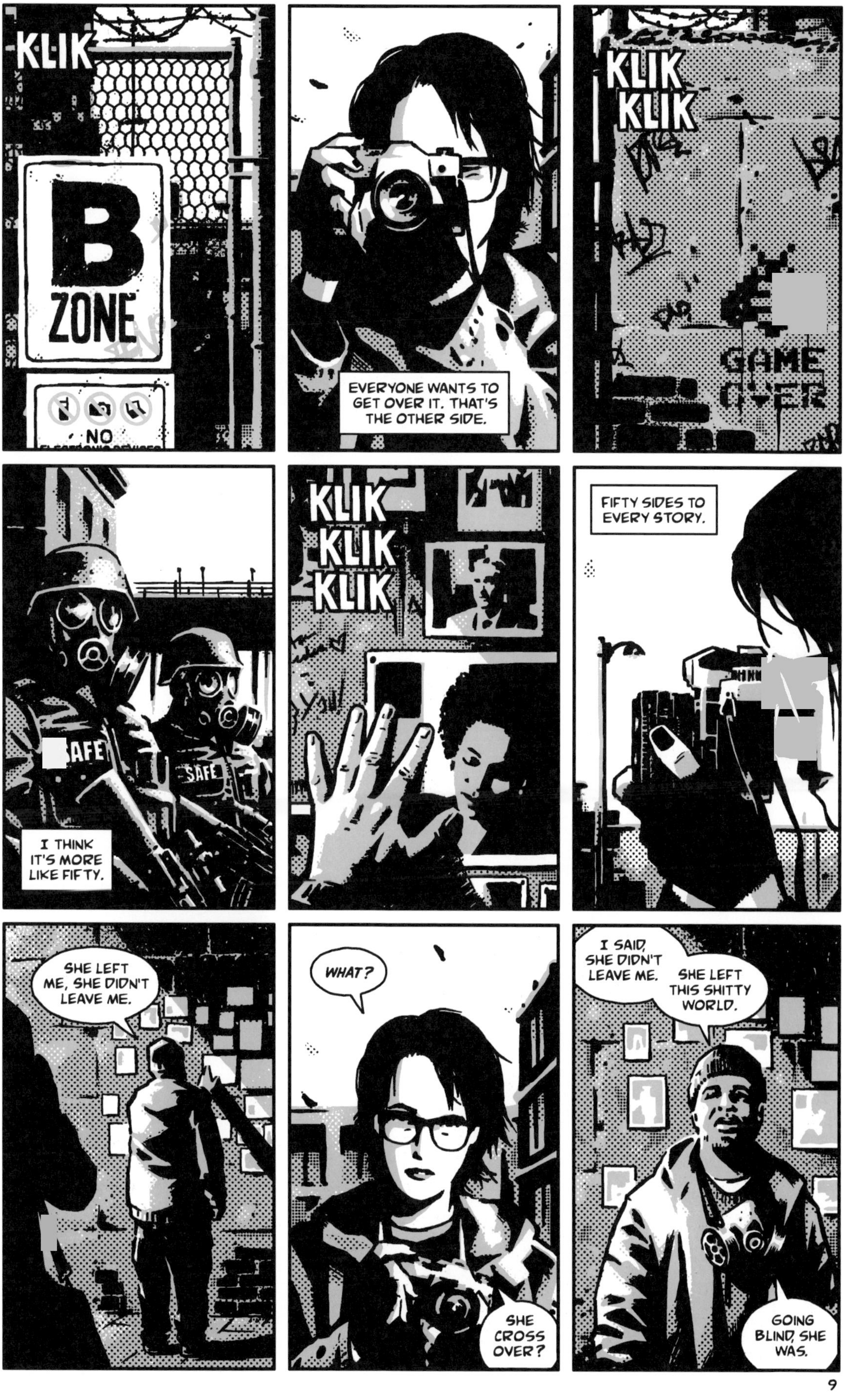
KLIK
B
ZONE
NO
EVERYONE WANTS TO GET OVER IT. THAT'S THE OTHER SIDE.
KLIK
KLIK
GAME OVER
SAFE
I THINK IT'S MORE LIKE FIFTY.
KLIK
KLIK
KLIK
FIFTY SIDES TO EVERY STORY.
SHE LEFT ME, SHE DIDN'T LEAVE ME.
WHAT?
SHE CROSS OVER?
I SAID, SHE DIDN'T LEAVE ME.
SHE LEFT THIS SHITTY WORLD.
GOING BLIND, SHE WAS.

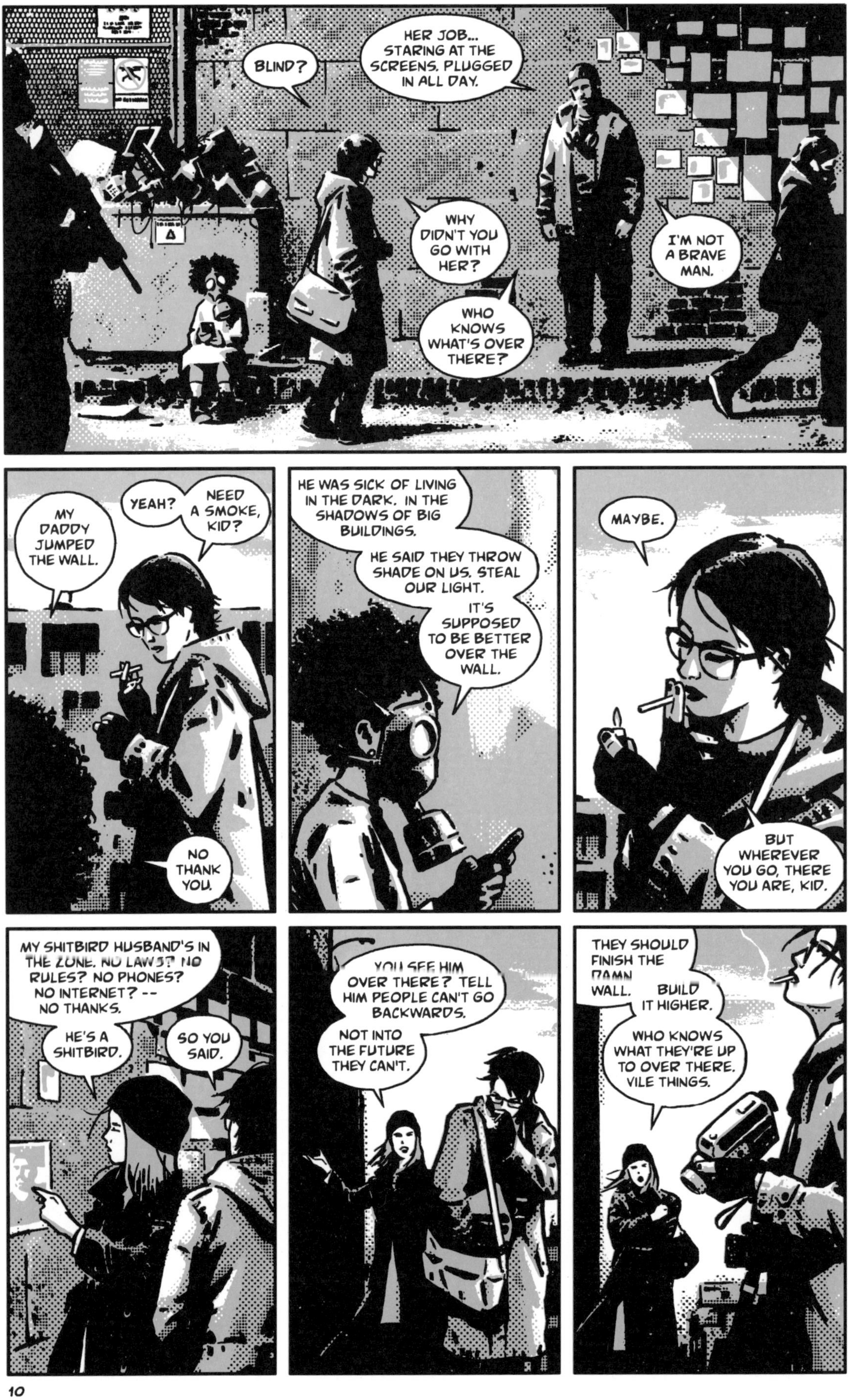
BLIND?
HER JOB... STARING AT THE SCREENS. PLUGGED IN ALL DAY.
WHY DIDN'T YOU GO WITH HER?
WHO KNOWS WHAT'S OVER THERE?
I'M NOT A BRAVE MAN.
MY DADDY JUMPED THE WALL.
YEAH?
NEED A SMOKE, KID?
NO THANK YOU.
HE WAS SICK OF LIVING IN THE DARK. IN THE SHADOWS OF BIG BUILDINGS.
HE SAID THEY THROW SHADE ON US. STEAL OUR LIGHT.
IT'S SUPPOSED TO BE BETTER OVER THE WALL.
MAYBE.
BUT WHEREVER YOU GO, THERE YOU ARE, KID.
MY SHITBIRD HUSBAND'S IN THE ZONE. NO LAWS? NO RULES? NO PHONES? NO INTERNET? -- NO THANKS.
HE'S A SHITBIRD.
SO YOU SAID.
YOU SEE HIM OVER THERE? TELL HIM PEOPLE CAN'T GO BACKWARDS.
NOT INTO THE FUTURE THEY CAN'T.
THEY SHOULD FINISH THE DAMN WALL.
BUILD IT HIGHER.
WHO KNOWS WHAT THEY'RE UP TO OVER THERE. VILE THINGS.

air quality alert. acid snow. zone b toxic. weaponized fallout. stay indoors. stay ssafe.

Alert!

Stay safe?

USER: ASTRA. ACTION: SEND FILES DK238 TO DK253 - UPLOAD TO GABRIELLE.

> Processing......
> In Cloud.
> Sending files...

ACTION: SEND TO SCOOP DROPBOX.

BOOK CAB. BARRIER ZONE B TO ZONE A.

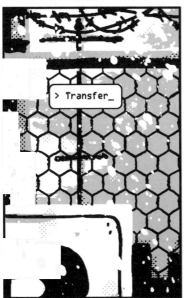

> Transfer_

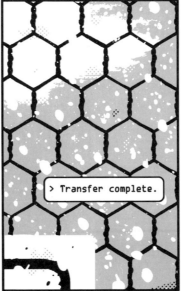

> Transfer complete.

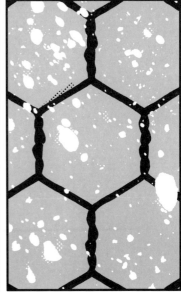

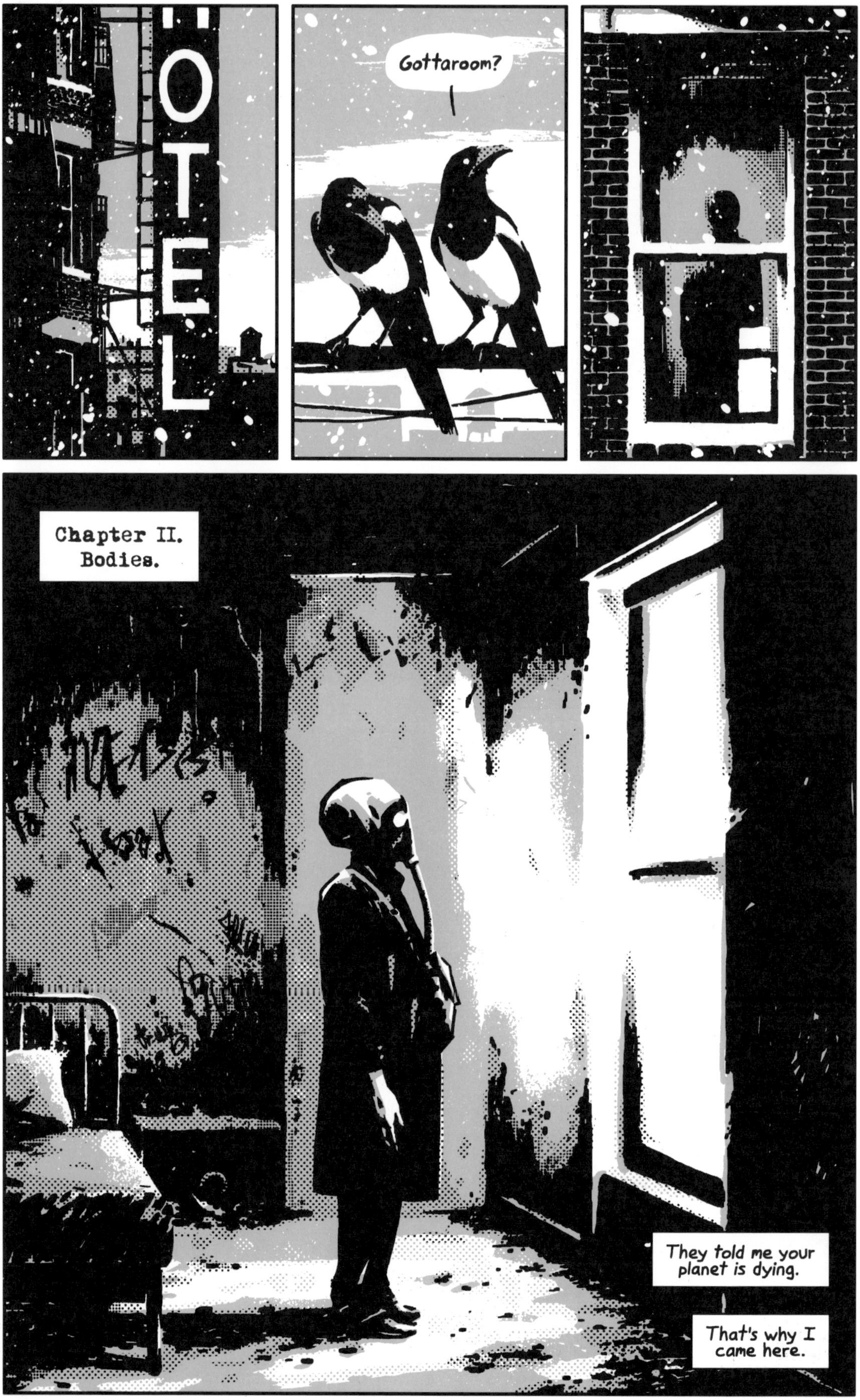
HOTEL
Gottaroom?
Chapter II.
Bodies.
They told me your planet is dying.
That's why I came here.

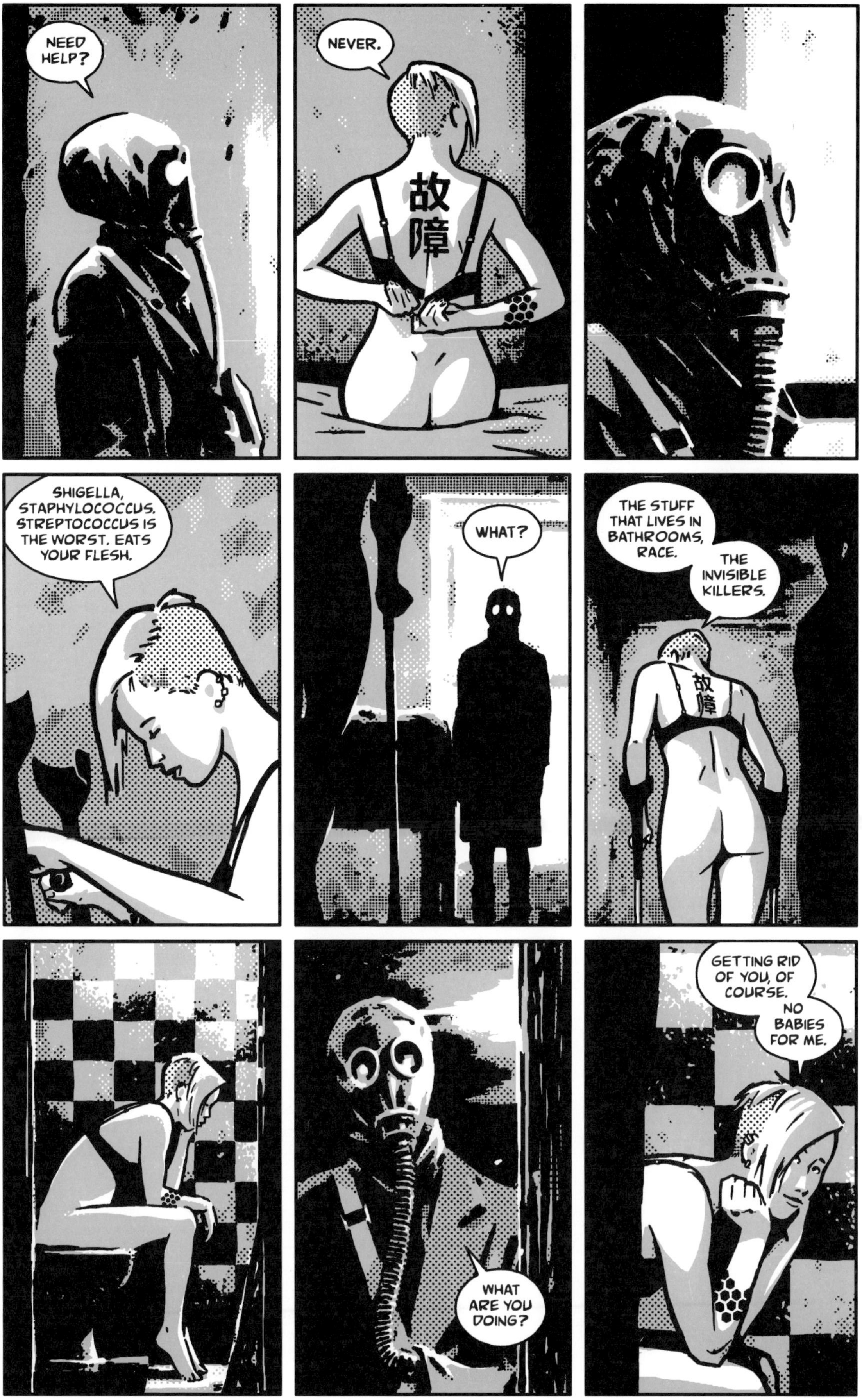
NEED HELP?
NEVER.
故障
SHIGELLA, STAPHYLOCOCCUS. STREPTOCOCCUS IS THE WORST. EATS YOUR FLESH.
WHAT?
THE STUFF THAT LIVES IN BATHROOMS, RACE.
THE INVISIBLE KILLERS.
故障
WHAT ARE YOU DOING?
GETTING RID OF YOU, OF COURSE.
NO BABIES FOR ME.

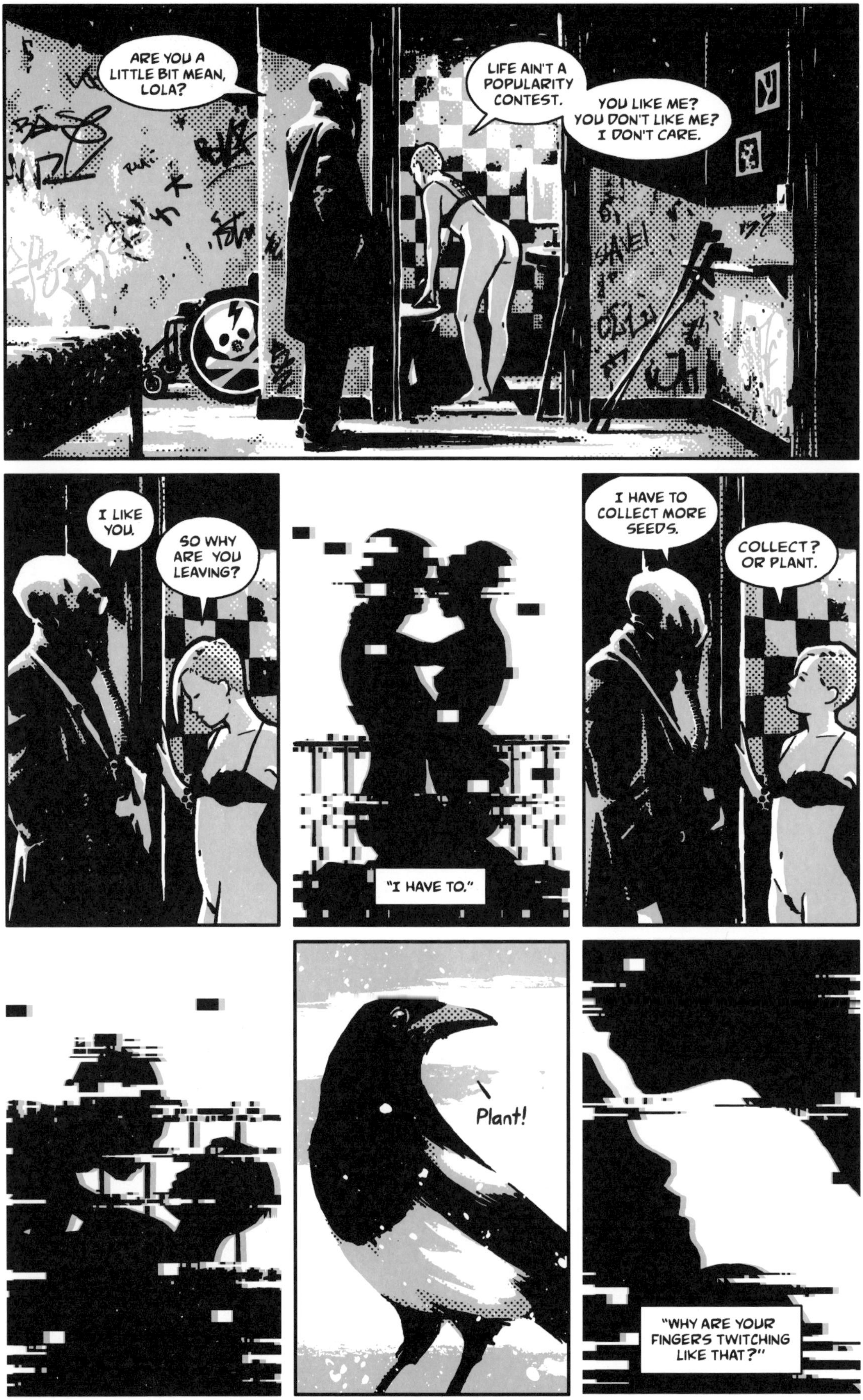
ARE YOU A LITTLE BIT MEAN, LOLA?
LIFE AIN'T A POPULARITY CONTEST.
YOU LIKE ME? YOU DON'T LIKE ME? I DON'T CARE.
I LIKE YOU.
SO WHY ARE YOU LEAVING?
"I HAVE TO."
I HAVE TO COLLECT MORE SEEDS.
COLLECT? OR PLANT.
Plant!
"WHY ARE YOUR FINGERS TWITCHING LIKE THAT?"

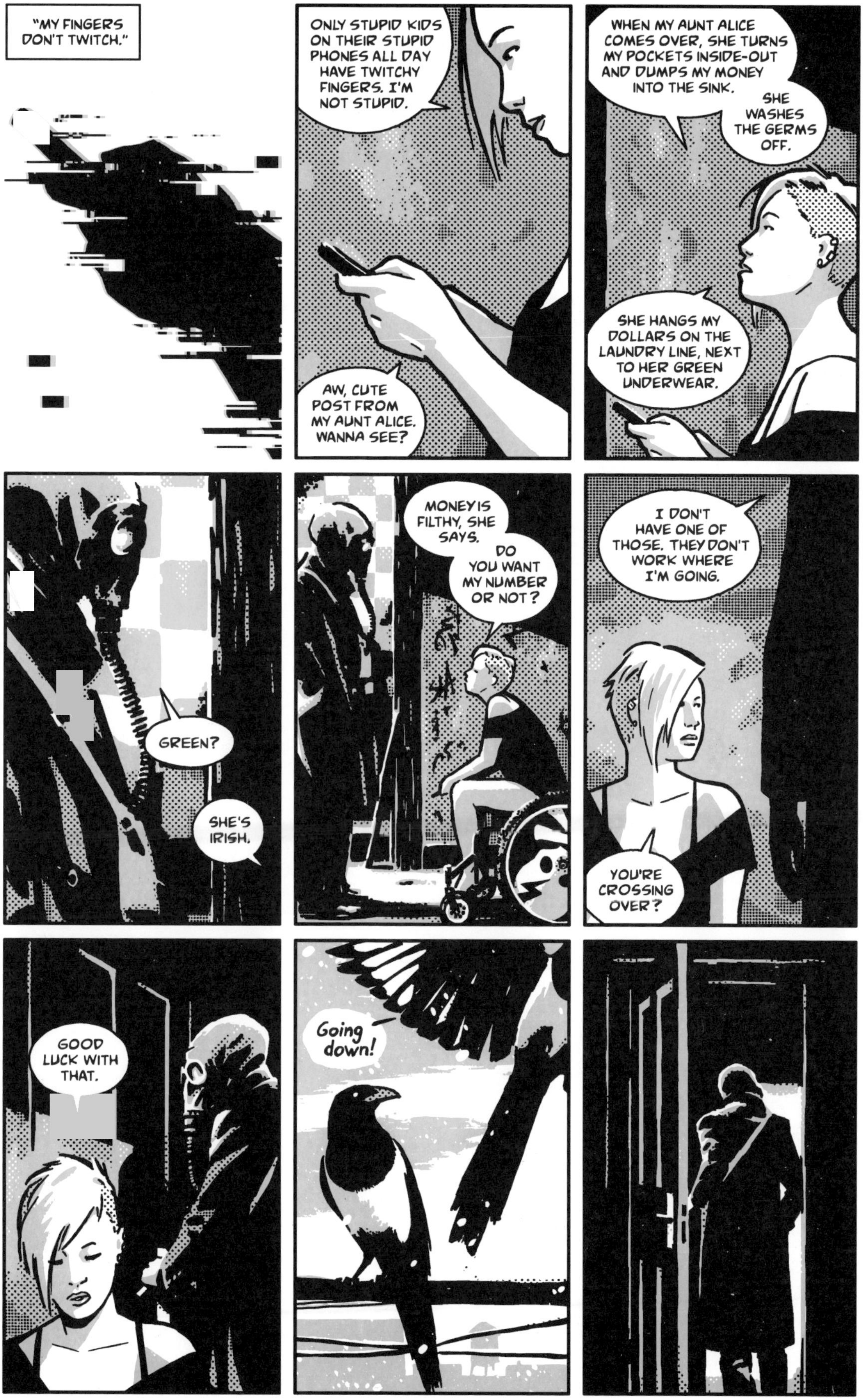
"MY FINGERS DON'T TWITCH."
ONLY STUPID KIDS ON THEIR STUPID PHONES ALL DAY HAVE TWITCHY FINGERS. I'M NOT STUPID.
AW, CUTE POST FROM MY AUNT ALICE. WANNA SEE?
WHEN MY AUNT ALICE COMES OVER, SHE TURNS MY POCKETS INSIDE-OUT AND DUMPS MY MONEY INTO THE SINK.
SHE WASHES THE GERMS OFF.
SHE HANGS MY DOLLARS ON THE LAUNDRY LINE, NEXT TO HER GREEN UNDERWEAR.
GREEN?
SHE'S IRISH.
MONEY IS FILTHY, SHE SAYS.
DO YOU WANT MY NUMBER OR NOT?
I DON'T HAVE ONE OF THOSE. THEY DON'T WORK WHERE I'M GOING.
YOU'RE CROSSING OVER?
GOOD LUCK WITH THAT.
Going down!

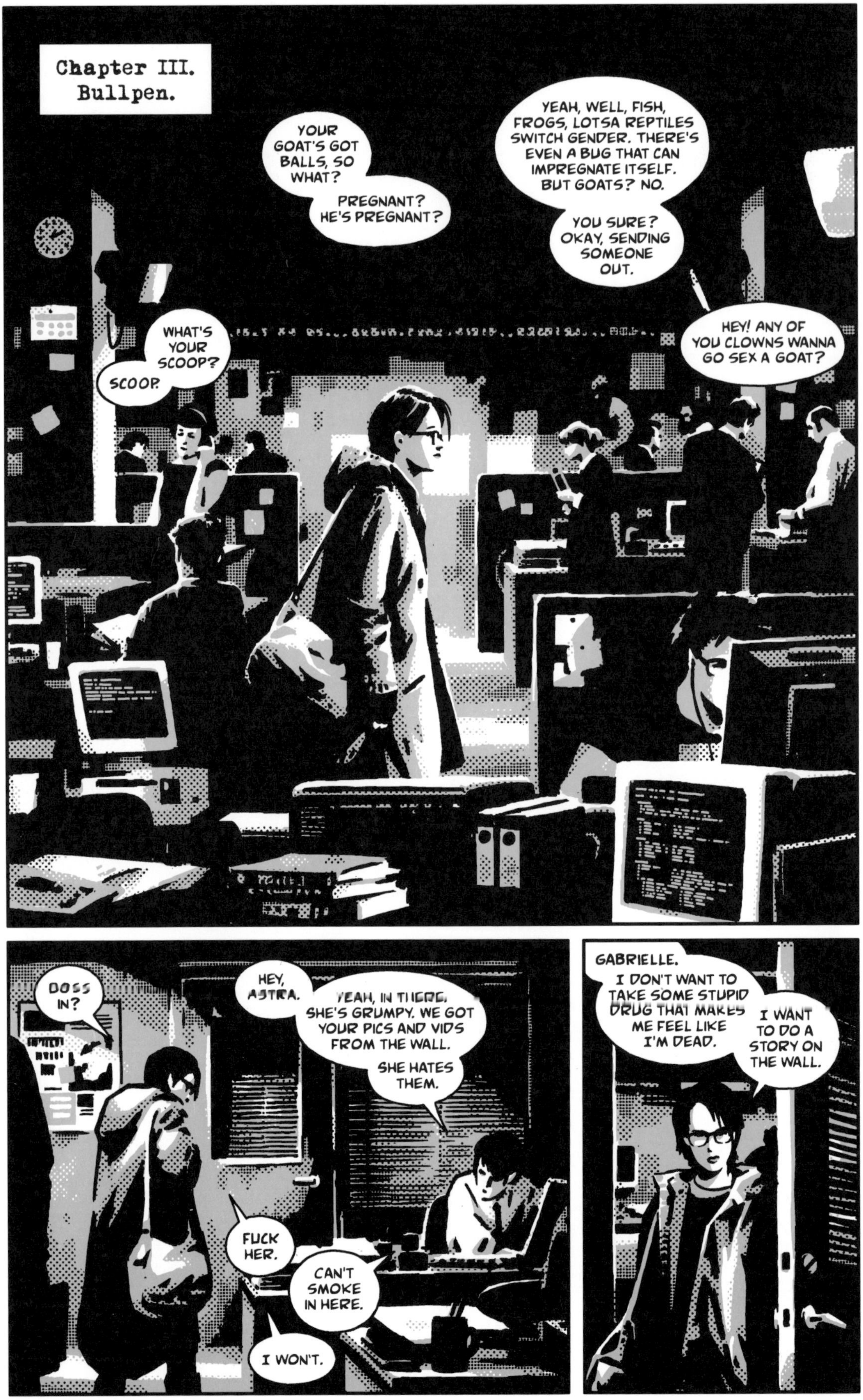
Chapter III.
Bullpen.
YOUR GOAT'S GOT BALLS, SO WHAT?
PREGNANT? HE'S PREGNANT?
YEAH, WELL, FISH, FROGS, LOTSA REPTILES SWITCH GENDER. THERE'S EVEN A BUG THAT CAN IMPREGNATE ITSELF. BUT GOATS? NO.
YOU SURE? OKAY, SENDING SOMEONE OUT.
WHAT'S YOUR SCOOP?
SCOOP.
HEY! ANY OF YOU CLOWNS WANNA GO SEX A GOAT?
BOSS IN?
HEY, ASTRA.
YEAH, IN THERE. SHE'S GRUMPY. WE GOT YOUR PICS AND VIDS FROM THE WALL.
SHE HATES THEM.
FUCK HER.
CAN'T SMOKE IN HERE.
I WON'T.
GABRIELLE.
I DON'T WANT TO TAKE SOME STUPID DRUG THAT MAKES ME FEEL LIKE I'M DEAD.
I WANT TO DO A STORY ON THE WALL.

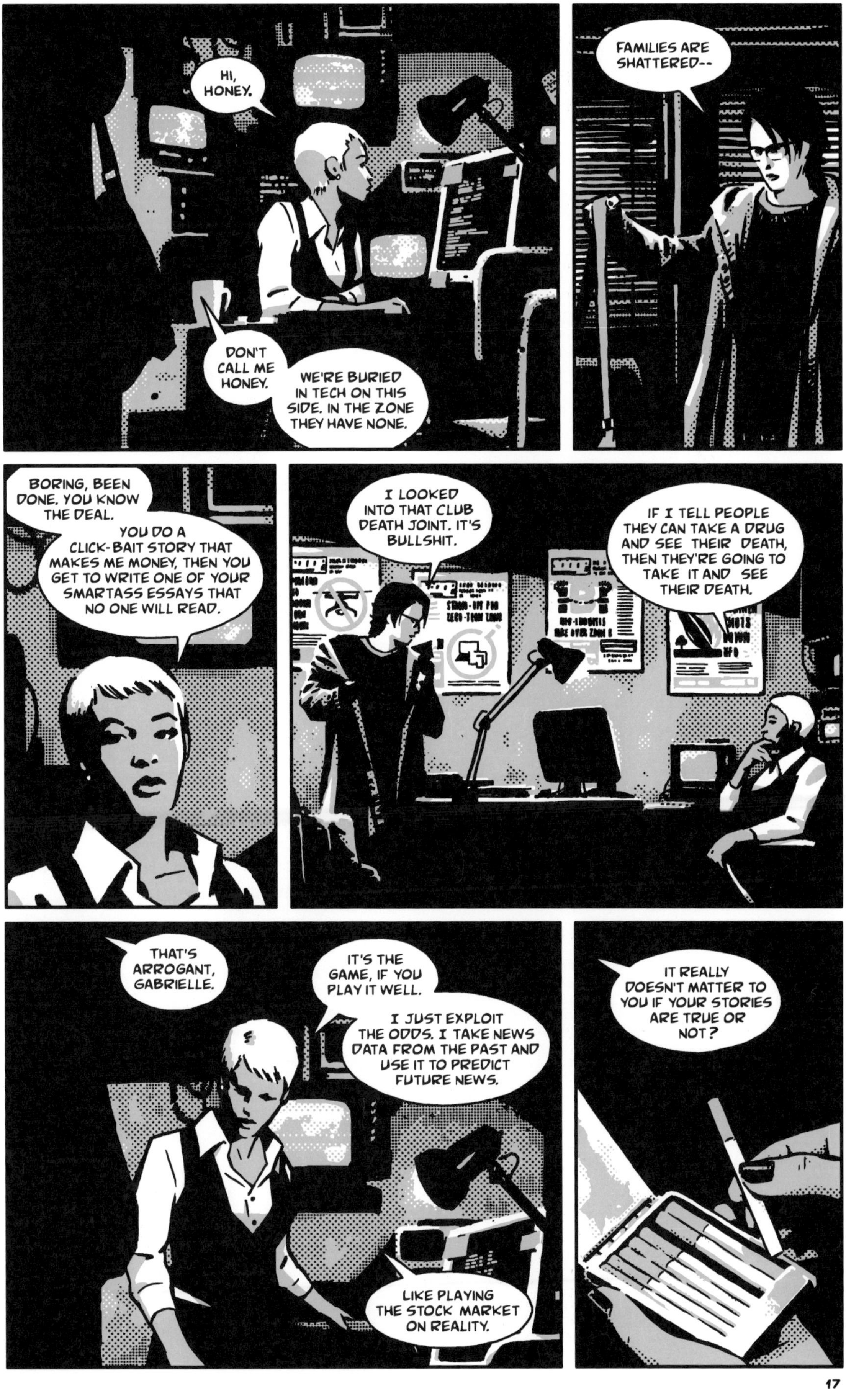
HI, HONEY.
DON'T CALL ME HONEY.
WE'RE BURIED IN TECH ON THIS SIDE. IN THE ZONE THEY HAVE NONE.
FAMILIES ARE SHATTERED--
BORING, BEEN DONE. YOU KNOW THE DEAL.
YOU DO A CLICK-BAIT STORY THAT MAKES ME MONEY, THEN YOU GET TO WRITE ONE OF YOUR SMARTASS ESSAYS THAT NO ONE WILL READ.
I LOOKED INTO THAT CLUB DEATH JOINT. IT'S BULLSHIT.
IF I TELL PEOPLE THEY CAN TAKE A DRUG AND SEE THEIR DEATH, THEN THEY'RE GOING TO TAKE IT AND SEE THEIR DEATH.
THAT'S ARROGANT, GABRIELLE.
IT'S THE GAME, IF YOU PLAY IT WELL.
I JUST EXPLOIT THE ODDS. I TAKE NEWS DATA FROM THE PAST AND USE IT TO PREDICT FUTURE NEWS.
LIKE PLAYING THE STOCK MARKET ON REALITY.
IT REALLY DOESN'T MATTER TO YOU IF YOUR STORIES ARE TRUE OR NOT?

WHO PREDICTED THE ANTI-TECH REVOLUTION? WHO PREDICTED THE ZONE? I DID. SCOOP OF THE CENTURY.

"WHEN I WAS IN HIGH SCHOOL, SOMEONE STARTED A RUMOR ABOUT ME.

"THAT I WAS A SLUT.

SCOOP WEEKLY

SKULL FOUND OF THE

DEMAND NO DRONE ZONE NOW!

"THAT I'D DO ANYBODY ANYWHERE."

IT WASN'T TRUE. I WAS SHY. BUT THE WHOLE SCHOOL BELIEVED I WAS A SLUT--

--SO I WAS ONE.

SLING MUD AND SOME DIRT STICKS.

THAT'S HORRIBLE.

YEAH, IT SUCKED. IT WAS A FAKE STORY... BUT IT CAME TRUE. I GOT SLUTTY AND LIKED IT.

THEY MAKE YOU THE THING, YOU MIGHT AS WELL BE THE THING.

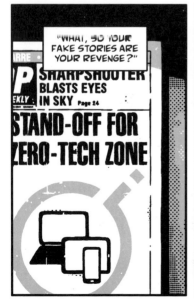

"WHAT, SO YOUR FAKE STORIES ARE YOUR REVENGE?"

SHARPSHOOTER BLASTS EYES IN SKY Page 24

STAND-OFF FOR ZERO-TECH ZONE

REPEAT A LIE OFTEN ENOUGH, IT TAKES ON THE ILLUSION OF TRUTH.

WALKE AS BLO

"YOU LIE 'TIL IT'S TRUE. BUT IT'S STILL... FALSE."

NEO-LUDDITES TAKE OVER ZONE

WORKERS SMASH JOB-STEALING BOTS Page 12

FU N0

"DON'T SPLIT HAIRS, HONEY."

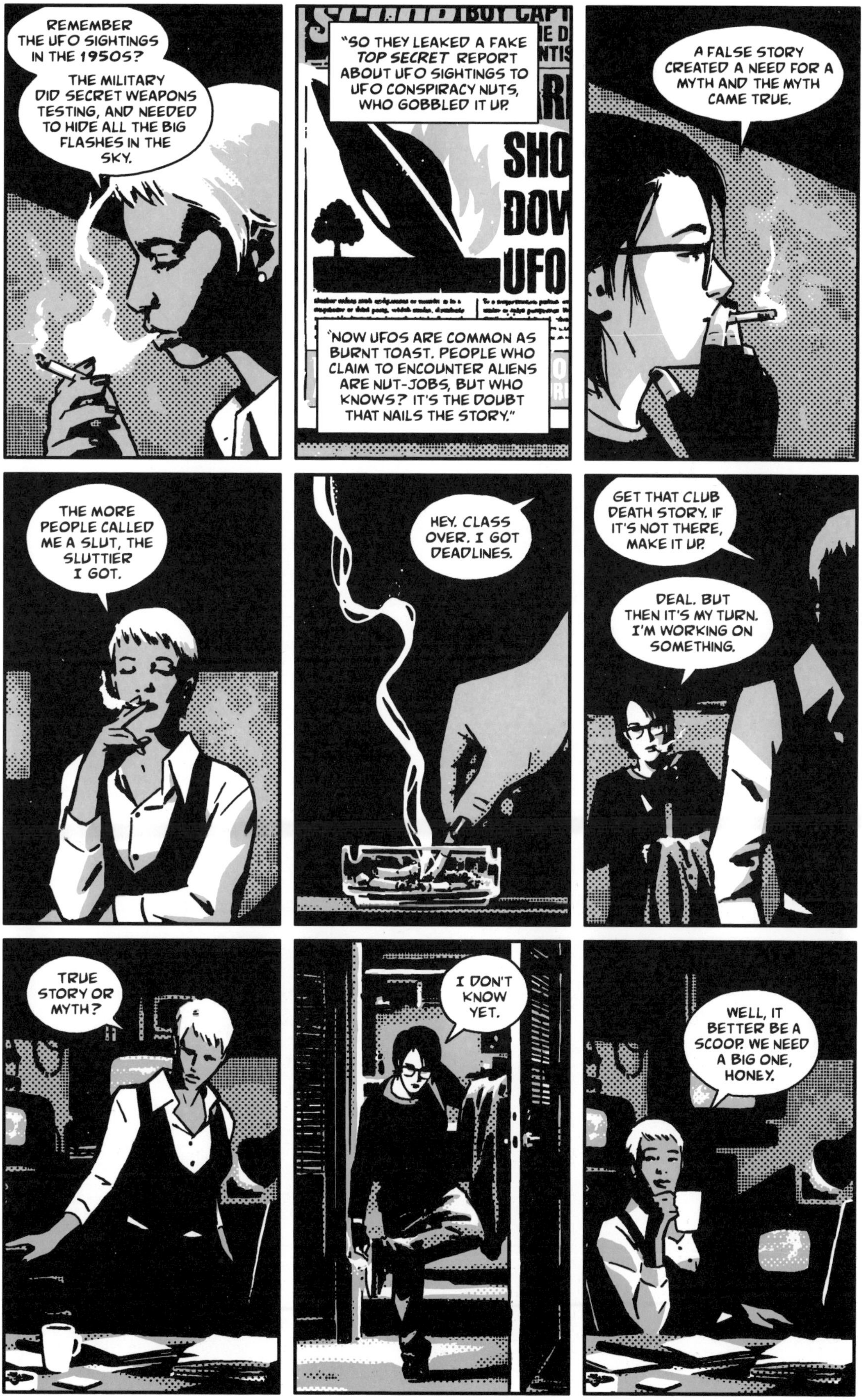

REMEMBER THE UFO SIGHTINGS IN THE 1950S?
THE MILITARY DID SECRET WEAPONS TESTING, AND NEEDED TO HIDE ALL THE BIG FLASHES IN THE SKY.
"SO THEY LEAKED A FAKE *TOP SECRET* REPORT ABOUT UFO SIGHTINGS TO UFO CONSPIRACY NUTS, WHO GOBBLED IT UP.
SHO DOW UFO
"NOW UFOS ARE COMMON AS BURNT TOAST. PEOPLE WHO CLAIM TO ENCOUNTER ALIENS ARE NUT-JOBS, BUT WHO KNOWS? IT'S THE DOUBT THAT NAILS THE STORY."
A FALSE STORY CREATED A NEED FOR A MYTH AND THE MYTH CAME TRUE.
THE MORE PEOPLE CALLED ME A SLUT, THE SLUTTIER I GOT.
HEY. CLASS OVER. I GOT DEADLINES.
GET THAT CLUB DEATH STORY. IF IT'S NOT THERE, MAKE IT UP.
DEAL. BUT THEN IT'S MY TURN. I'M WORKING ON SOMETHING.
TRUE STORY OR MYTH?
I DON'T KNOW YET.
WELL, IT BETTER BE A SCOOP. WE NEED A BIG ONE, HONEY.

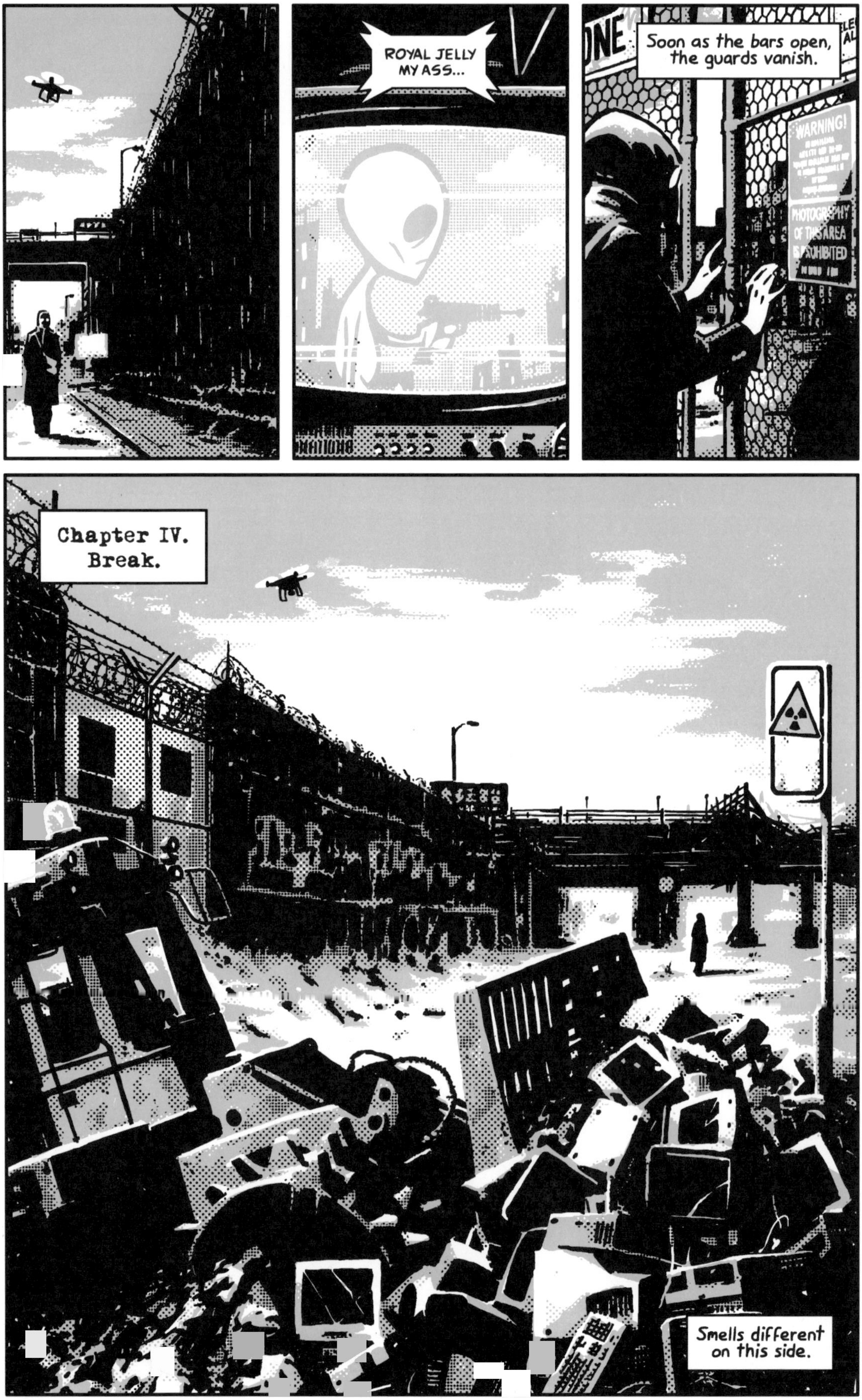
ROYAL JELLY MY ASS...
Soon as the bars open, the guards vanish.
WARNING!
PHOTOGRAPHY OF THIS AREA IS PROHIBITED
Chapter IV. Break.
Smells different on this side.

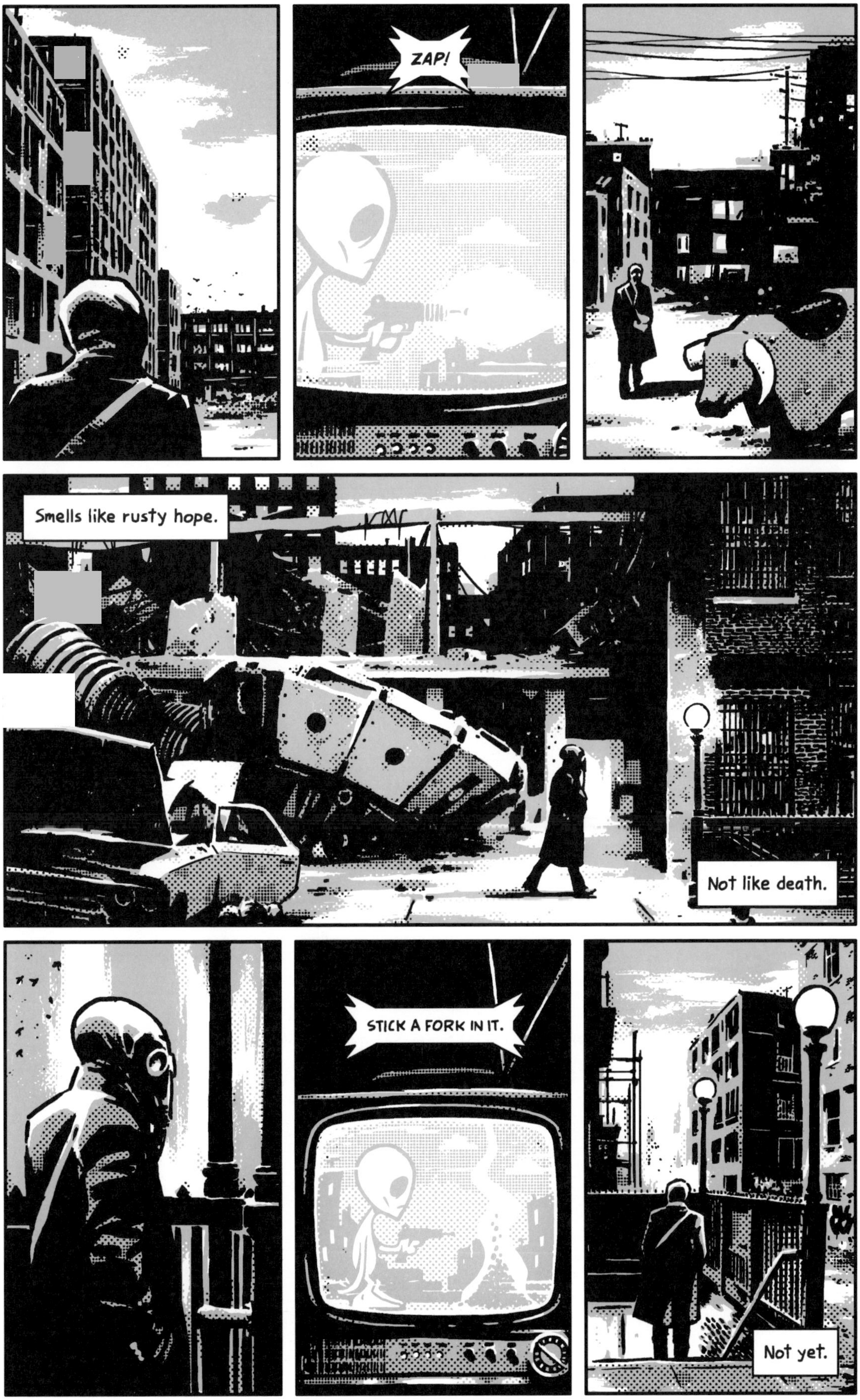
ZAP!
Smells like rusty hope.
Not like death.
STICK A FORK IN IT.
Not yet.

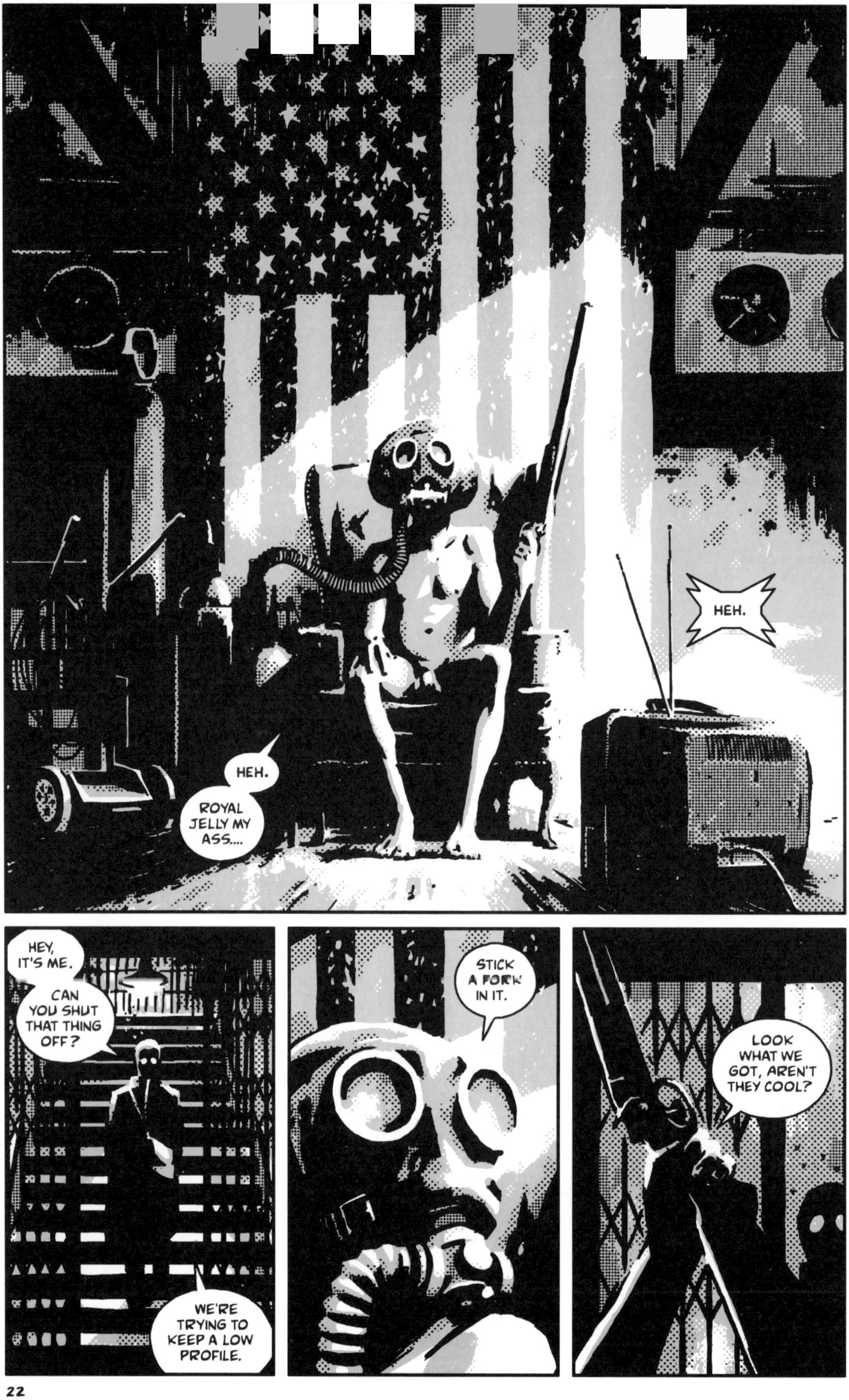
HEH.
HEH.
ROYAL JELLY MY ASS....
HEY, IT'S ME.
CAN YOU SHUT THAT THING OFF?
WE'RE TRYING TO KEEP A LOW PROFILE.
STICK A FORK IN IT.
LOOK WHAT WE GOT, AREN'T THEY COOL?

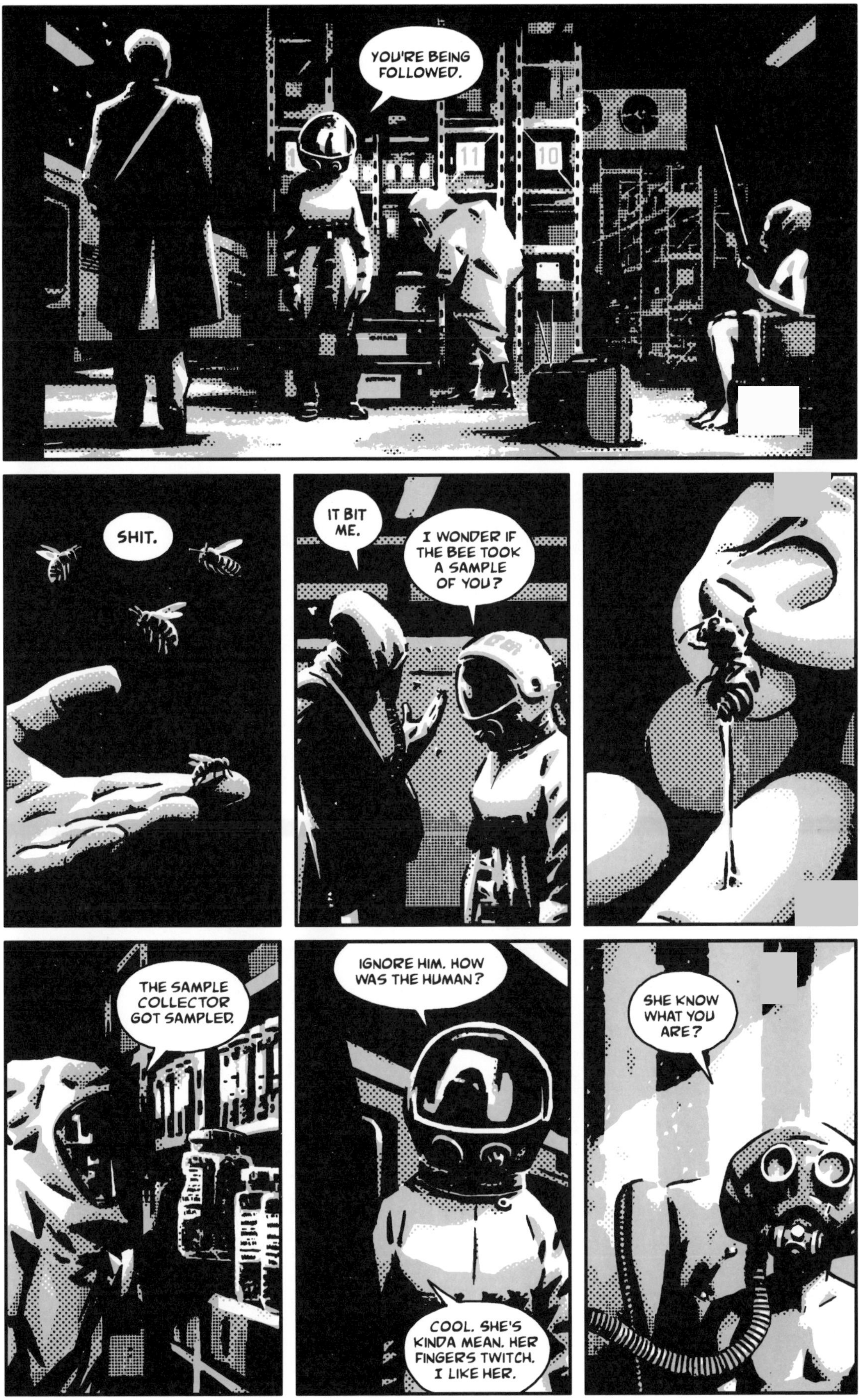
YOU'RE BEING FOLLOWED.
11
10
SHIT.
IT BIT ME.
I WONDER IF THE BEE TOOK A SAMPLE OF YOU?
THE SAMPLE COLLECTOR GOT SAMPLED.
IGNORE HIM. HOW WAS THE HUMAN?
COOL. SHE'S KINDA MEAN. HER FINGERS TWITCH. I LIKE HER.
SHE KNOW WHAT YOU ARE?

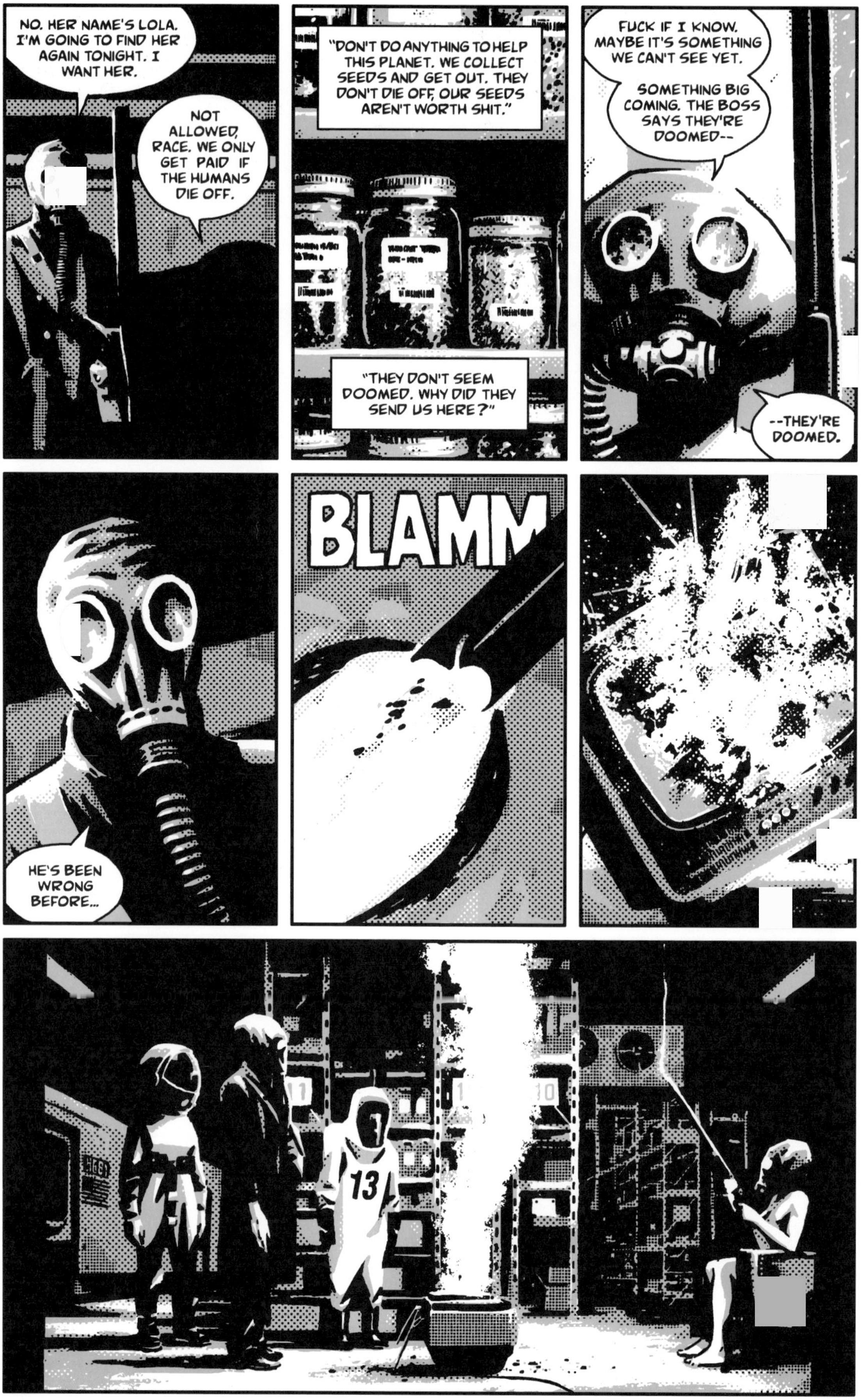
NO. HER NAME'S LOLA. I'M GOING TO FIND HER AGAIN TONIGHT. I WANT HER.
NOT ALLOWED, RACE. WE ONLY GET PAID IF THE HUMANS DIE OFF.
"DON'T DO ANYTHING TO HELP THIS PLANET. WE COLLECT SEEDS AND GET OUT. THEY DON'T DIE OFF, OUR SEEDS AREN'T WORTH SHIT."
"THEY DON'T SEEM DOOMED. WHY DID THEY SEND US HERE?"
FUCK IF I KNOW. MAYBE IT'S SOMETHING WE CAN'T SEE YET.
SOMETHING BIG COMING. THE BOSS SAYS THEY'RE DOOMED--
--THEY'RE DOOMED.
HE'S BEEN WRONG BEFORE...
BLAMM
13

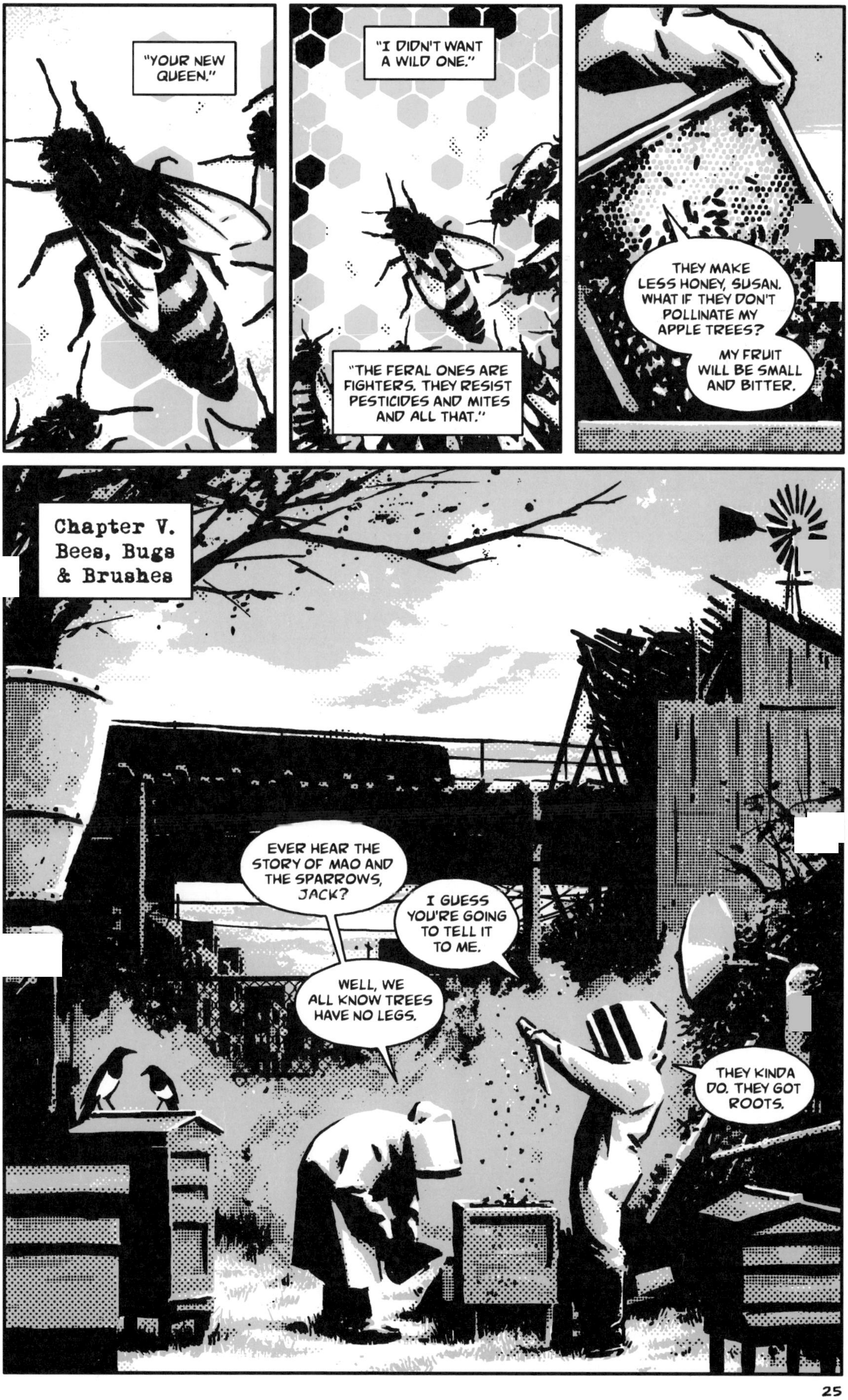
"YOUR NEW QUEEN."
"I DIDN'T WANT A WILD ONE."
"THE FERAL ONES ARE FIGHTERS. THEY RESIST PESTICIDES AND MITES AND ALL THAT."
THEY MAKE LESS HONEY, SUSAN. WHAT IF THEY DON'T POLLINATE MY APPLE TREES?
MY FRUIT WILL BE SMALL AND BITTER.
Chapter V. Bees, Bugs & Brushes
EVER HEAR THE STORY OF MAO AND THE SPARROWS, JACK?
I GUESS YOU'RE GOING TO TELL IT TO ME.
WELL, WE ALL KNOW TREES HAVE NO LEGS.
THEY KINDA DO. THEY GOT ROOTS.

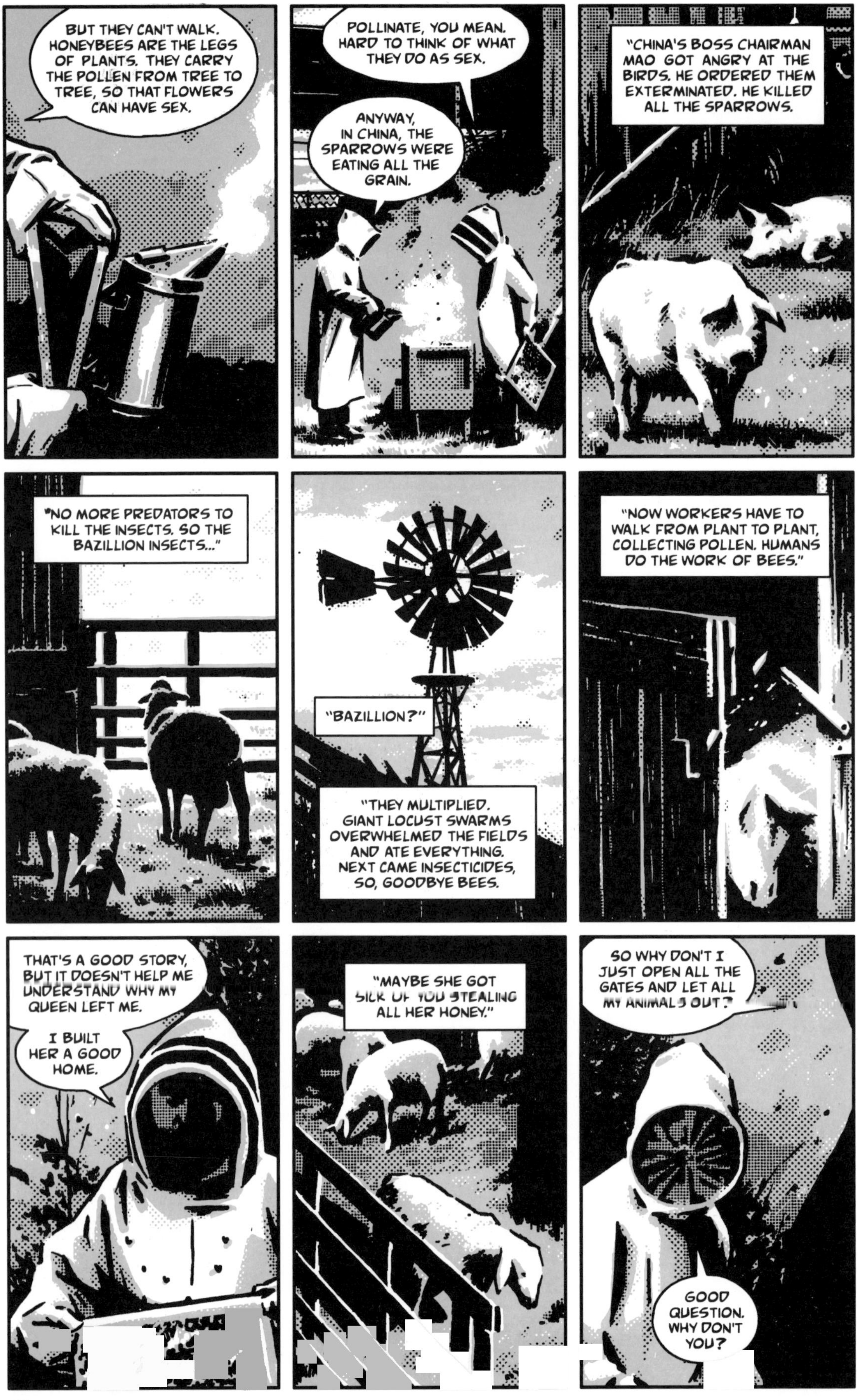

BUT THEY CAN'T WALK. HONEYBEES ARE THE LEGS OF PLANTS. THEY CARRY THE POLLEN FROM TREE TO TREE, SO THAT FLOWERS CAN HAVE SEX.
POLLINATE, YOU MEAN. HARD TO THINK OF WHAT THEY DO AS SEX.
ANYWAY, IN CHINA, THE SPARROWS WERE EATING ALL THE GRAIN.
"CHINA'S BOSS CHAIRMAN MAO GOT ANGRY AT THE BIRDS. HE ORDERED THEM EXTERMINATED. HE KILLED ALL THE SPARROWS.
"NO MORE PREDATORS TO KILL THE INSECTS. SO THE BAZILLION INSECTS..."
"BAZILLION?"
"THEY MULTIPLIED. GIANT LOCUST SWARMS OVERWHELMED THE FIELDS AND ATE EVERYTHING. NEXT CAME INSECTICIDES, SO, GOODBYE BEES.
"NOW WORKERS HAVE TO WALK FROM PLANT TO PLANT, COLLECTING POLLEN. HUMANS DO THE WORK OF BEES."
THAT'S A GOOD STORY, BUT IT DOESN'T HELP ME UNDERSTAND WHY MY QUEEN LEFT ME.
I BUILT HER A GOOD HOME.
"MAYBE SHE GOT SICK OF YOU STEALING ALL HER HONEY."
SO WHY DON'T I JUST OPEN ALL THE GATES AND LET ALL MY ANIMALS OUT?
GOOD QUESTION. WHY DON'T YOU?

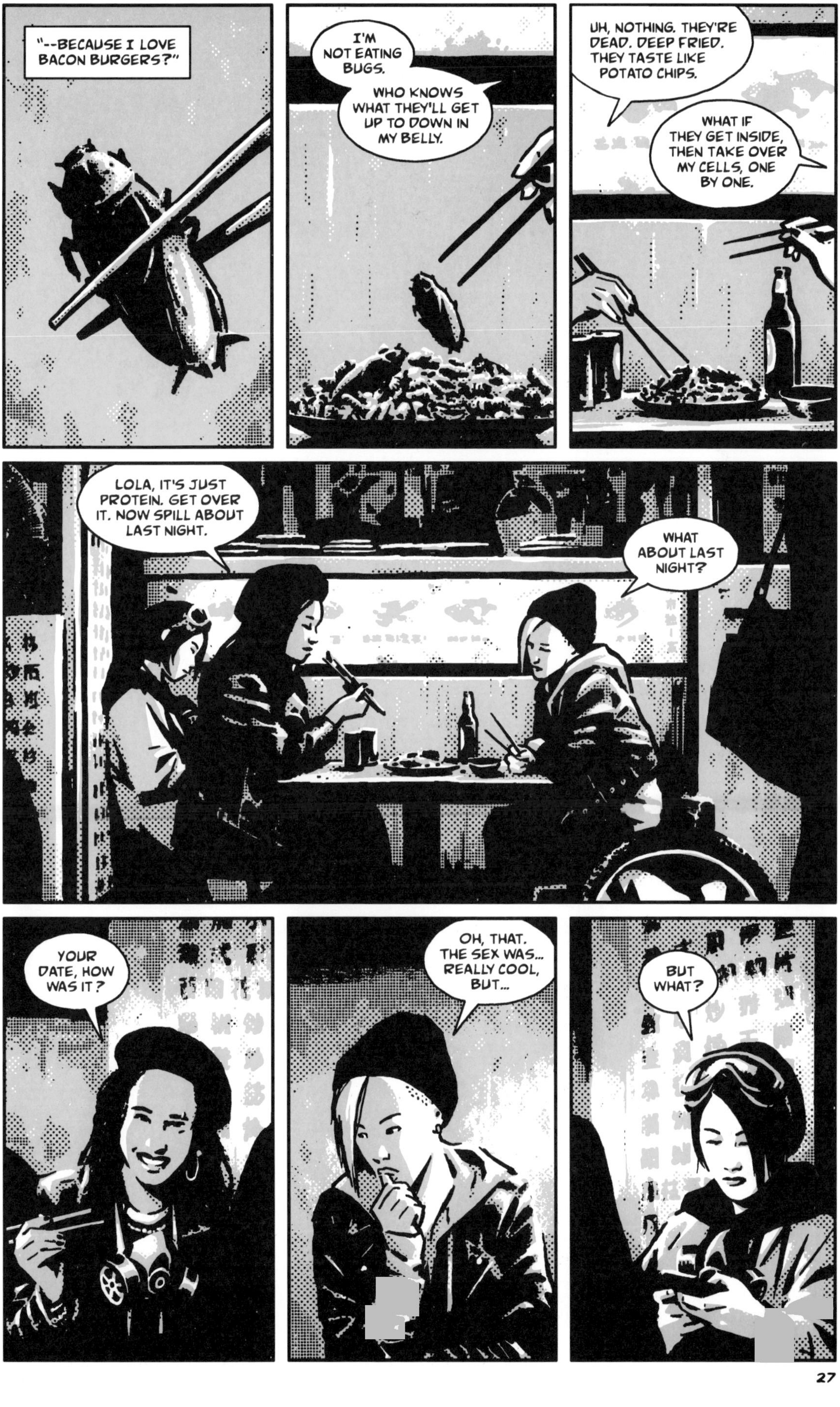
"--BECAUSE I LOVE BACON BURGERS?"
I'M NOT EATING BUGS.
WHO KNOWS WHAT THEY'LL GET UP TO DOWN IN MY BELLY.
UH, NOTHING. THEY'RE DEAD. DEEP FRIED. THEY TASTE LIKE POTATO CHIPS.
WHAT IF THEY GET INSIDE, THEN TAKE OVER MY CELLS, ONE BY ONE.
LOLA, IT'S JUST PROTEIN. GET OVER IT. NOW SPILL ABOUT LAST NIGHT.
WHAT ABOUT LAST NIGHT?
YOUR DATE, HOW WAS IT?
OH, THAT. THE SEX WAS... REALLY COOL, BUT...
BUT WHAT?

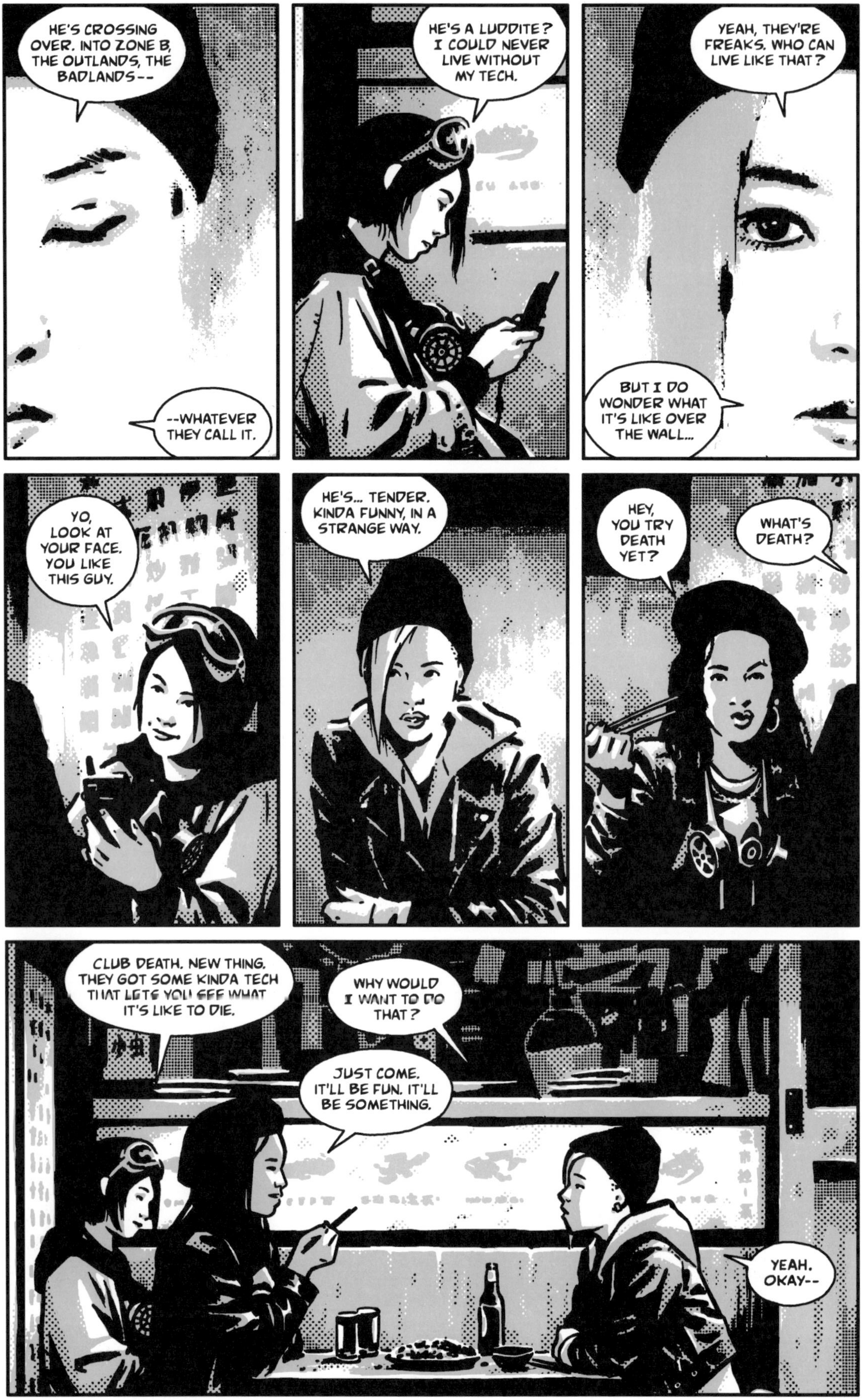
HE'S CROSSING OVER. INTO ZONE B, THE OUTLANDS, THE BADLANDS--
--WHATEVER THEY CALL IT.
HE'S A LUDDITE? I COULD NEVER LIVE WITHOUT MY TECH.
YEAH, THEY'RE FREAKS. WHO CAN LIVE LIKE THAT?
BUT I DO WONDER WHAT IT'S LIKE OVER THE WALL...
YO, LOOK AT YOUR FACE. YOU LIKE THIS GUY.
HE'S... TENDER. KINDA FUNNY, IN A STRANGE WAY.
HEY, YOU TRY DEATH YET?
WHAT'S DEATH?
CLUB DEATH. NEW THING. THEY GOT SOME KINDA TECH THAT LETS YOU SEE WHAT IT'S LIKE TO DIE.
WHY WOULD I WANT TO DO THAT?
JUST COME. IT'LL BE FUN. IT'LL BE SOMETHING.
YEAH. OKAY--

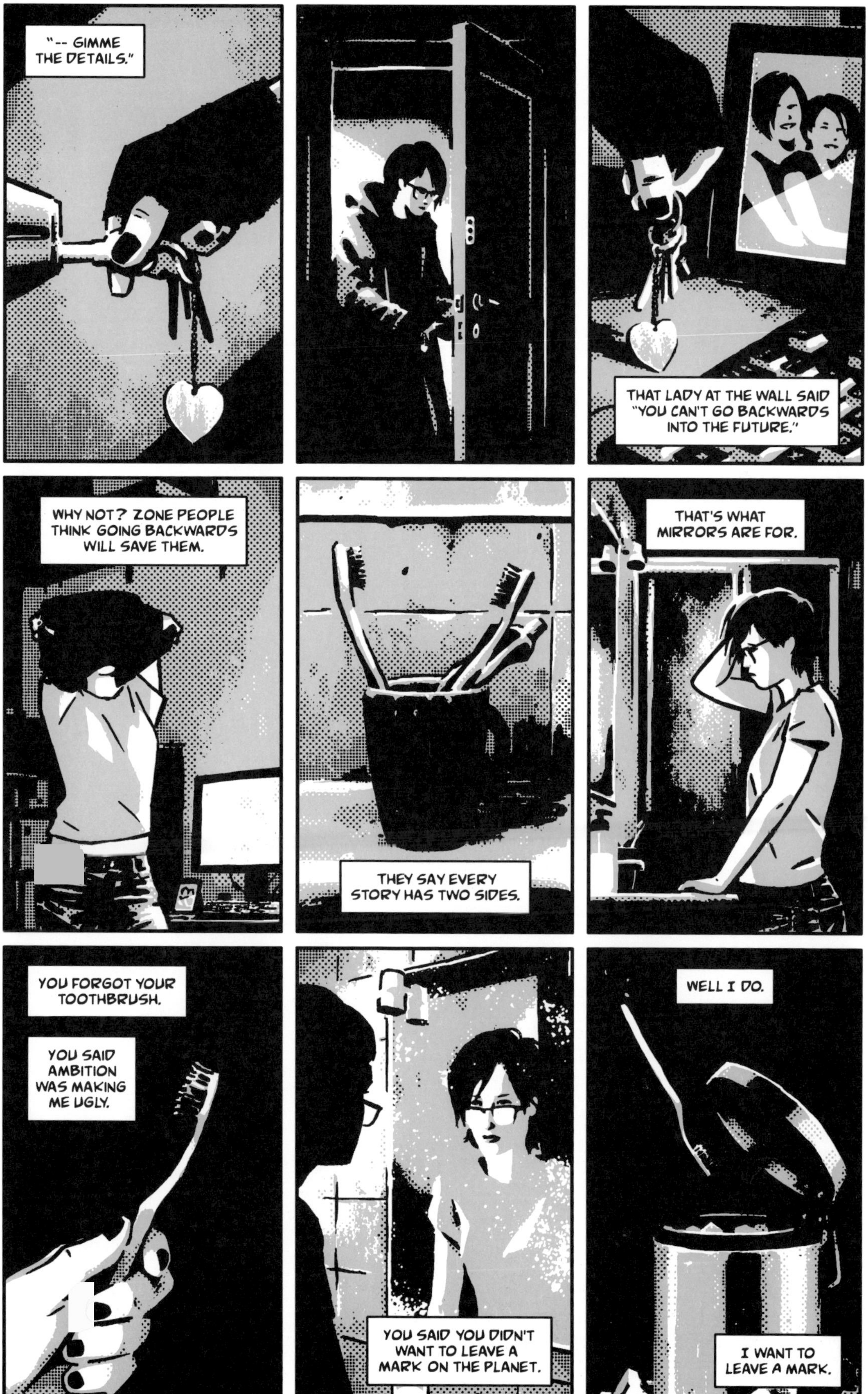
"-- GIMME THE DETAILS."
THAT LADY AT THE WALL SAID "YOU CAN'T GO BACKWARDS INTO THE FUTURE."
WHY NOT? ZONE PEOPLE THINK GOING BACKWARDS WILL SAVE THEM.
THEY SAY EVERY STORY HAS TWO SIDES.
THAT'S WHAT MIRRORS ARE FOR.
YOU FORGOT YOUR TOOTHBRUSH.
YOU SAID AMBITION WAS MAKING ME UGLY.
YOU SAID YOU DIDN'T WANT TO LEAVE A MARK ON THE PLANET.
WELL I DO.
I WANT TO LEAVE A MARK.

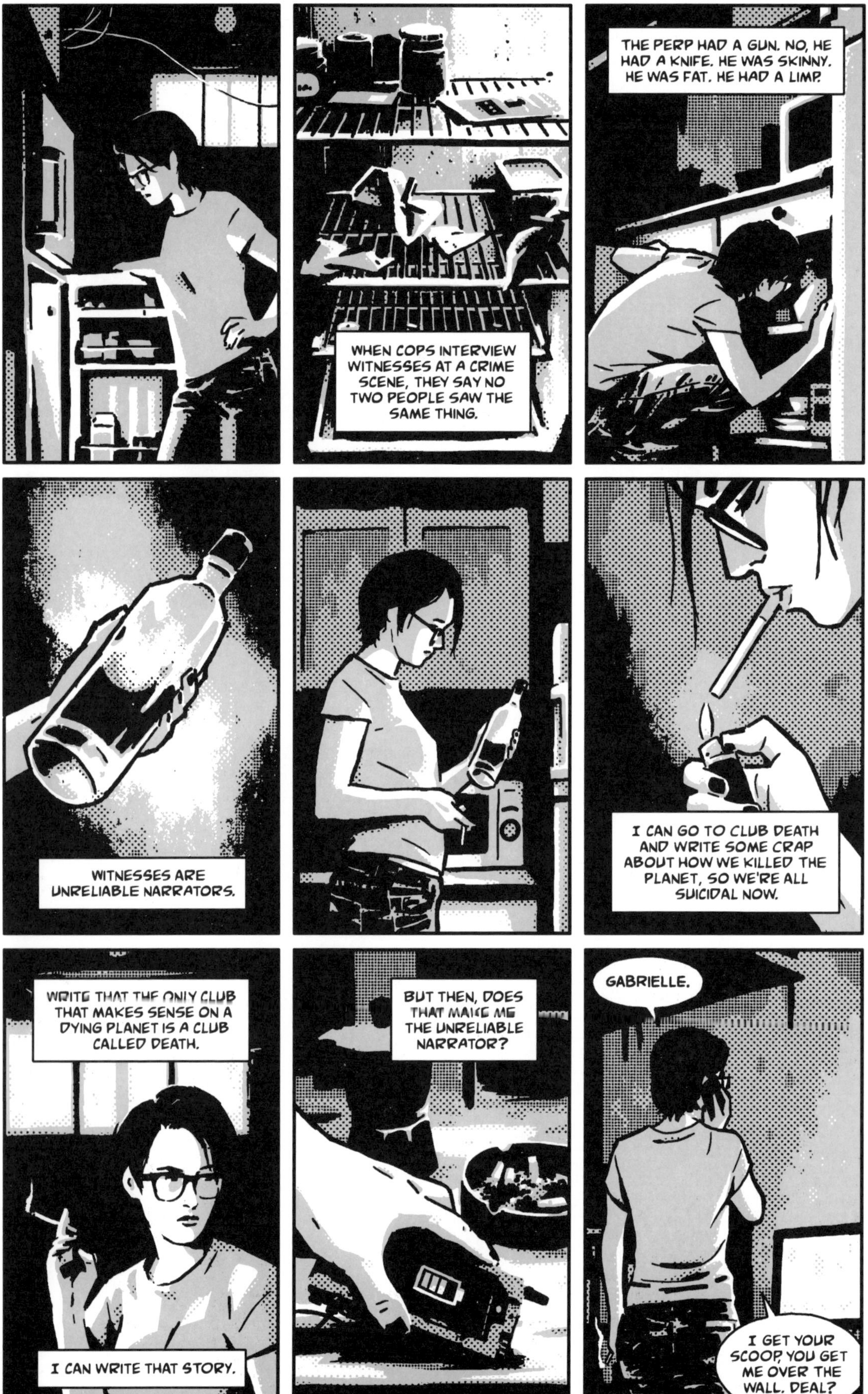
WHEN COPS INTERVIEW WITNESSES AT A CRIME SCENE, THEY SAY NO TWO PEOPLE SAW THE SAME THING.
THE PERP HAD A GUN. NO, HE HAD A KNIFE. HE WAS SKINNY. HE WAS FAT. HE HAD A LIMP.
WITNESSES ARE UNRELIABLE NARRATORS.
I CAN GO TO CLUB DEATH AND WRITE SOME CRAP ABOUT HOW WE KILLED THE PLANET, SO WE'RE ALL SUICIDAL NOW.
WRITE THAT THE ONLY CLUB THAT MAKES SENSE ON A DYING PLANET IS A CLUB CALLED DEATH.
I CAN WRITE THAT STORY.
BUT THEN, DOES THAT MAKE ME THE UNRELIABLE NARRATOR?
GABRIELLE.
I GET YOUR SCOOP, YOU GET ME OVER THE WALL. DEAL?

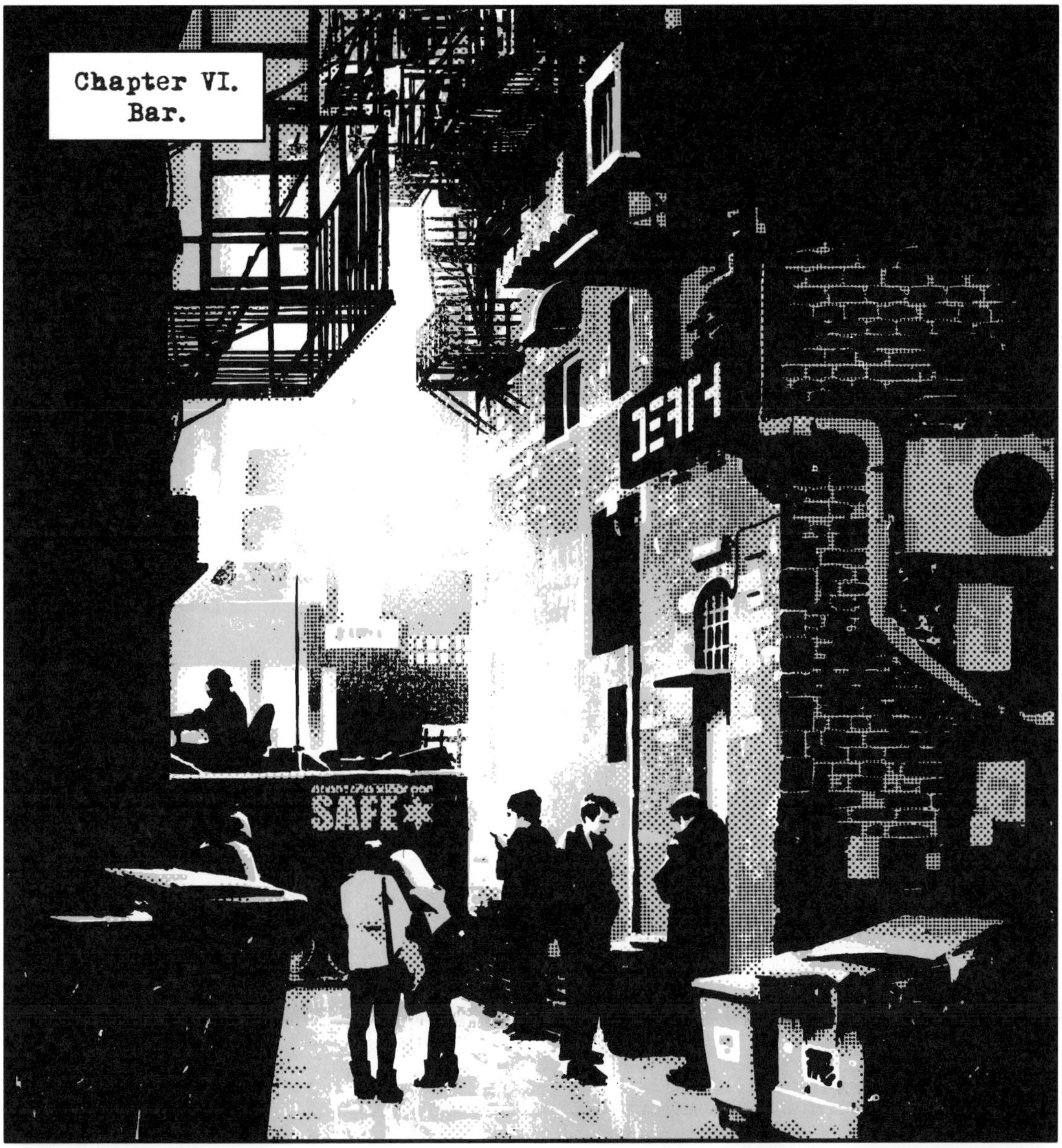
Chapter VI.
Bar.
SAFE

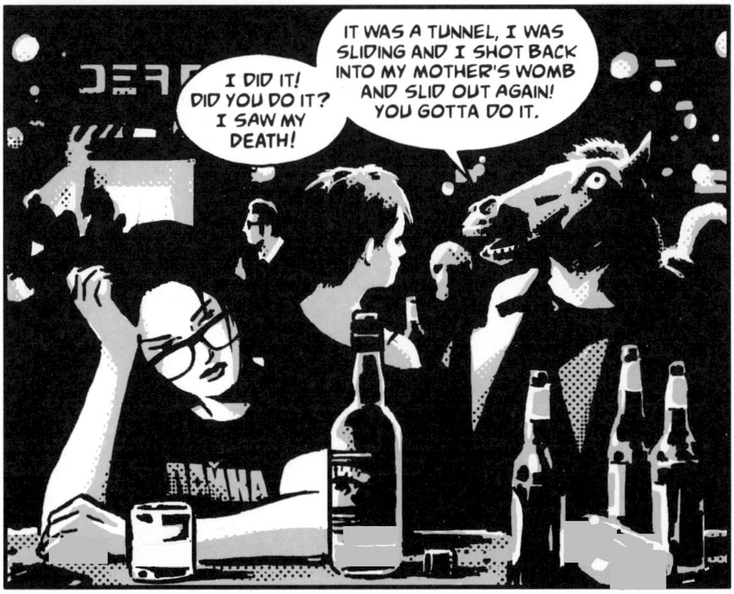
I DID IT! DID YOU DO IT? I SAW MY DEATH!
IT WAS A TUNNEL, I WAS SLIDING AND I SHOT BACK INTO MY MOTHER'S WOMB AND SLID OUT AGAIN! YOU GOTTA DO IT.

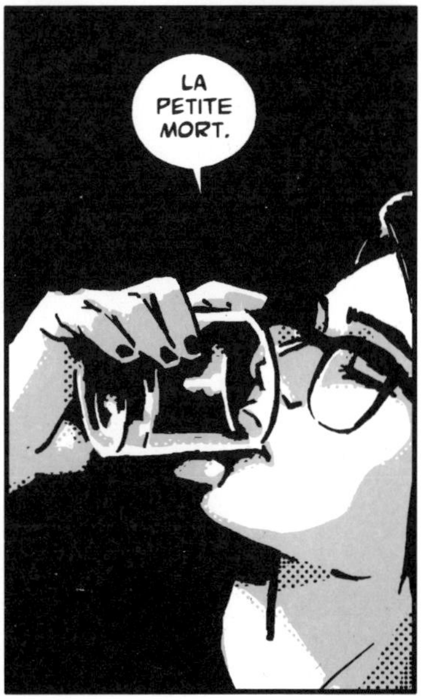
LA PETITE MORT.

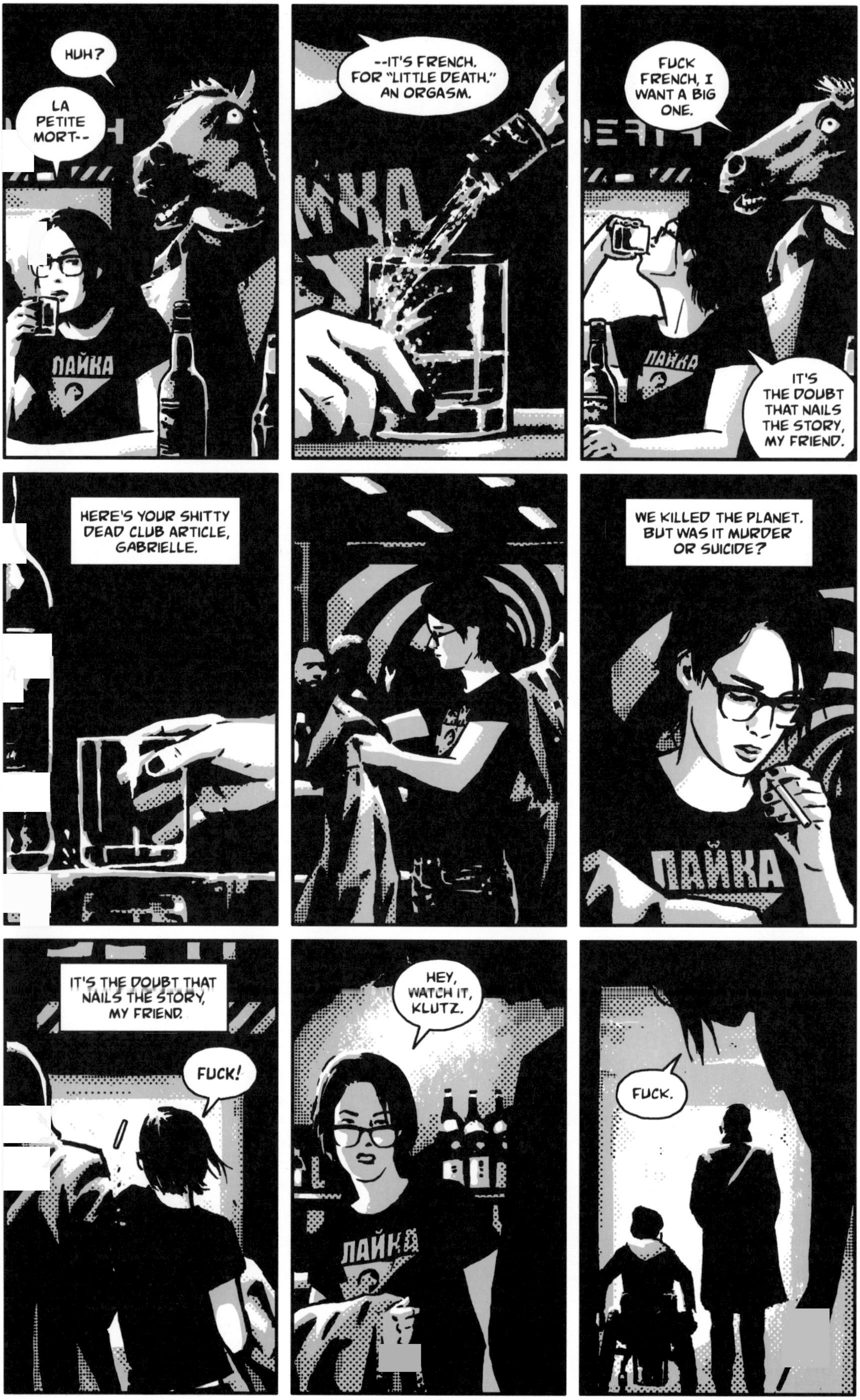
HUH?
LA PETITE MORT--
--IT'S FRENCH. FOR "LITTLE DEATH." AN ORGASM.
FUCK FRENCH, I WANT A BIG ONE.
IT'S THE DOUBT THAT NAILS THE STORY, MY FRIEND.
HERE'S YOUR SHITTY DEAD CLUB ARTICLE, GABRIELLE.
WE KILLED THE PLANET. BUT WAS IT MURDER OR SUICIDE?
IT'S THE DOUBT THAT NAILS THE STORY, MY FRIEND.
FUCK!
HEY, WATCH IT, KLUTZ.
FUCK.

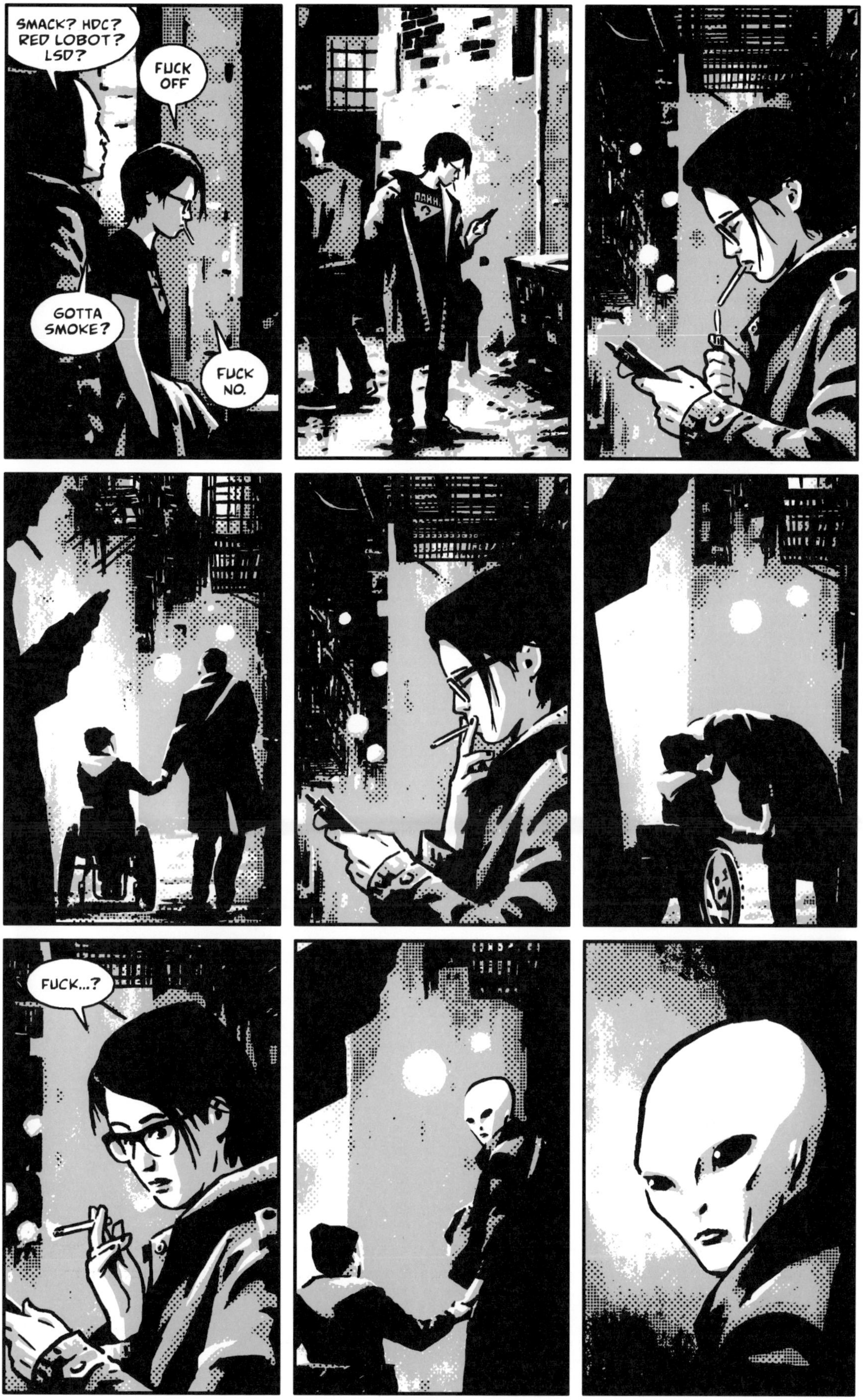
SMACK? HDC? RED LOBOT? LSD?
FUCK OFF
GOTTA SMOKE?
FUCK NO.
FUCK...?

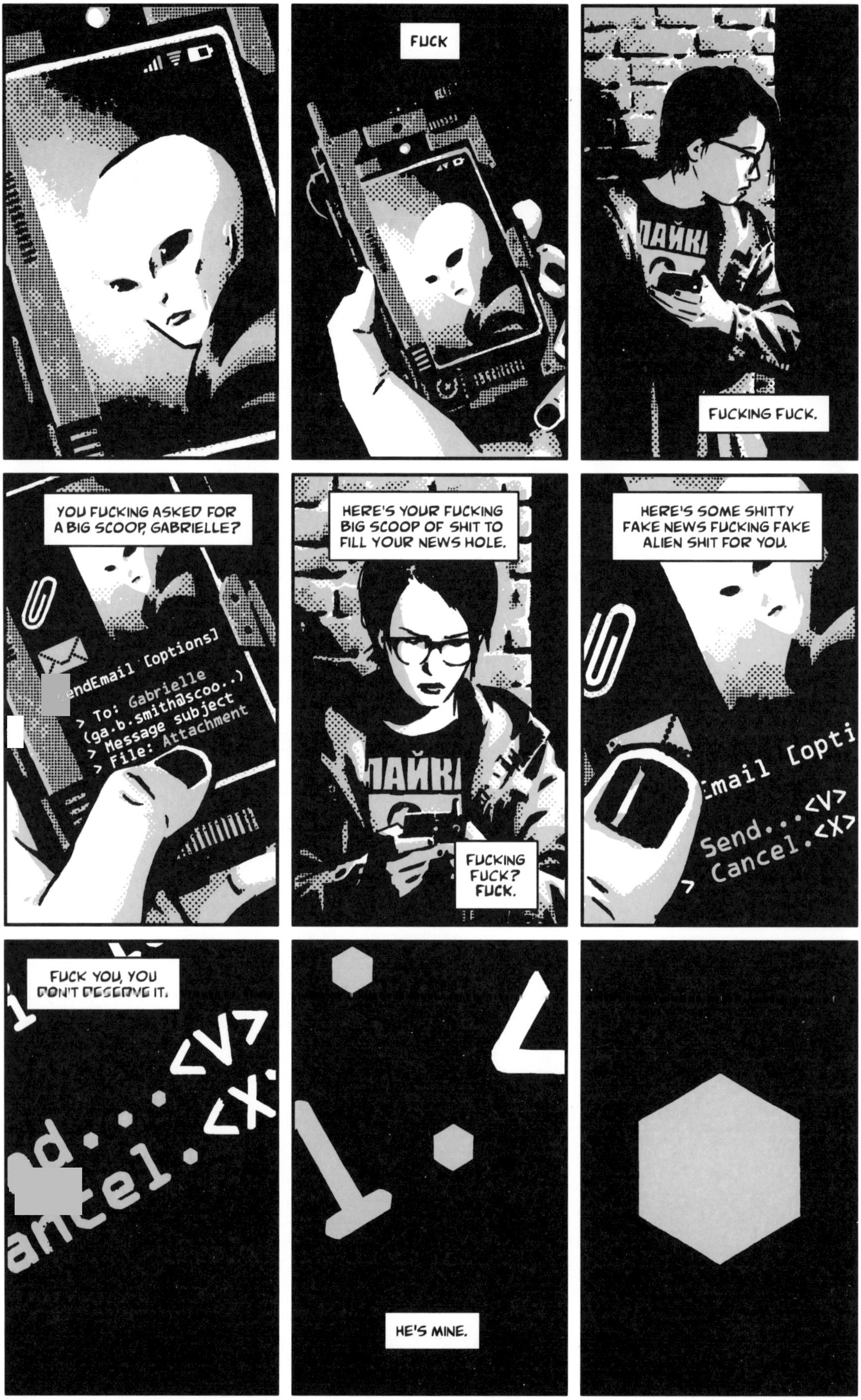
FUCK
FUCKING FUCK.
YOU FUCKING ASKED FOR A BIG SCOOP, GABRIELLE?
endEmail [options]
> To: Gabrielle
(ga.b.smith@scoo..)
> Message subject
> File: Attachment
HERE'S YOUR FUCKING BIG SCOOP OF SHIT TO FILL YOUR NEWS HOLE.
FUCKING FUCK? FUCK.
HERE'S SOME SHITTY FAKE NEWS FUCKING FAKE ALIEN SHIT FOR YOU.
Email [opti
Send...<V>
> Cancel.<X>
FUCK YOU, YOU DON'T DESERVE IT.
HE'S MINE.

[2. Metafork.]

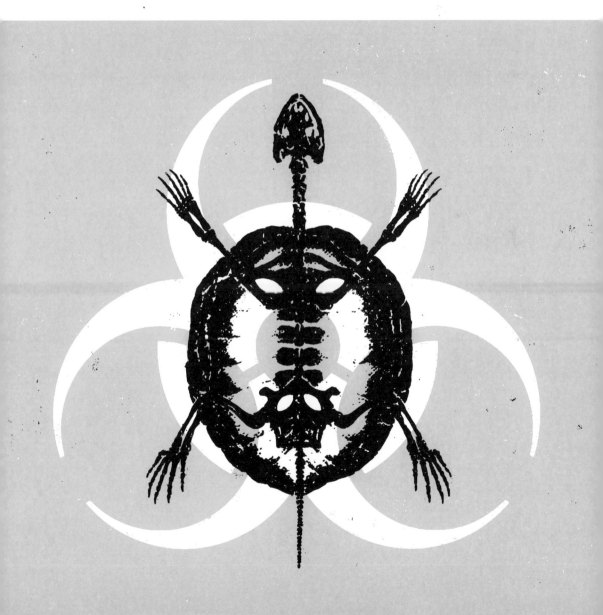

Fig.2

"If you're not at the
table, you're on
the menu."

- modern proverb

"...that frozen moment
when everyone sees
what's on the end of
every fork."

- William S. Burroughs

"YOU SURE, LOLA?"

"NO."

"I HEAR THERE'S NO WATER OUT THERE.

"YOU HAVE TO CRAWL A MILE FOR A DRINK."

"SO."

"I HEAR THEY USE CAR BATTERIES FOR POWER.

"PATHETIC.

"WHAT IF YOUR WHEELCHAIR BREAKS?"

"I DUNNO."

"YOU REALLY LIKE THIS GUY."

"YEAH."

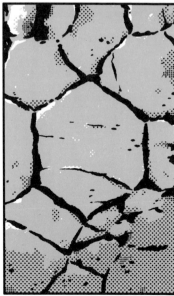

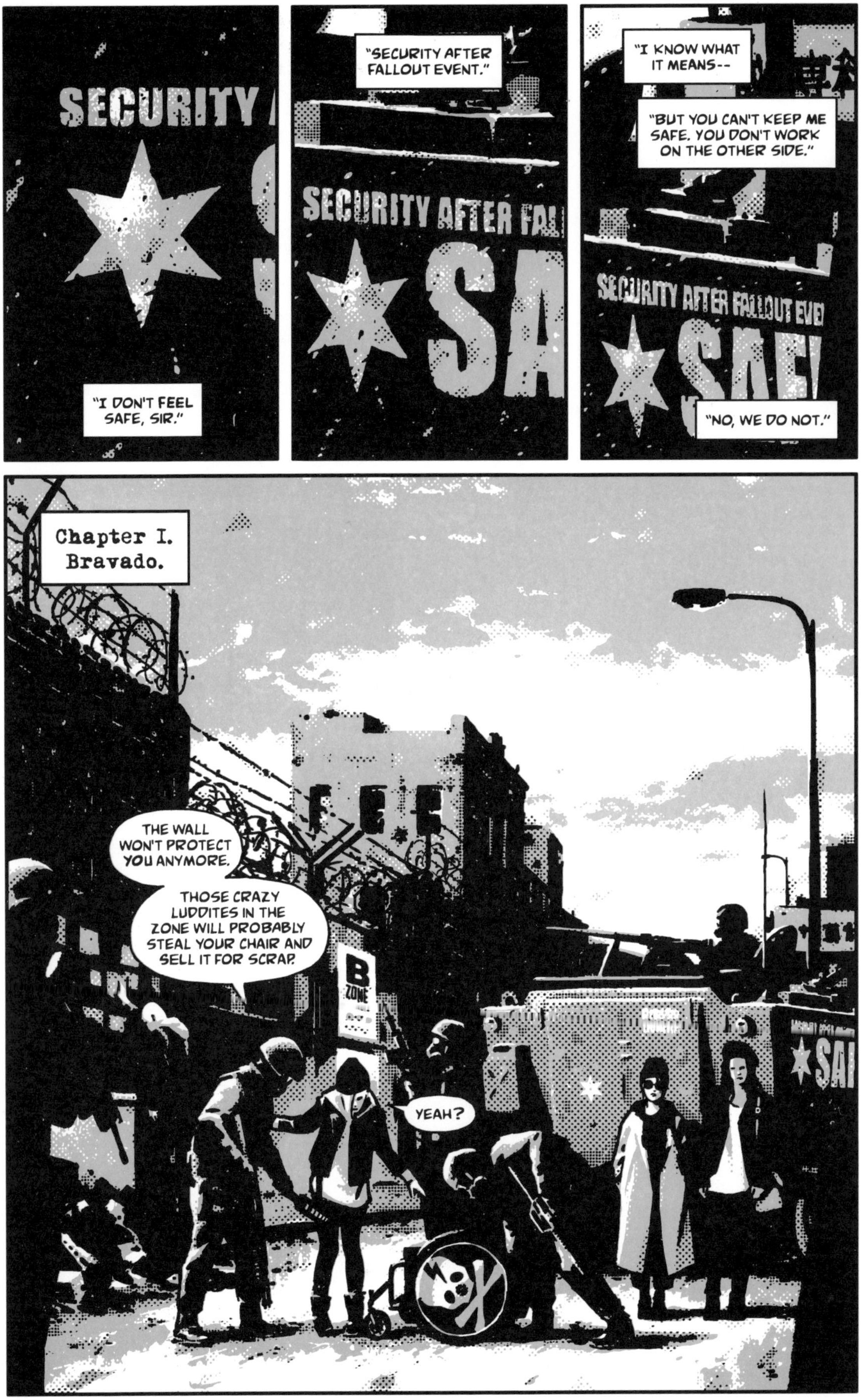
SECURITY
"I DON'T FEEL SAFE, SIR."
"SECURITY AFTER FALLOUT EVENT."
SECURITY AFTER FAL
SA
"I KNOW WHAT IT MEANS--
"BUT YOU CAN'T KEEP ME SAFE. YOU DON'T WORK ON THE OTHER SIDE."
SECURITY AFTER FALLOUT EVE
SAF
"NO, WE DO NOT."
Chapter I. Bravado.
THE WALL WON'T PROTECT YOU ANYMORE.
THOSE CRAZY LUDDITES IN THE ZONE WILL PROBABLY STEAL YOUR CHAIR AND SELL IT FOR SCRAP.
B ZONE
YEAH?
SAF

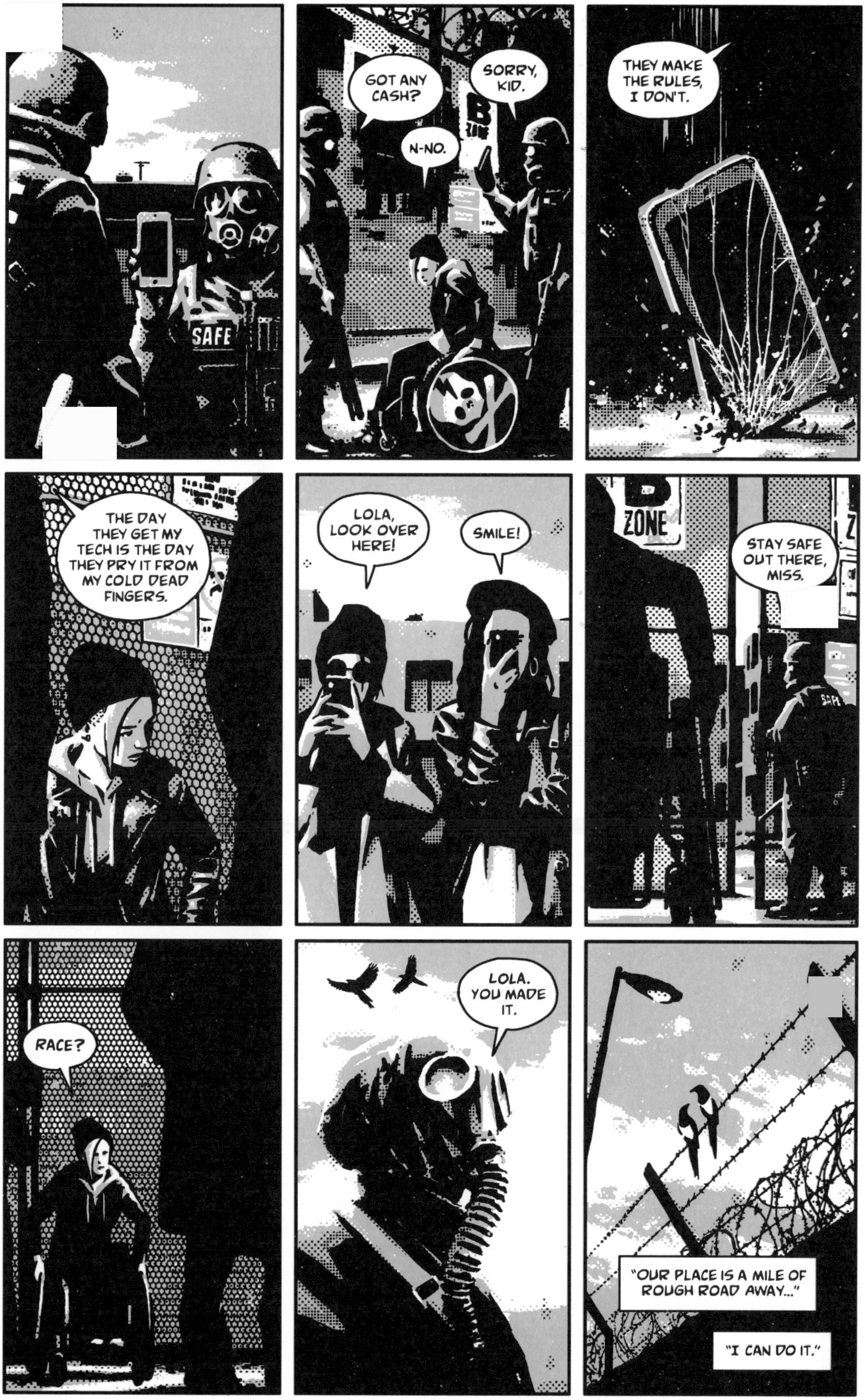
GOT ANY CASH?
SORRY, KID.
N-NO.
THEY MAKE THE RULES, I DON'T.
THE DAY THEY GET MY TECH IS THE DAY THEY PRY IT FROM MY COLD DEAD FINGERS.
LOLA, LOOK OVER HERE!
SMILE!
B ZONE
STAY SAFE OUT THERE, MISS.
RACE?
LOLA. YOU MADE IT.
"OUR PLACE IS A MILE OF ROUGH ROAD AWAY..."
"I CAN DO IT."

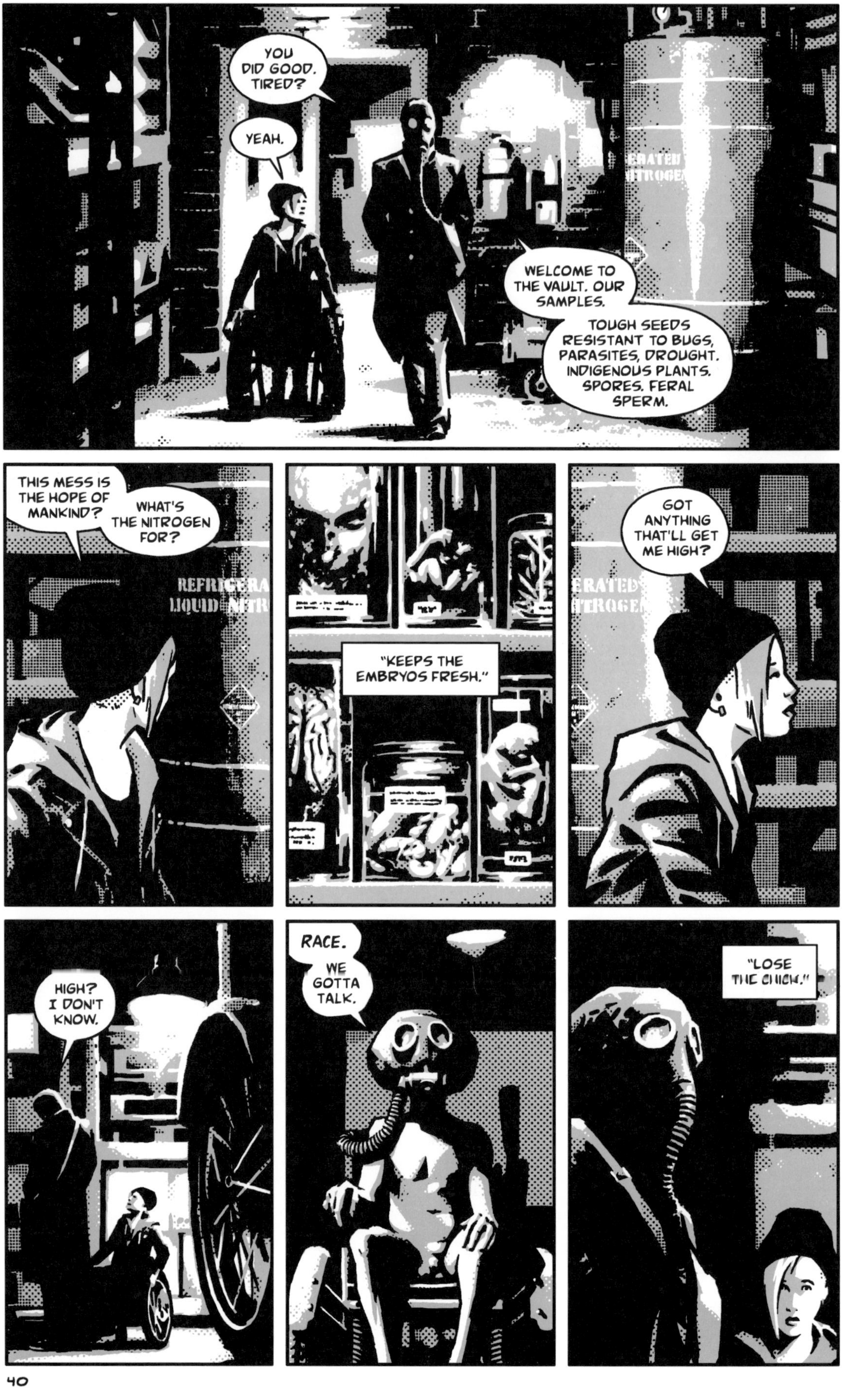
YOU DID GOOD. TIRED?
YEAH.
WELCOME TO THE VAULT. OUR SAMPLES.
TOUGH SEEDS RESISTANT TO BUGS, PARASITES, DROUGHT. INDIGENOUS PLANTS. SPORES. FERAL SPERM.
THIS MESS IS THE HOPE OF MANKIND?
WHAT'S THE NITROGEN FOR?
"KEEPS THE EMBRYOS FRESH."
GOT ANYTHING THAT'LL GET ME HIGH?
HIGH? I DON'T KNOW.
RACE.
WE GOTTA TALK.
"LOSE THE CHICK."

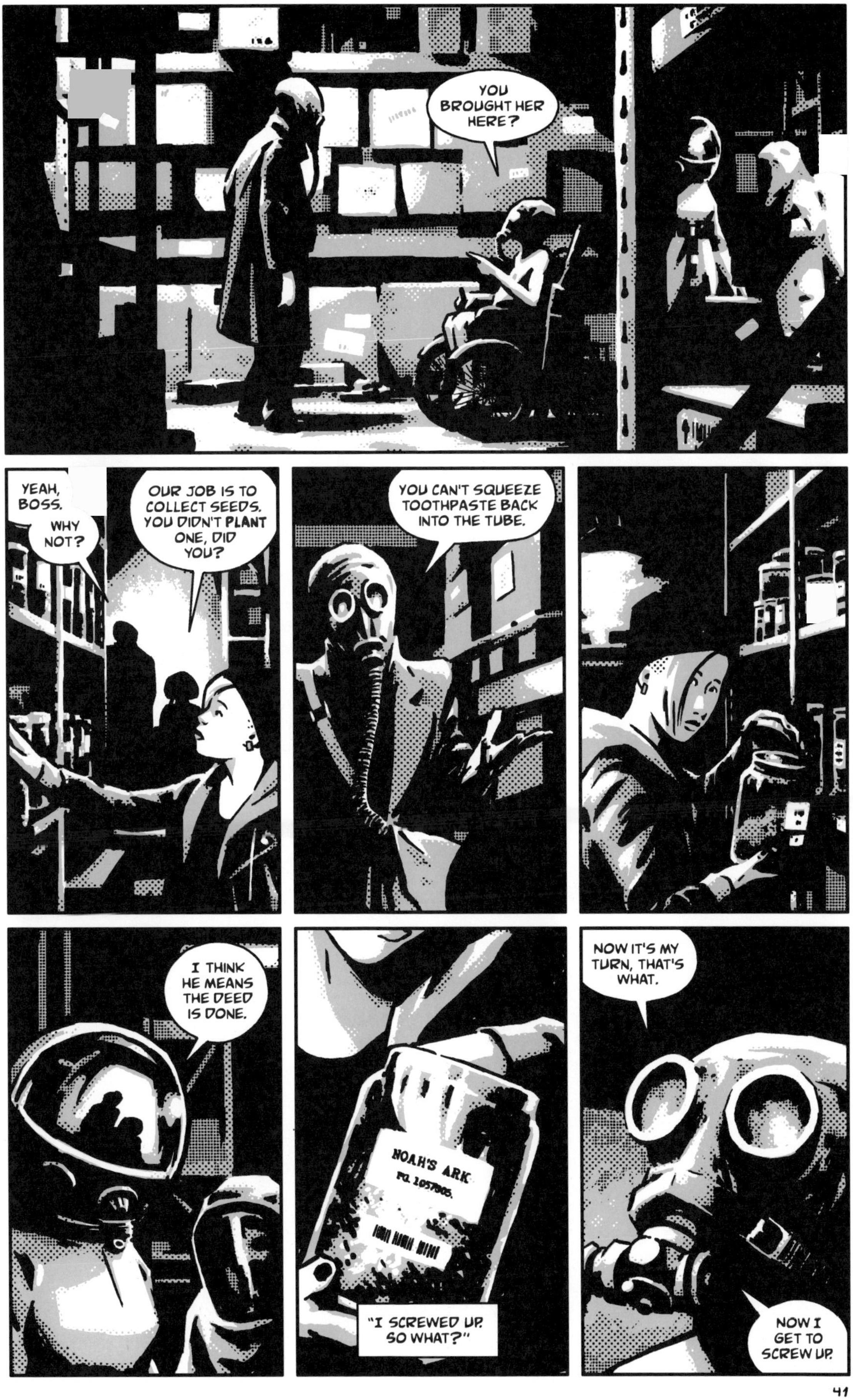
YOU BROUGHT HER HERE?
YEAH, BOSS.
WHY NOT?
OUR JOB IS TO COLLECT SEEDS. YOU DIDN'T PLANT ONE, DID YOU?
YOU CAN'T SQUEEZE TOOTHPASTE BACK INTO THE TUBE.
I THINK HE MEANS THE DEED IS DONE.
NOAH'S ARK
"I SCREWED UP. SO WHAT?"
NOW IT'S MY TURN, THAT'S WHAT.
NOW I GET TO SCREW UP.

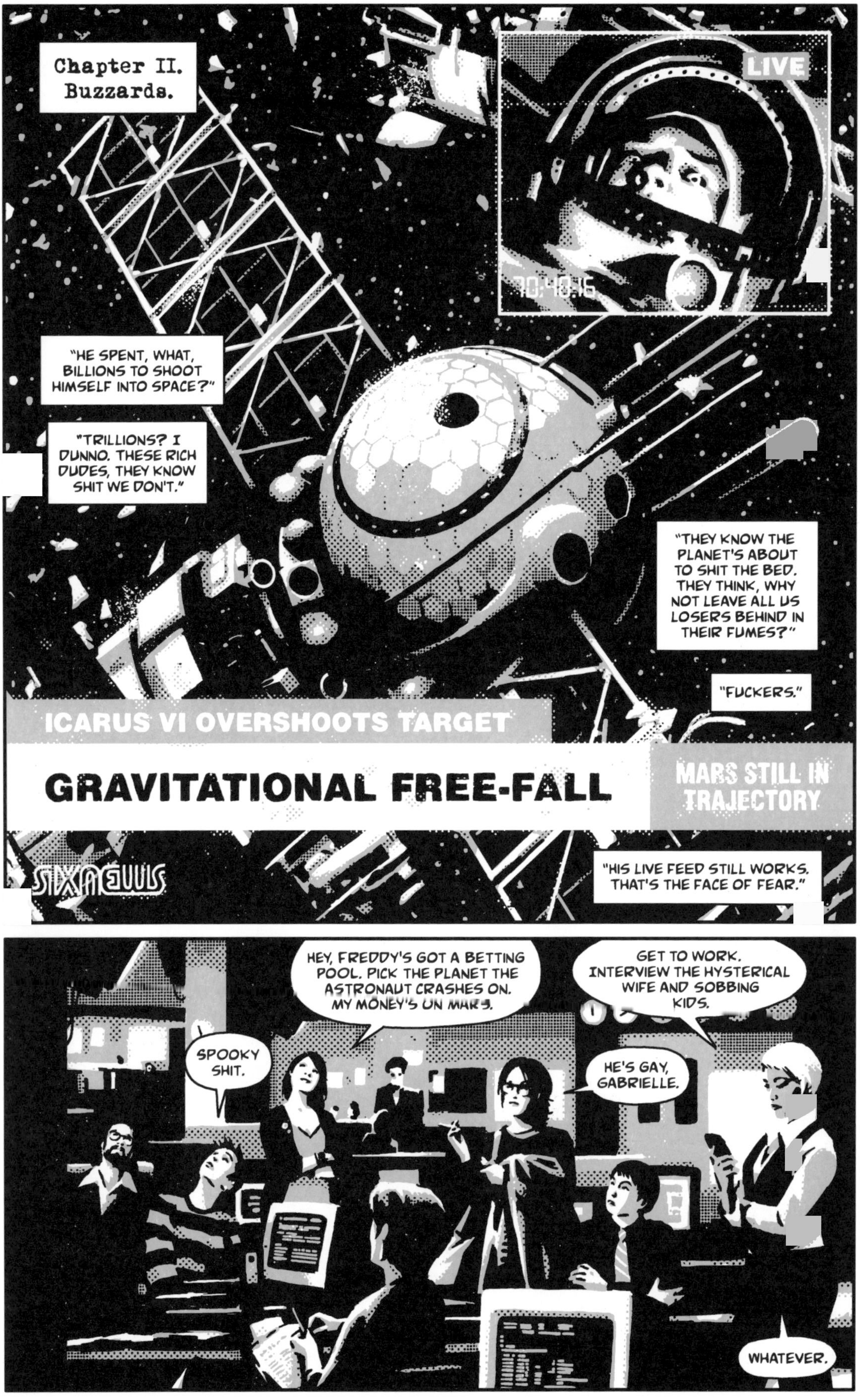
Chapter II.
Buzzards.
LIVE
70:48:16
"HE SPENT, WHAT, BILLIONS TO SHOOT HIMSELF INTO SPACE?"
"TRILLIONS? I DUNNO. THESE RICH DUDES, THEY KNOW SHIT WE DON'T."
"THEY KNOW THE PLANET'S ABOUT TO SHIT THE BED. THEY THINK, WHY NOT LEAVE ALL US LOSERS BEHIND IN THEIR FUMES?"
"FUCKERS."
ICARUS VI OVERSHOOTS TARGET
GRAVITATIONAL FREE-FALL
MARS STILL IN TRAJECTORY
"HIS LIVE FEED STILL WORKS. THAT'S THE FACE OF FEAR."
SPOOKY SHIT.
HEY, FREDDY'S GOT A BETTING POOL. PICK THE PLANET THE ASTRONAUT CRASHES ON. MY MONEY'S ON MARS.
GET TO WORK. INTERVIEW THE HYSTERICAL WIFE AND SOBBING KIDS.
HE'S GAY, GABRIELLE.
WHATEVER.

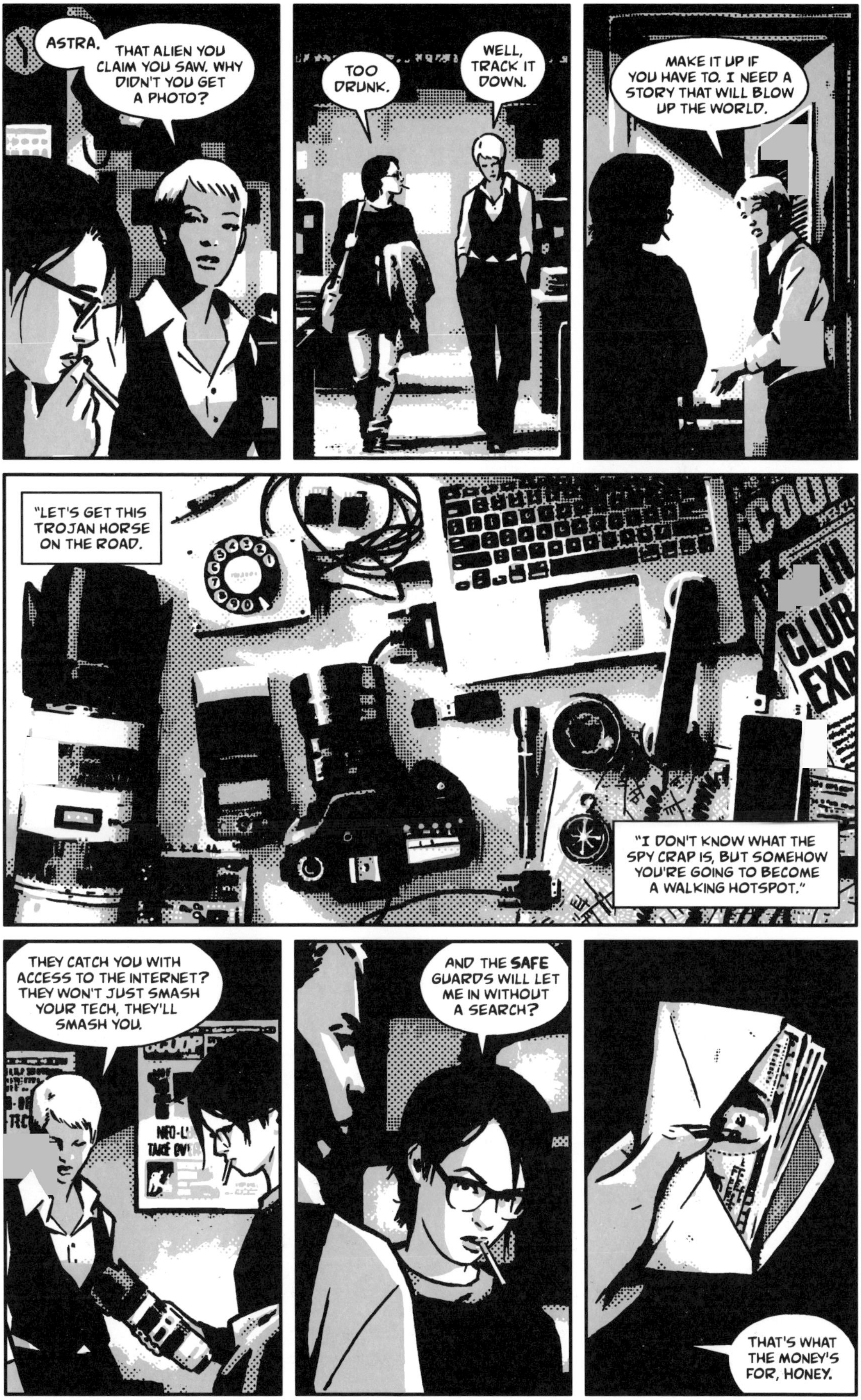
ASTRA.
THAT ALIEN YOU CLAIM YOU SAW. WHY DIDN'T YOU GET A PHOTO?
TOO DRUNK.
WELL, TRACK IT DOWN.
MAKE IT UP IF YOU HAVE TO. I NEED A STORY THAT WILL BLOW UP THE WORLD.
"LET'S GET THIS TROJAN HORSE ON THE ROAD.
"I DON'T KNOW WHAT THE SPY CRAP IS, BUT SOMEHOW YOU'RE GOING TO BECOME A WALKING HOTSPOT."
THEY CATCH YOU WITH ACCESS TO THE INTERNET? THEY WON'T JUST SMASH YOUR TECH, THEY'LL SMASH YOU.
AND THE SAFE GUARDS WILL LET ME IN WITHOUT A SEARCH?
THAT'S WHAT THE MONEY'S FOR, HONEY.

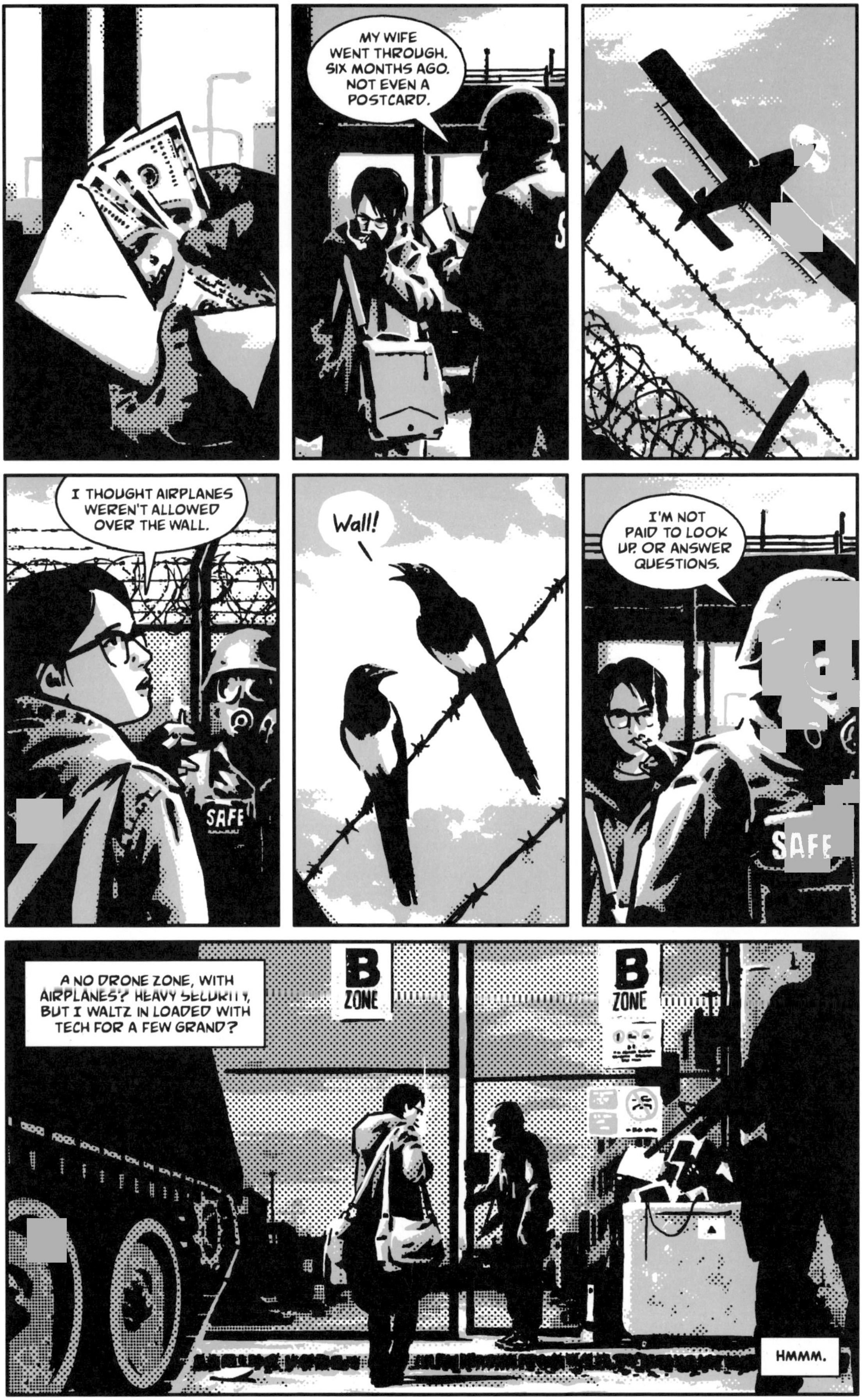
MY WIFE WENT THROUGH. SIX MONTHS AGO. NOT EVEN A POSTCARD.
I THOUGHT AIRPLANES WEREN'T ALLOWED OVER THE WALL.
Wall!
I'M NOT PAID TO LOOK UP. OR ANSWER QUESTIONS.
SAFE
A NO DRONE ZONE, WITH AIRPLANES? HEAVY SECURITY, BUT I WALTZ IN LOADED WITH TECH FOR A FEW GRAND?
B ZONE
B ZONE
HMMM.

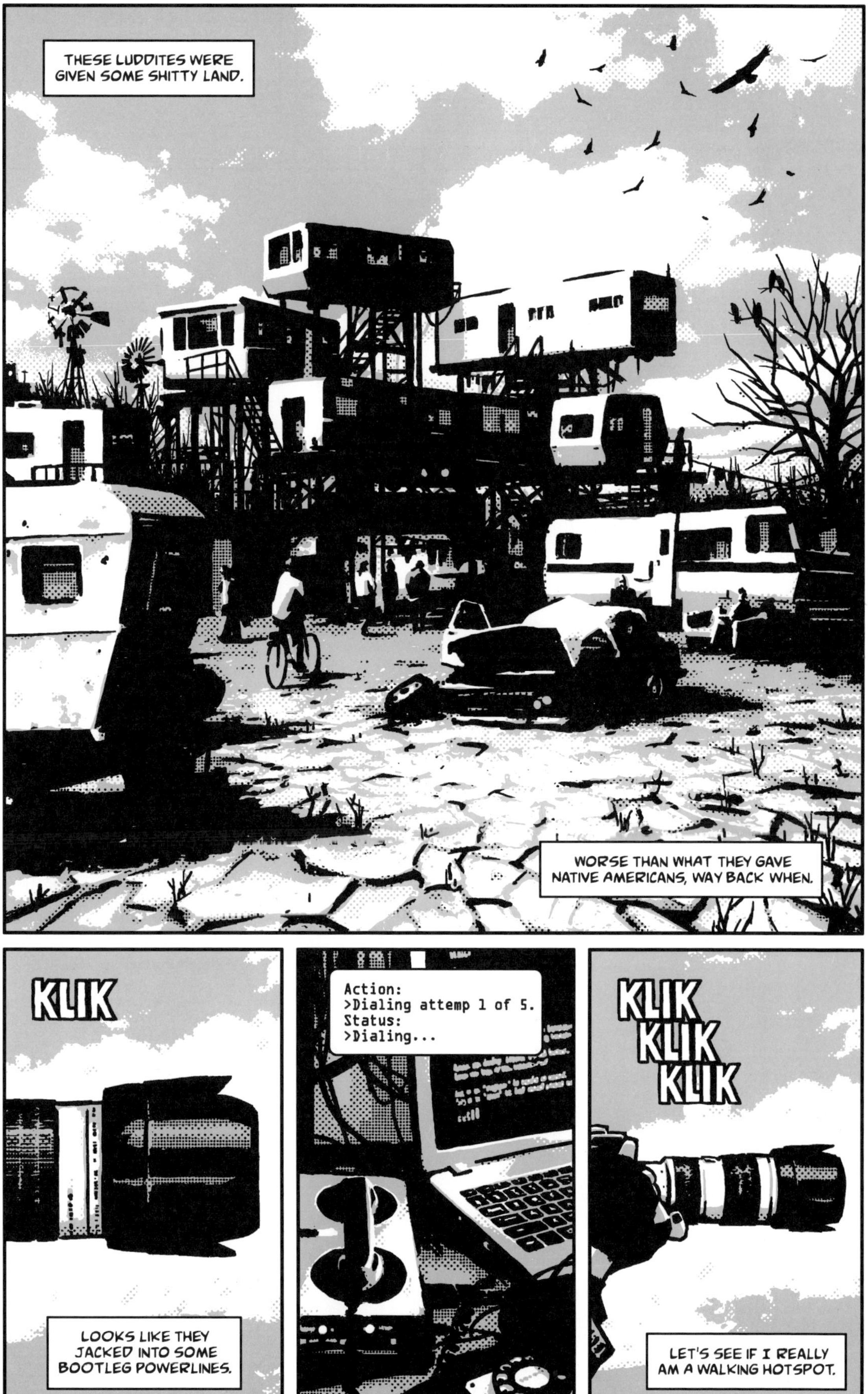
THESE LUDDITES WERE GIVEN SOME SHITTY LAND.
WORSE THAN WHAT THEY GAVE NATIVE AMERICANS, WAY BACK WHEN.
KLIK
LOOKS LIKE THEY JACKED INTO SOME BOOTLEG POWERLINES.
Action:
>Dialing attemp 1 of 5.
Status:
>Dialing...
KLIK
KLIK
KLIK
LET'S SEE IF I REALLY AM A WALKING HOTSPOT.

GABRIELLE. I'M IN.

ASTRA? SEND ME A TEASE.

HOW CAN I TEASE A STORY BEFORE I'VE WRITTEN IT?

TAIL WAGGING THE DOG, GABRIELLE.

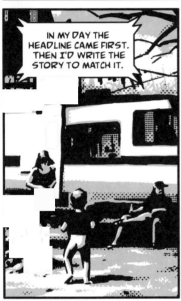

IN MY DAY THE HEADLINE CAME FIRST. THEN I'D WRITE THE STORY TO MATCH IT.

I ONCE WROTE A BLOODY GREAT HEADLINE ABOUT A VAMPIRE CULT, AND TO PROVE THE HEADLINE--

--HAD TO START THE CULT MYSELF.

YOU MAY WANT TO PREDICT NEWS, GABRIELLE, BUT I'D RATHER FIND THE REAL THING.

NO BALLS. THAT'S YOUR PROBLEM, ASTRA.

GO FIND THAT ALIEN. PRETEND TO BE AN ALIEN IF YOU HAVE TO.

I SUCKED A LOT OF BLOOD IN MY DAY. YOUR TURN.

WHAT IF THE HUMAN AND ALIEN LOVE EACH OTHER?

WHY EXPOSE THEM AND WRECK THEIR LIVES?

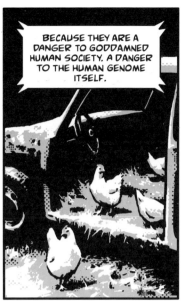

BECAUSE THEY ARE A DANGER TO GODDAMNED HUMAN SOCIETY. A DANGER TO THE HUMAN GENOME ITSELF.

THE PUBLIC HAS A RIGHT TO KNOW IF ALIENS ARE FUCKING HUMANS.

MAYBE NOT.

MAYBE THAT'S THE POINT OF THE ZONE. BEING ABLE TO SCREW WHATEVER YOU WANT.

YOU THINK SO, HONEY?

WHAT IF EVIL ALIEN BABIES POP OUT?

DON'T CALL ME HONEY.

SO LONG, BOSS.

MY TURN.

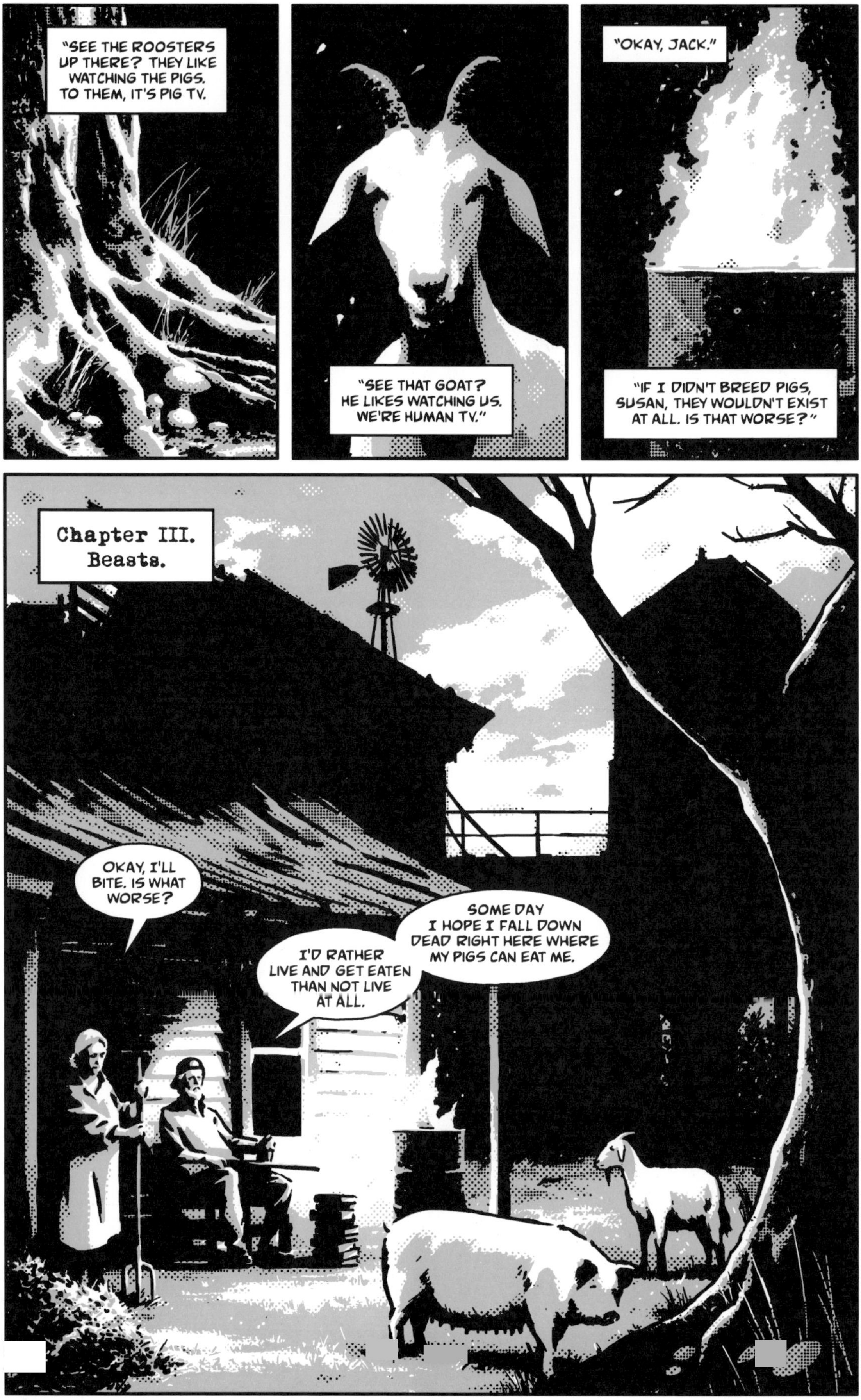
"SEE THE ROOSTERS UP THERE? THEY LIKE WATCHING THE PIGS. TO THEM, IT'S PIG TV.
"SEE THAT GOAT? HE LIKES WATCHING US. WE'RE HUMAN TV."
"OKAY, JACK."
"IF I DIDN'T BREED PIGS, SUSAN, THEY WOULDN'T EXIST AT ALL. IS THAT WORSE?"
Chapter III. Beasts.
OKAY, I'LL BITE. IS WHAT WORSE?
I'D RATHER LIVE AND GET EATEN THAN NOT LIVE AT ALL.
SOME DAY I HOPE I FALL DOWN DEAD RIGHT HERE WHERE MY PIGS CAN EAT ME.

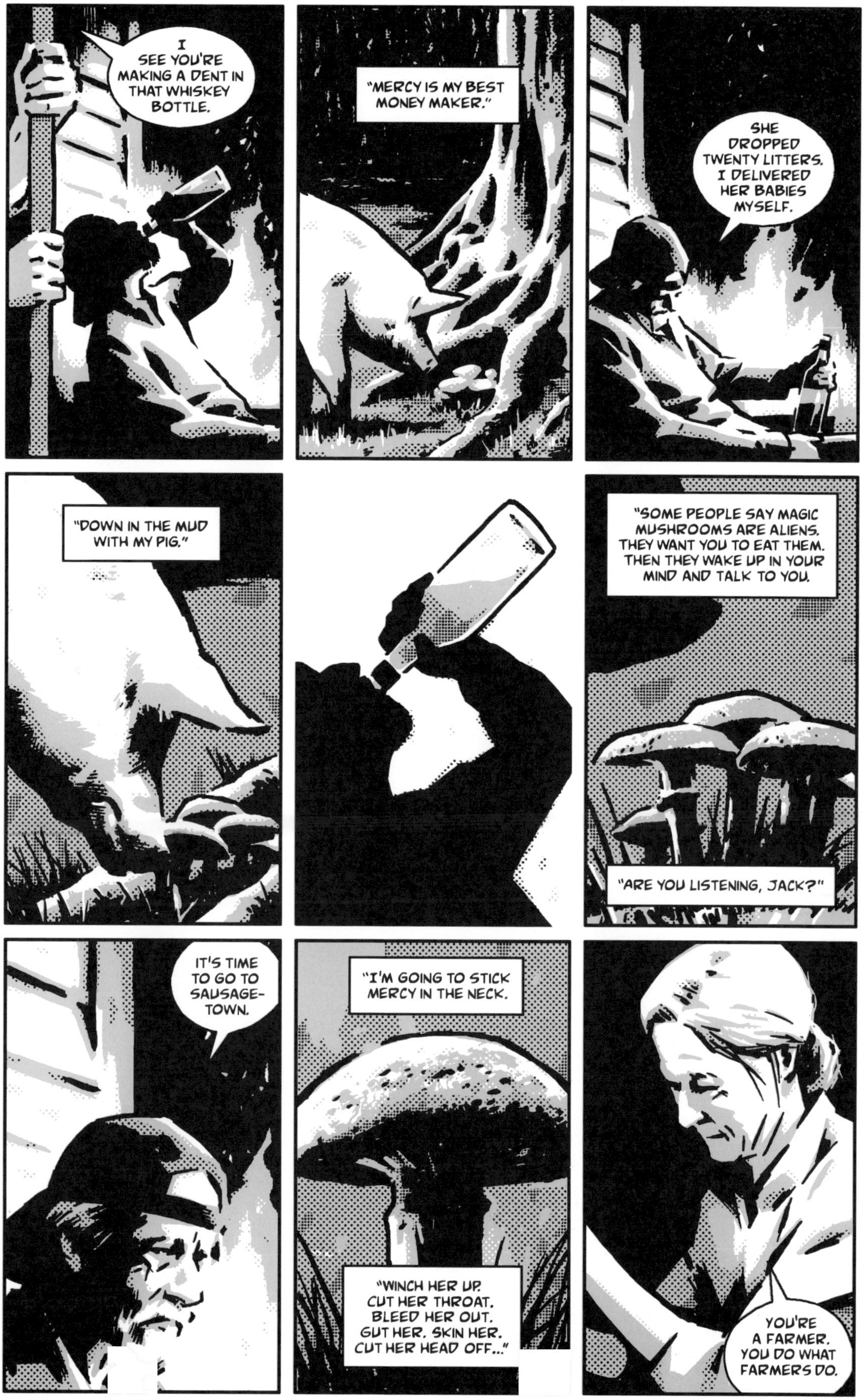

I SEE YOU'RE MAKING A DENT IN THAT WHISKEY BOTTLE.
"MERCY IS MY BEST MONEY MAKER."
SHE DROPPED TWENTY LITTERS. I DELIVERED HER BABIES MYSELF.
"DOWN IN THE MUD WITH MY PIG."
"SOME PEOPLE SAY MAGIC MUSHROOMS ARE ALIENS. THEY WANT YOU TO EAT THEM. THEN THEY WAKE UP IN YOUR MIND AND TALK TO YOU.
"ARE YOU LISTENING, JACK?"
IT'S TIME TO GO TO SAUSAGE-TOWN.
"I'M GOING TO STICK MERCY IN THE NECK.
"WINCH HER UP. CUT HER THROAT. BLEED HER OUT. GUT HER. SKIN HER. CUT HER HEAD OFF..."
YOU'RE A FARMER. YOU DO WHAT FARMERS DO.

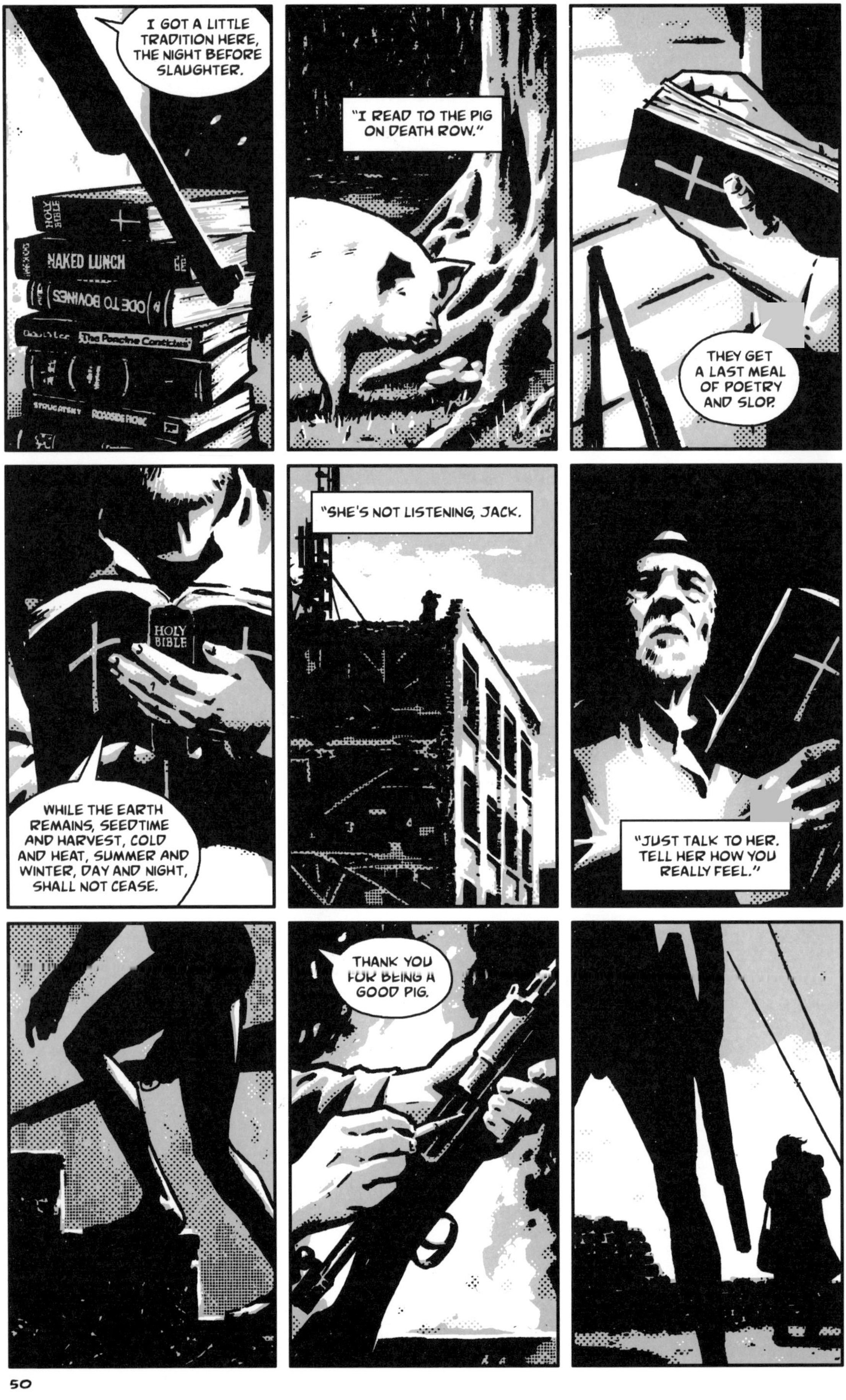
I GOT A LITTLE TRADITION HERE, THE NIGHT BEFORE SLAUGHTER.
HOLY BIBLE
NAKED LUNCH
ODE TO BOVINES
The Porcine Canticles
ROADSIDE PICNIC
"I READ TO THE PIG ON DEATH ROW."
THEY GET A LAST MEAL OF POETRY AND SLOP.
HOLY BIBLE
WHILE THE EARTH REMAINS, SEEDTIME AND HARVEST, COLD AND HEAT, SUMMER AND WINTER, DAY AND NIGHT, SHALL NOT CEASE.
"SHE'S NOT LISTENING, JACK.
"JUST TALK TO HER. TELL HER HOW YOU REALLY FEEL."
THANK YOU FOR BEING A GOOD PIG.

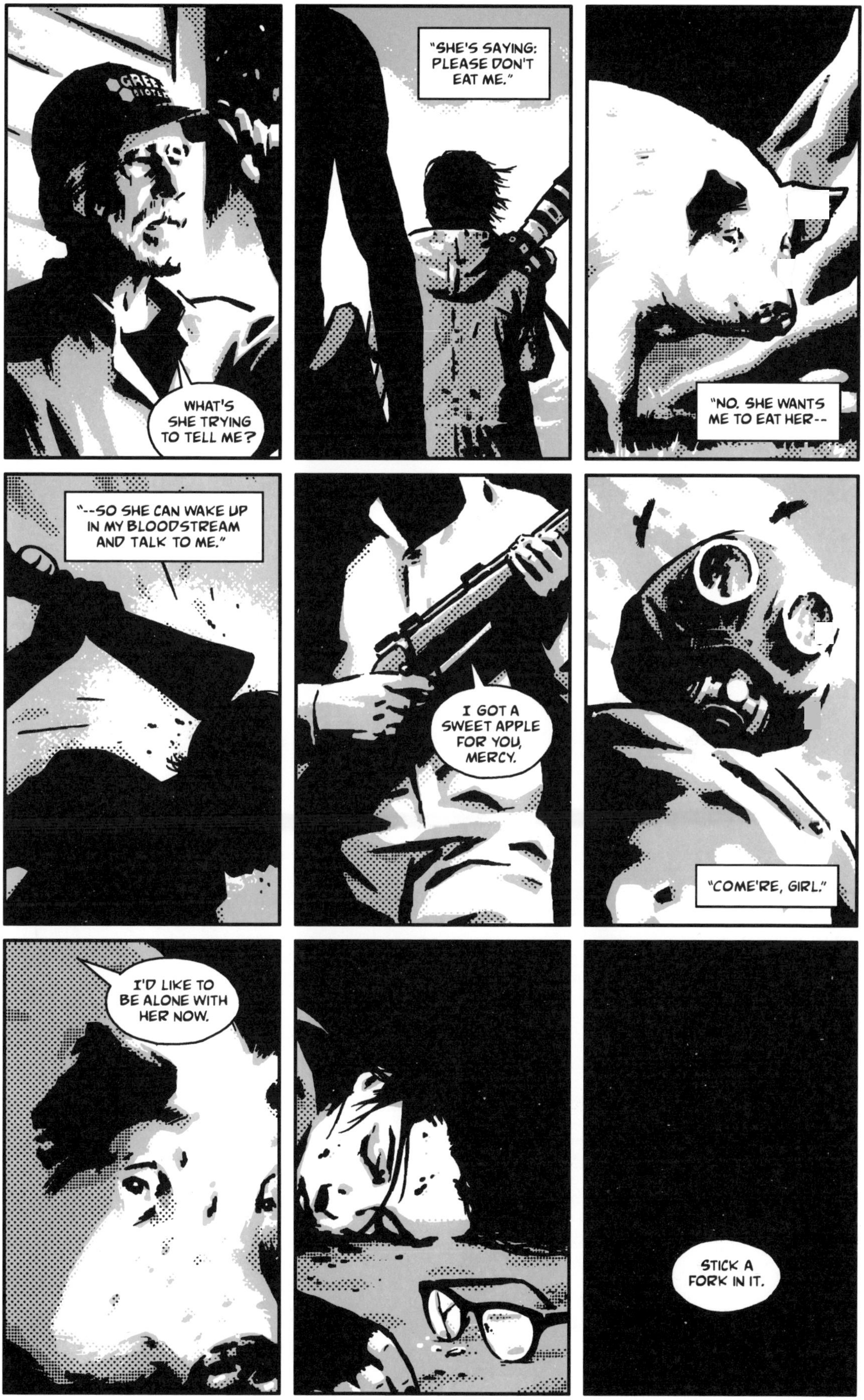
WHAT'S SHE TRYING TO TELL ME?
"SHE'S SAYING: PLEASE DON'T EAT ME."
"NO. SHE WANTS ME TO EAT HER--
"--SO SHE CAN WAKE UP IN MY BLOODSTREAM AND TALK TO ME."
I GOT A SWEET APPLE FOR YOU, MERCY.
"COME'RE, GIRL."
I'D LIKE TO BE ALONE WITH HER NOW.
STICK A FORK IN IT.

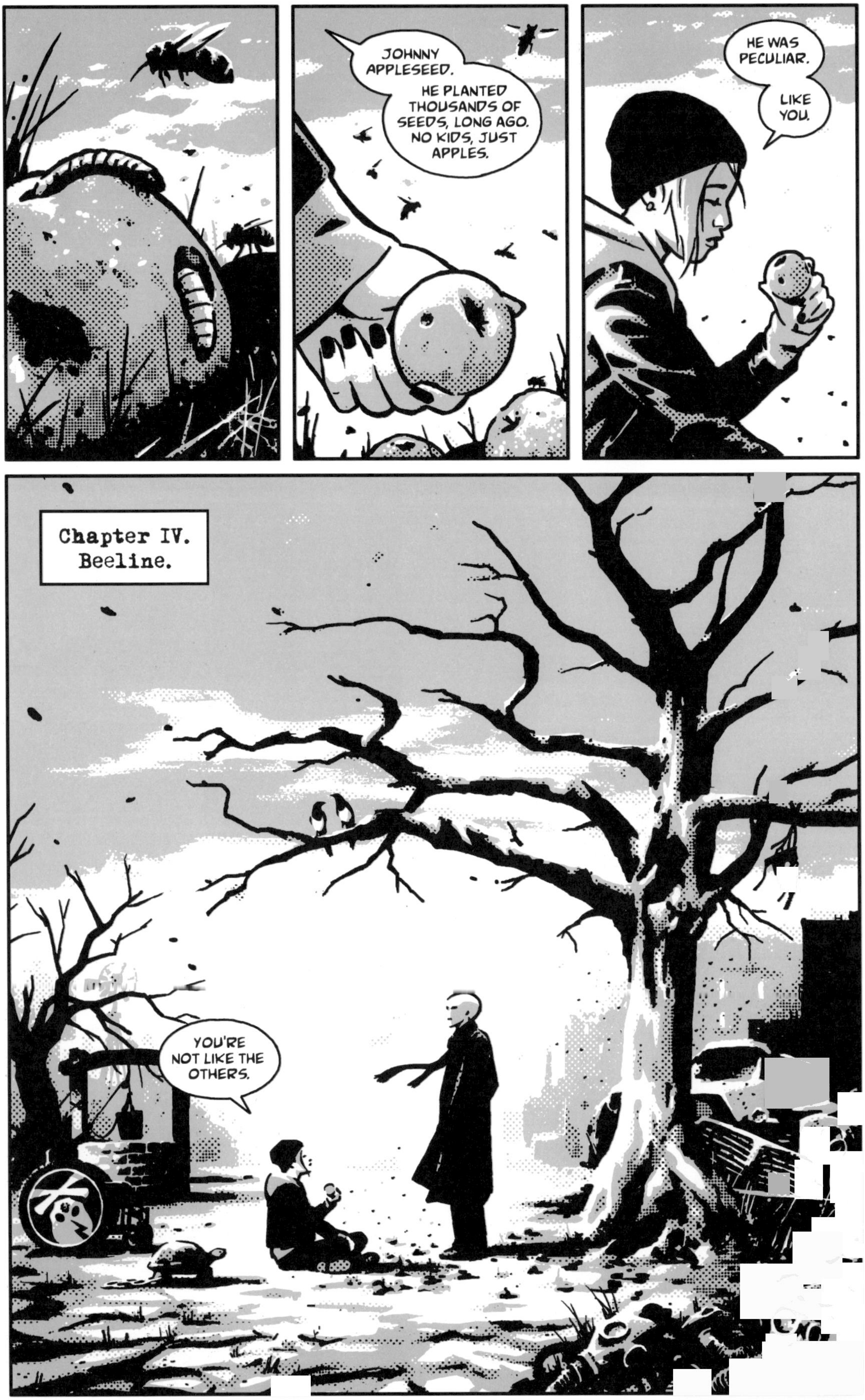
JOHNNY APPLESEED.
HE PLANTED THOUSANDS OF SEEDS, LONG AGO. NO KIDS, JUST APPLES.
HE WAS PECULIAR.
LIKE YOU.
Chapter IV. Beeline.
YOU'RE NOT LIKE THE OTHERS.

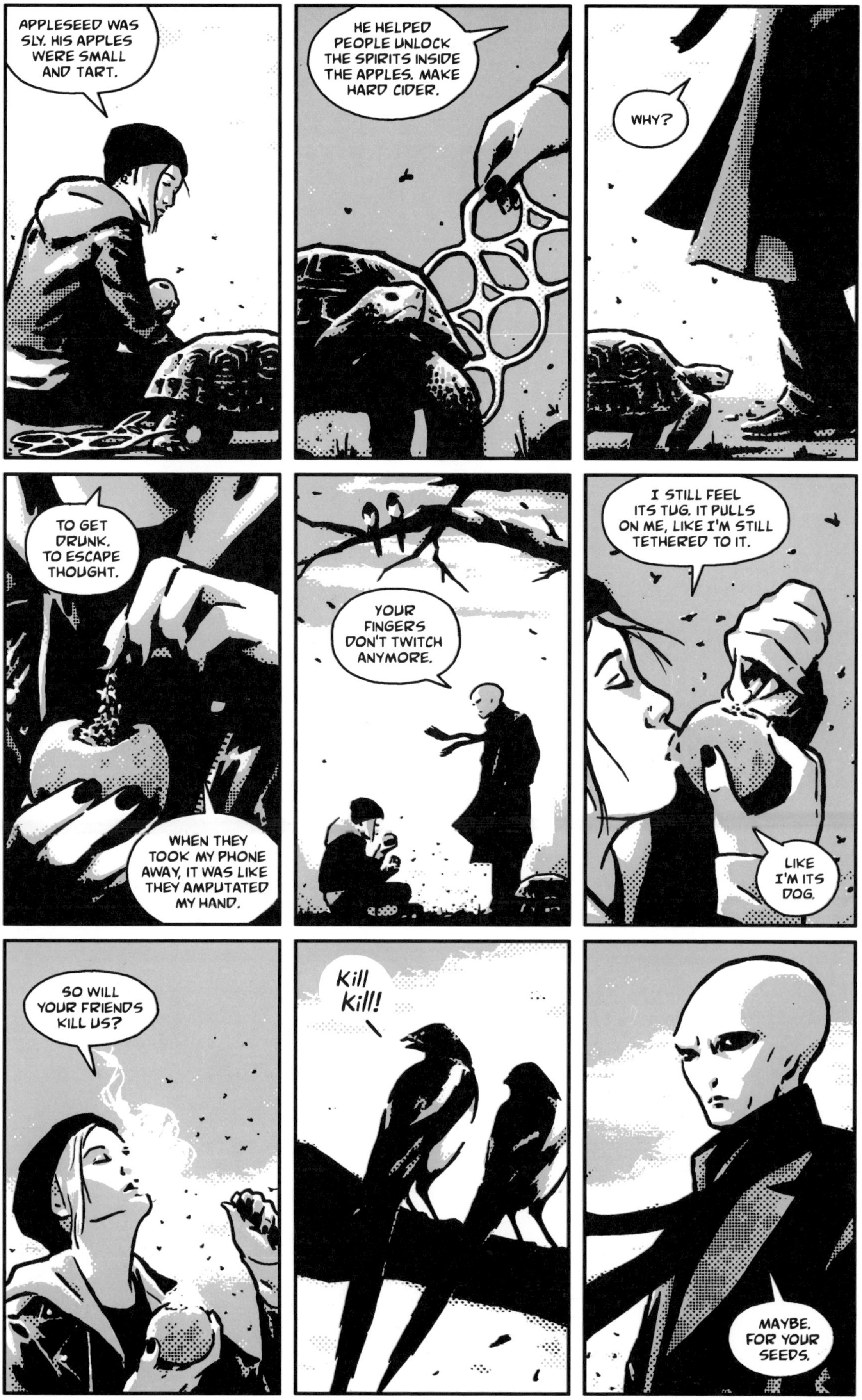
APPLESEED WAS SLY. HIS APPLES WERE SMALL AND TART.
HE HELPED PEOPLE UNLOCK THE SPIRITS INSIDE THE APPLES. MAKE HARD CIDER.
WHY?
TO GET DRUNK. TO ESCAPE THOUGHT.
WHEN THEY TOOK MY PHONE AWAY, IT WAS LIKE THEY AMPUTATED MY HAND.
YOUR FINGERS DON'T TWITCH ANYMORE.
I STILL FEEL ITS TUG. IT PULLS ON ME, LIKE I'M STILL TETHERED TO IT.
LIKE I'M ITS DOG.
SO WILL YOUR FRIENDS KILL US?
Kill Kill!
MAYBE. FOR YOUR SEEDS.

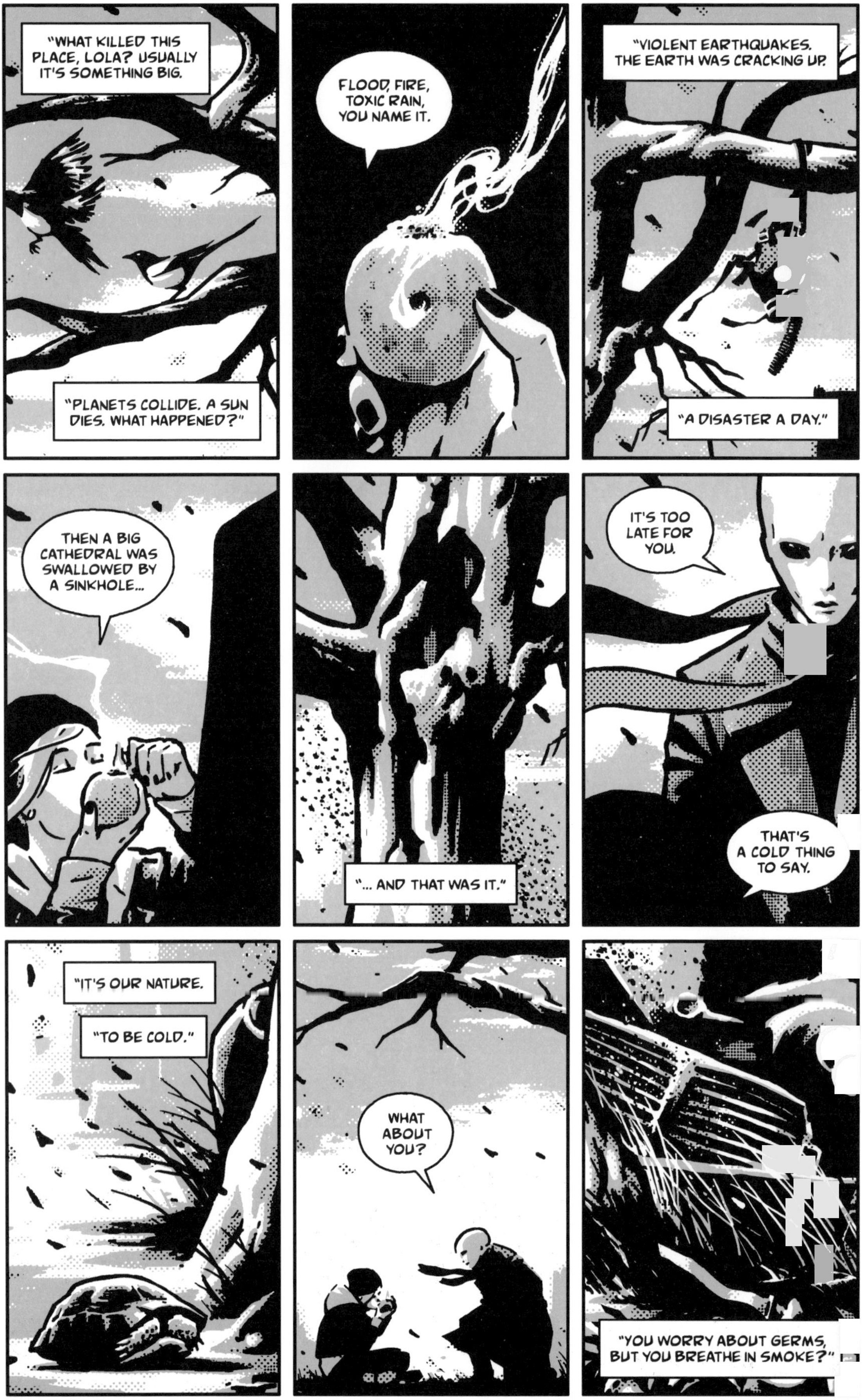
"WHAT KILLED THIS PLACE, LOLA? USUALLY IT'S SOMETHING BIG.
"PLANETS COLLIDE. A SUN DIES. WHAT HAPPENED?"
FLOOD, FIRE, TOXIC RAIN, YOU NAME IT.
"VIOLENT EARTHQUAKES. THE EARTH WAS CRACKING UP.
"A DISASTER A DAY."
THEN A BIG CATHEDRAL WAS SWALLOWED BY A SINKHOLE...
"... AND THAT WAS IT."
IT'S TOO LATE FOR YOU.
THAT'S A COLD THING TO SAY.
"IT'S OUR NATURE.
"TO BE COLD."
WHAT ABOUT YOU?
"YOU WORRY ABOUT GERMS, BUT YOU BREATHE IN SMOKE?"

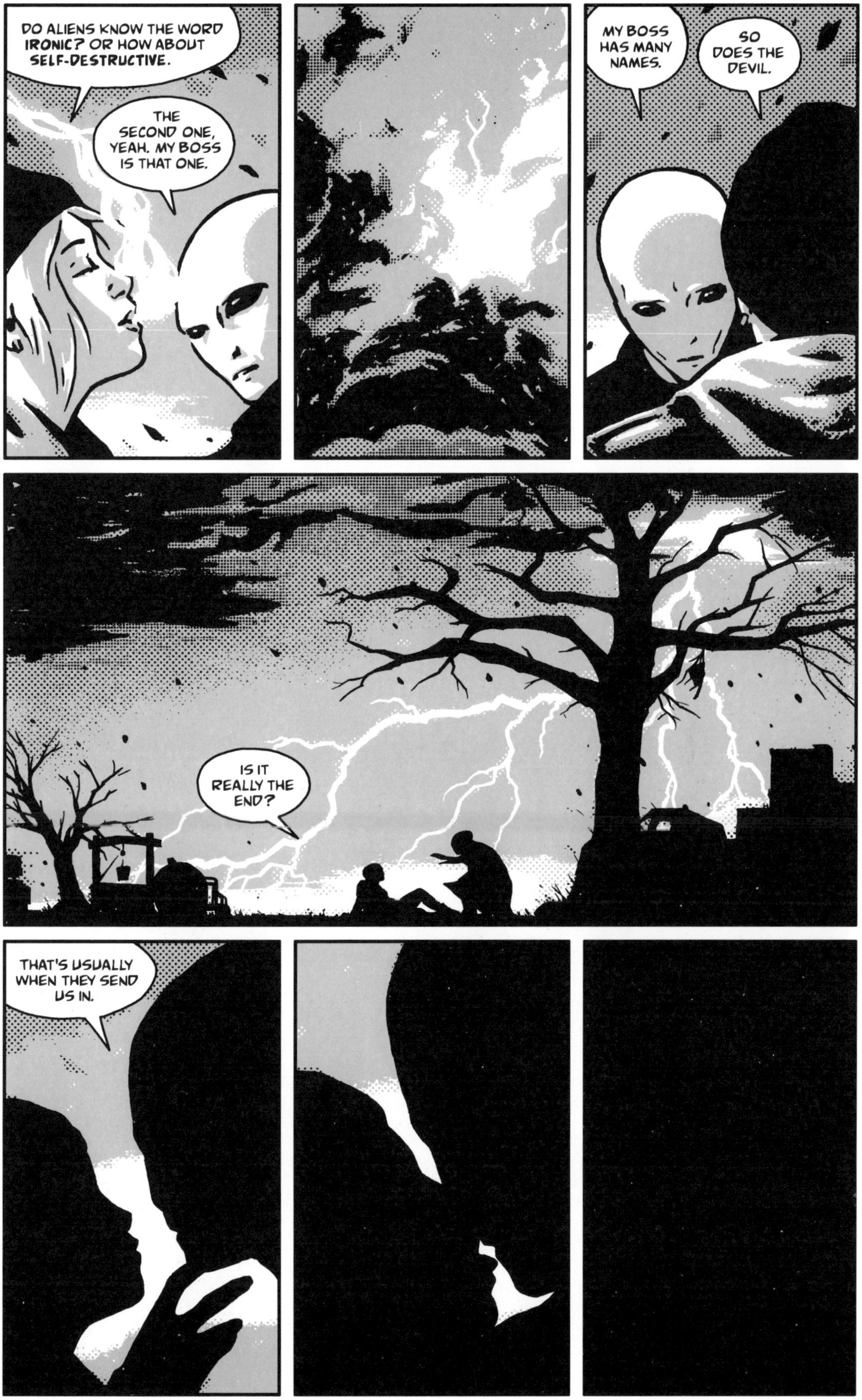
DO ALIENS KNOW THE WORD IRONIC? OR HOW ABOUT SELF-DESTRUCTIVE.
THE SECOND ONE, YEAH. MY BOSS IS THAT ONE.
MY BOSS HAS MANY NAMES.
SO DOES THE DEVIL.
IS IT REALLY THE END?
THAT'S USUALLY WHEN THEY SEND US IN.

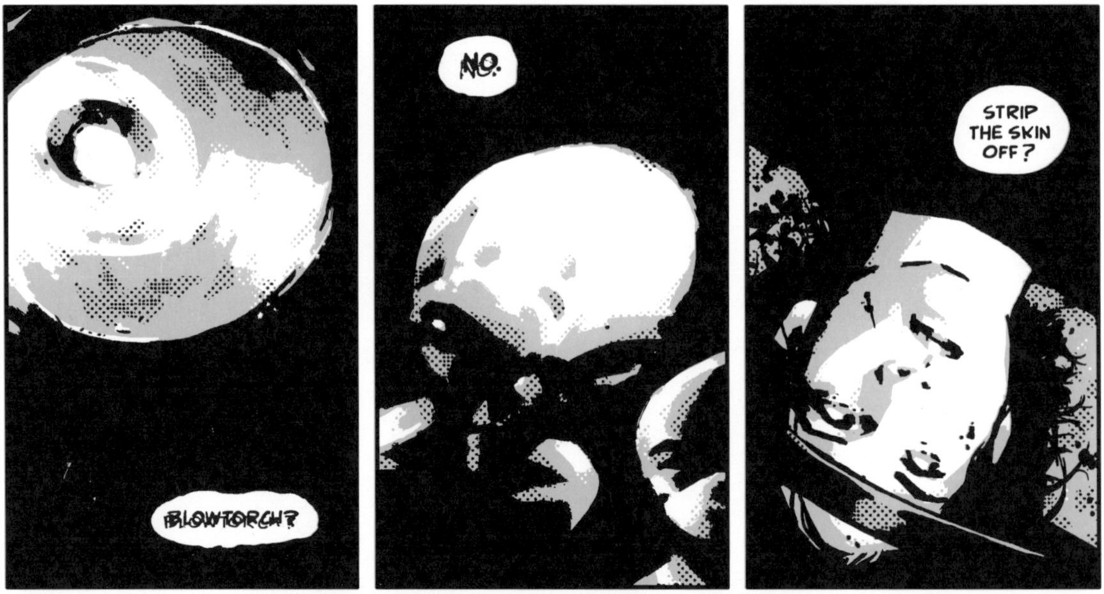
BLOWTORCH?
NO.
STRIP THE SKIN OFF?

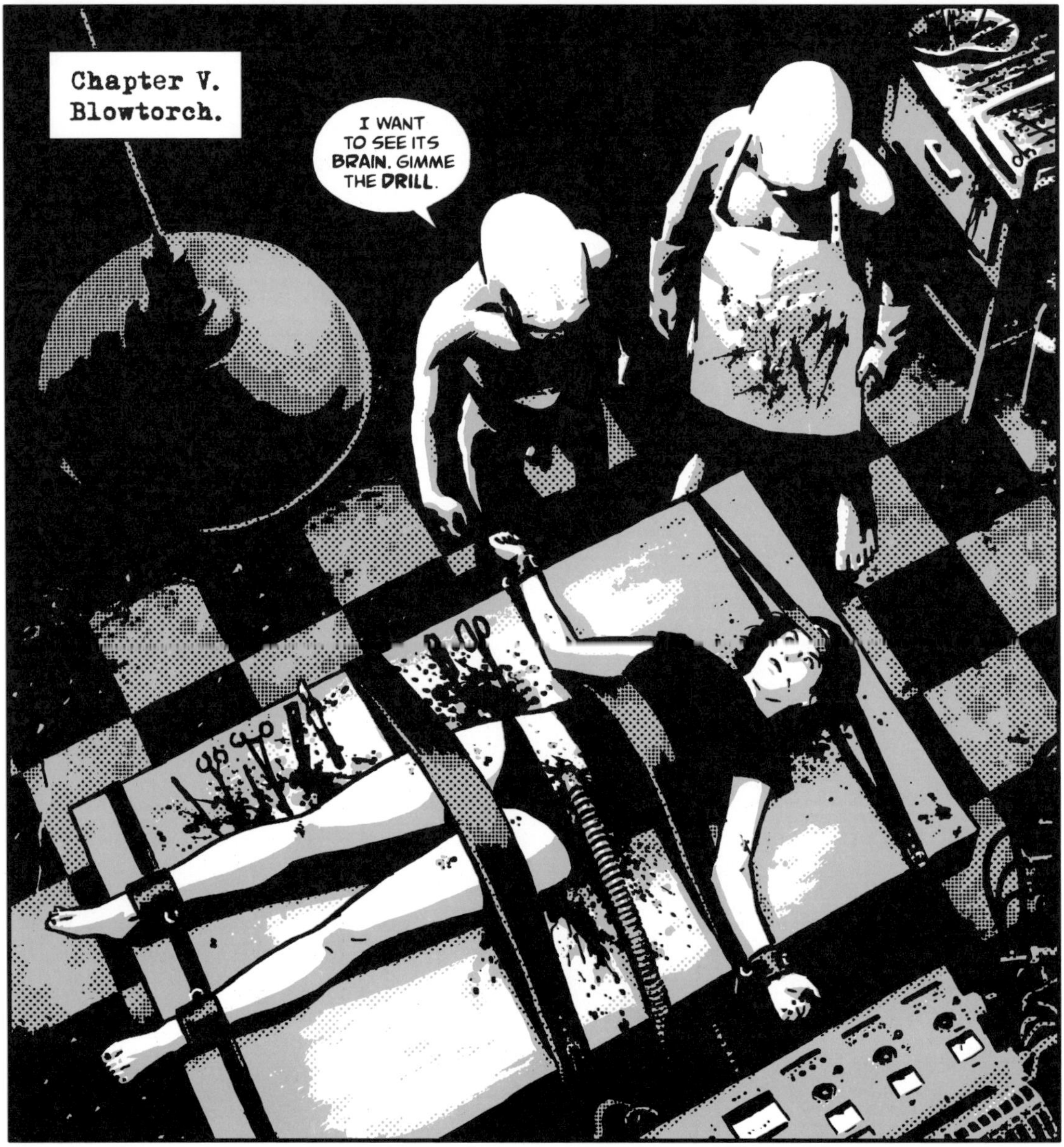
Chapter V.
Blowtorch.
I WANT TO SEE ITS BRAIN. GIMME THE DRILL.

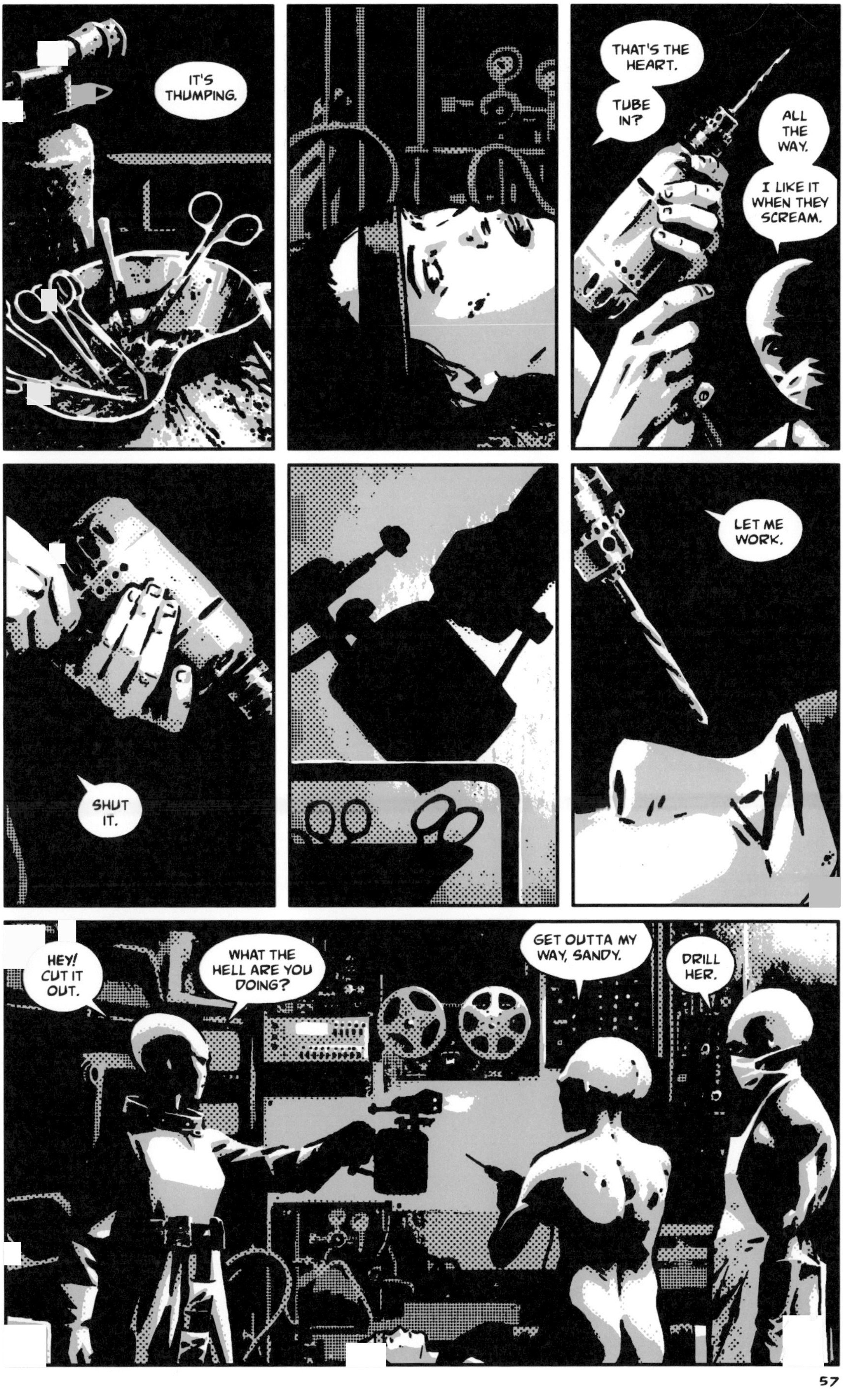
IT'S THUMPING.
THAT'S THE HEART.
TUBE IN?
ALL THE WAY.
I LIKE IT WHEN THEY SCREAM.
SHUT IT.
LET ME WORK.
HEY! CUT IT OUT.
WHAT THE HELL ARE YOU DOING?
GET OUTTA MY WAY, SANDY.
DRILL HER.

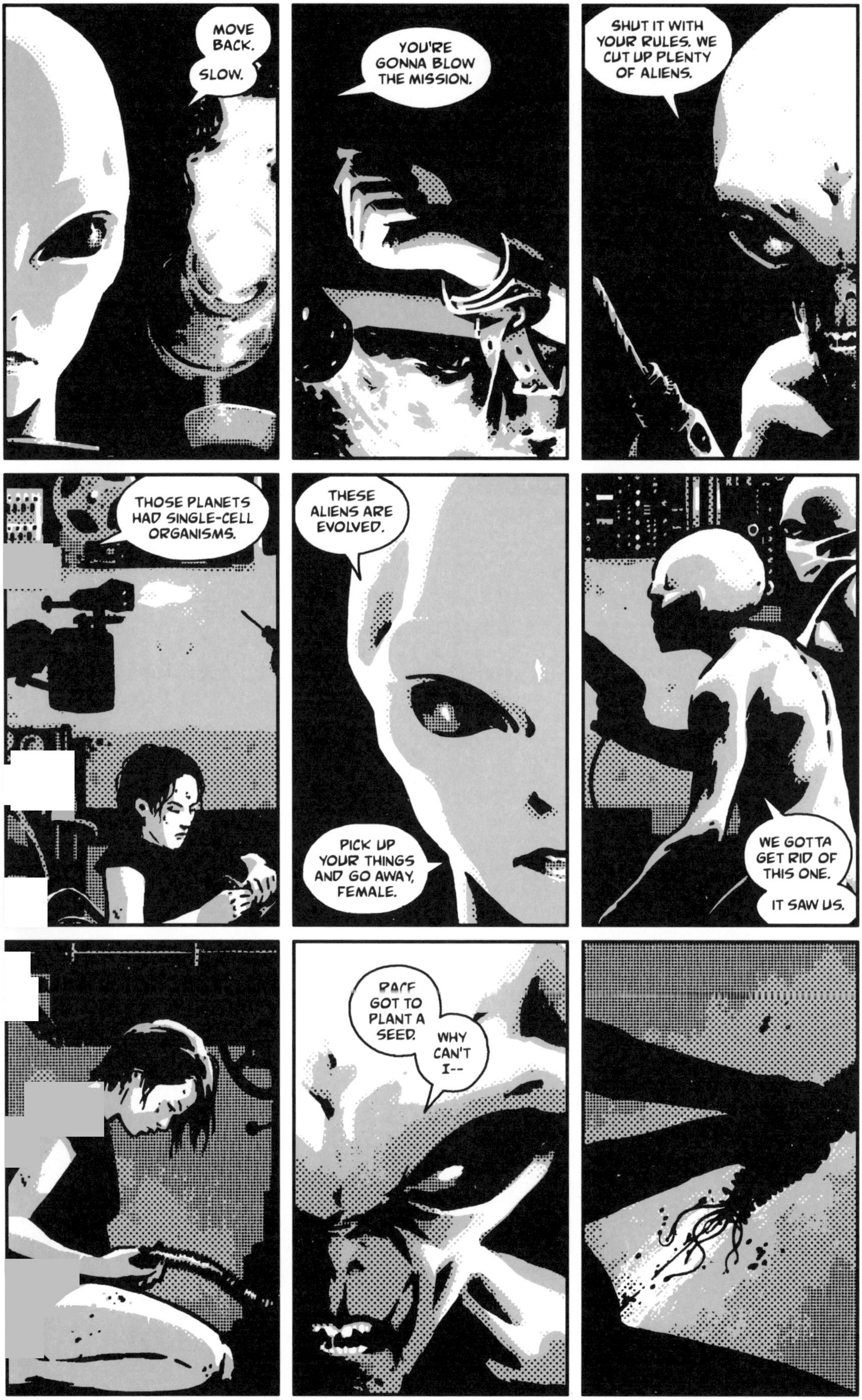
MOVE BACK.
SLOW.
YOU'RE GONNA BLOW THE MISSION.
SHUT IT WITH YOUR RULES. WE CUT UP PLENTY OF ALIENS.
THOSE PLANETS HAD SINGLE-CELL ORGANISMS.
THESE ALIENS ARE EVOLVED.
PICK UP YOUR THINGS AND GO AWAY, FEMALE.
WE GOTTA GET RID OF THIS ONE.
IT SAW US.
RACE GOT TO PLANT A SEED.
WHY CAN'T I--

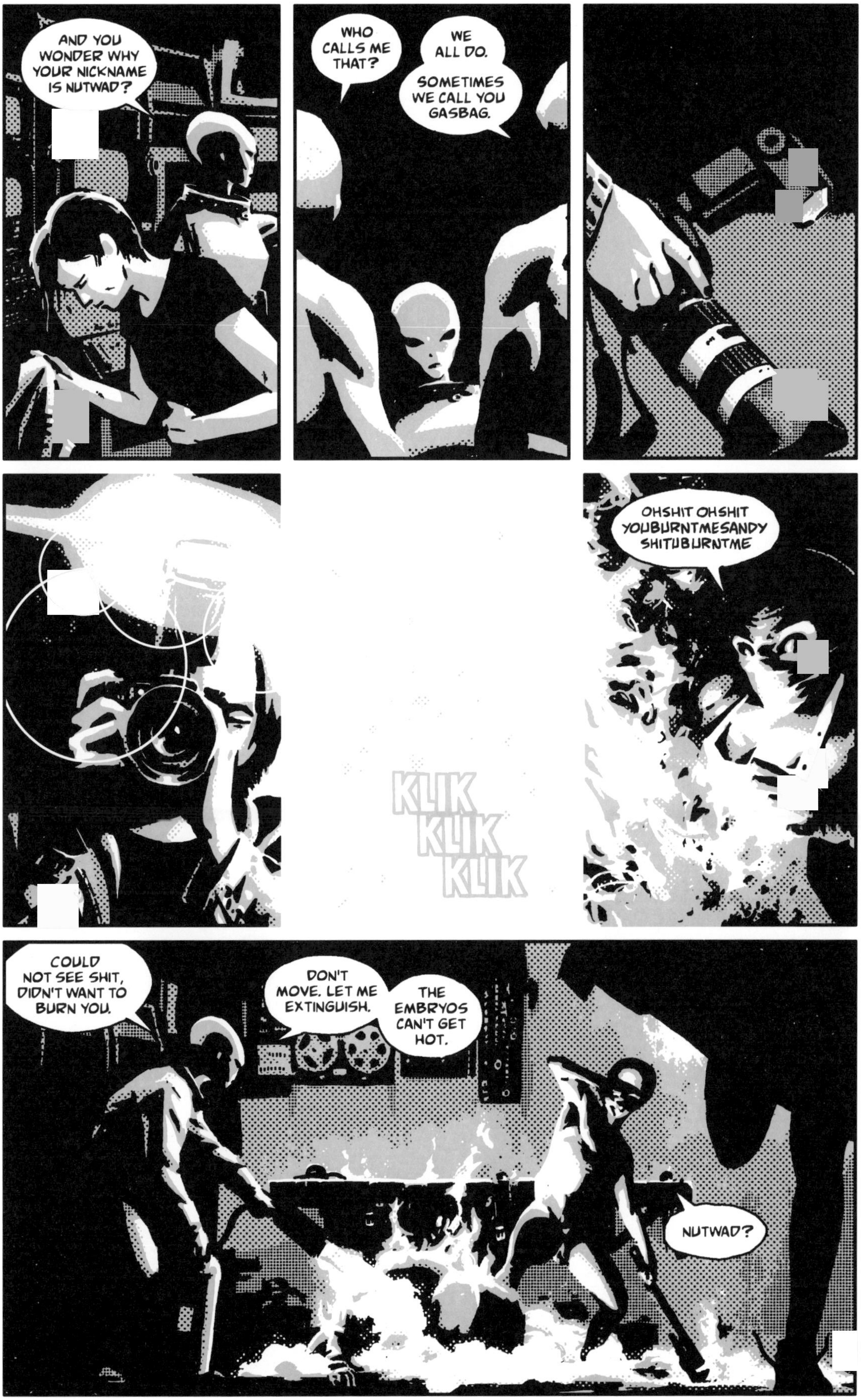
AND YOU WONDER WHY YOUR NICKNAME IS NUTWAD?
WHO CALLS ME THAT?
WE ALL DO.
SOMETIMES WE CALL YOU GASBAG.
KLIK KLIK KLIK
OHSHIT OHSHIT YOUBURNTMESANDY SHITUBURNTME
COULD NOT SEE SHIT, DIDN'T WANT TO BURN YOU.
DON'T MOVE. LET ME EXTINGUISH.
THE EMBRYOS CAN'T GET HOT.
NUTWAD?

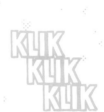

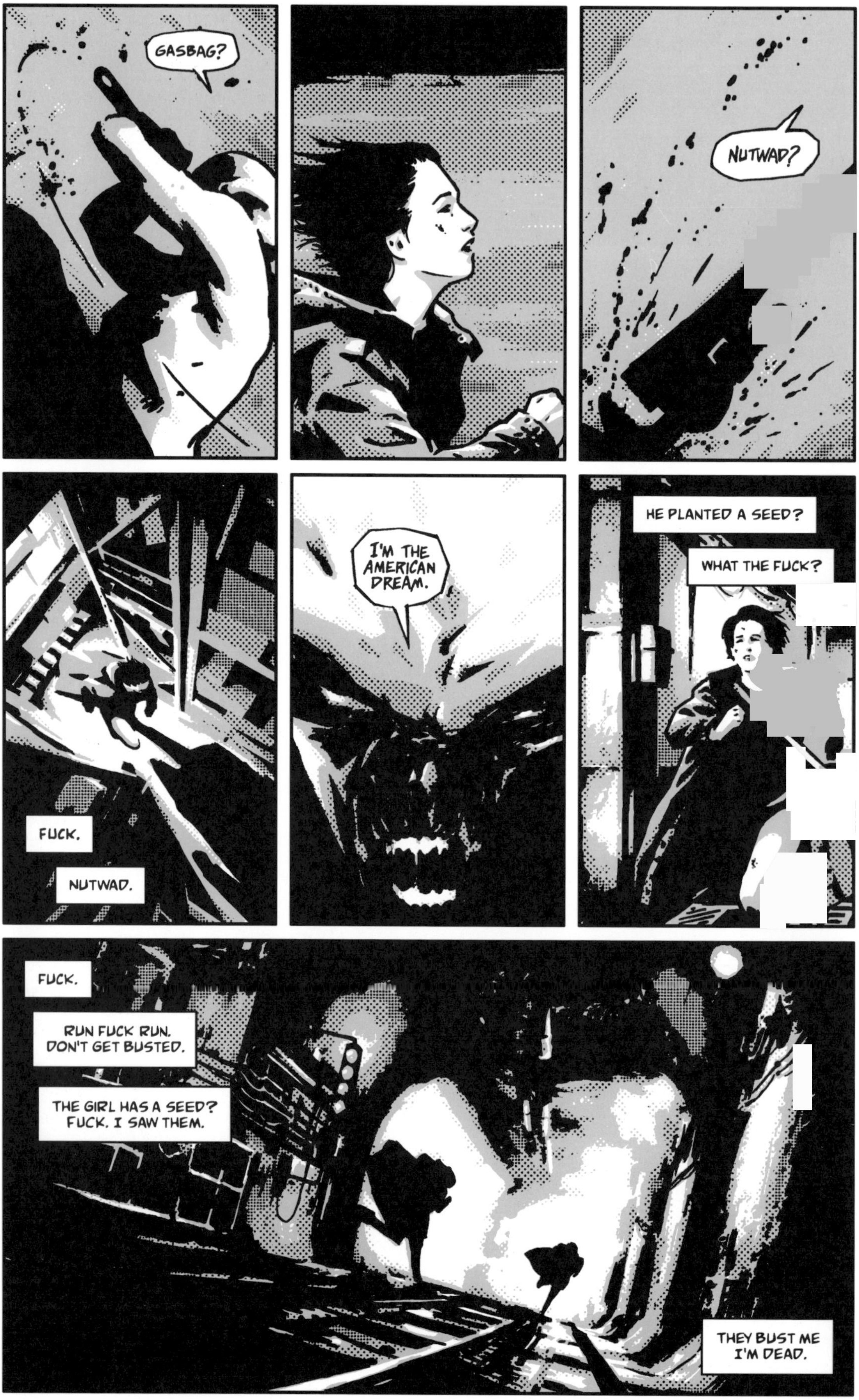
GASBAG?
NUTWAD?
FUCK.
NUTWAD.
I'M THE AMERICAN DREAM.
HE PLANTED A SEED?
WHAT THE FUCK?
FUCK.
RUN FUCK RUN. DON'T GET BUSTED.
THE GIRL HAS A SEED? FUCK. I SAW THEM.
THEY BUST ME I'M DEAD.

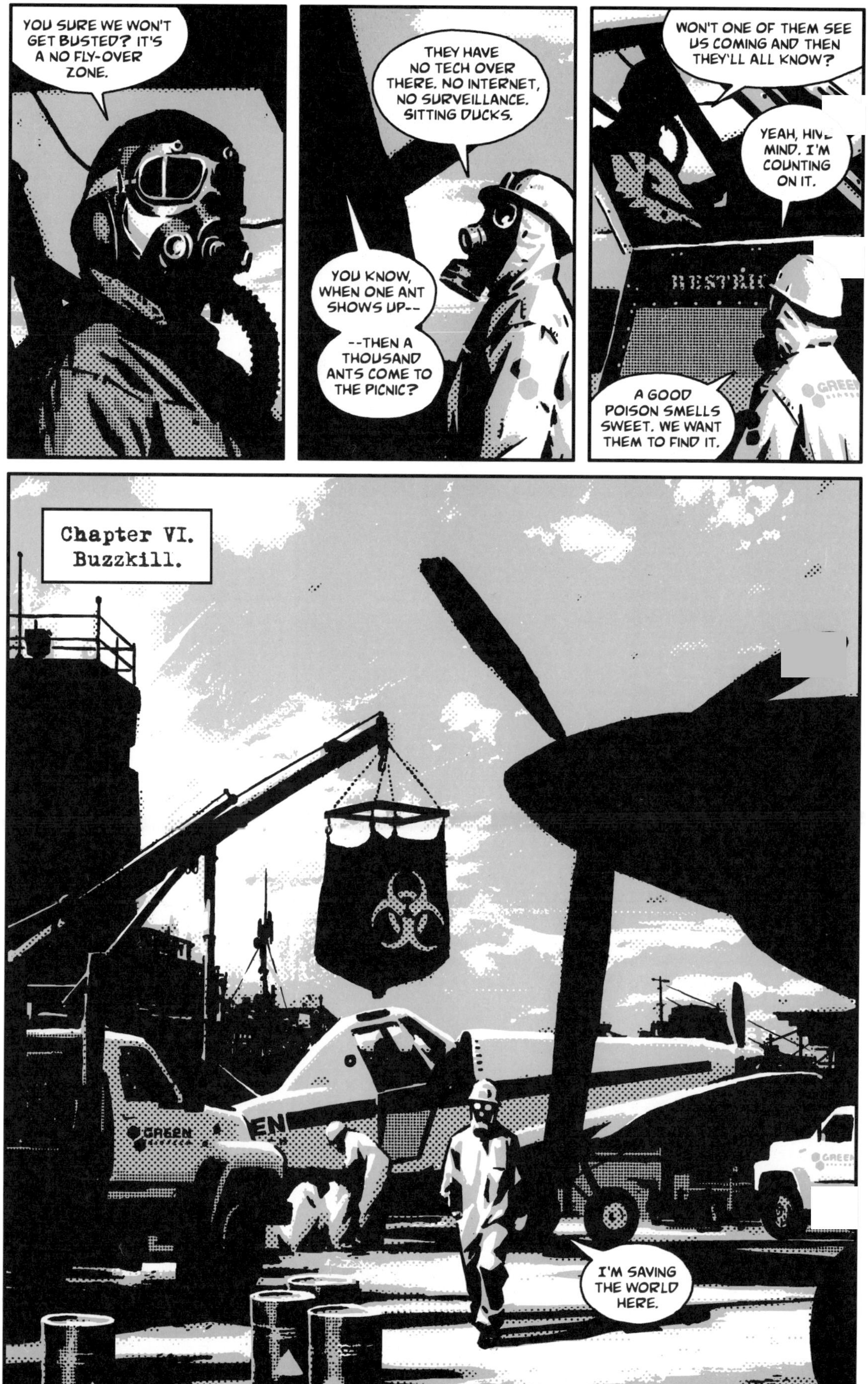
YOU SURE WE WON'T GET BUSTED? IT'S A NO FLY-OVER ZONE.
THEY HAVE NO TECH OVER THERE. NO INTERNET, NO SURVEILLANCE. SITTING DUCKS.
YOU KNOW, WHEN ONE ANT SHOWS UP--
--THEN A THOUSAND ANTS COME TO THE PICNIC?
WON'T ONE OF THEM SEE US COMING AND THEN THEY'LL ALL KNOW?
YEAH, HIVE MIND. I'M COUNTING ON IT.
A GOOD POISON SMELLS SWEET. WE WANT THEM TO FIND IT.
Chapter VI.
Buzzkill.
I'M SAVING THE WORLD HERE.

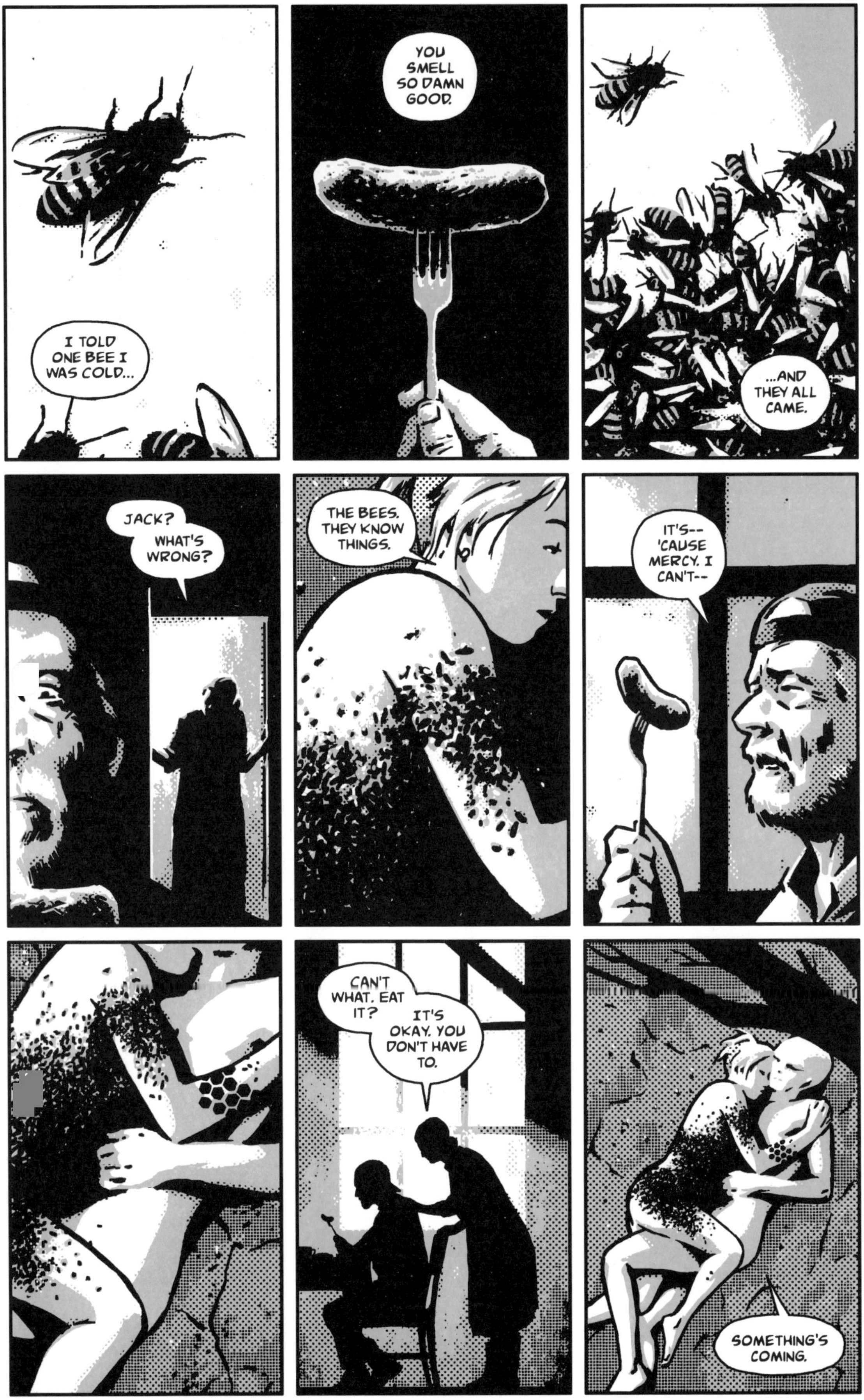
I TOLD ONE BEE I WAS COLD...
YOU SMELL SO DAMN GOOD.
...AND THEY ALL CAME.
JACK? WHAT'S WRONG?
THE BEES. THEY KNOW THINGS.
IT'S-- 'CAUSE MERCY. I CAN'T--
CAN'T WHAT. EAT IT?
IT'S OKAY. YOU DON'T HAVE TO.
SOMETHING'S COMING.

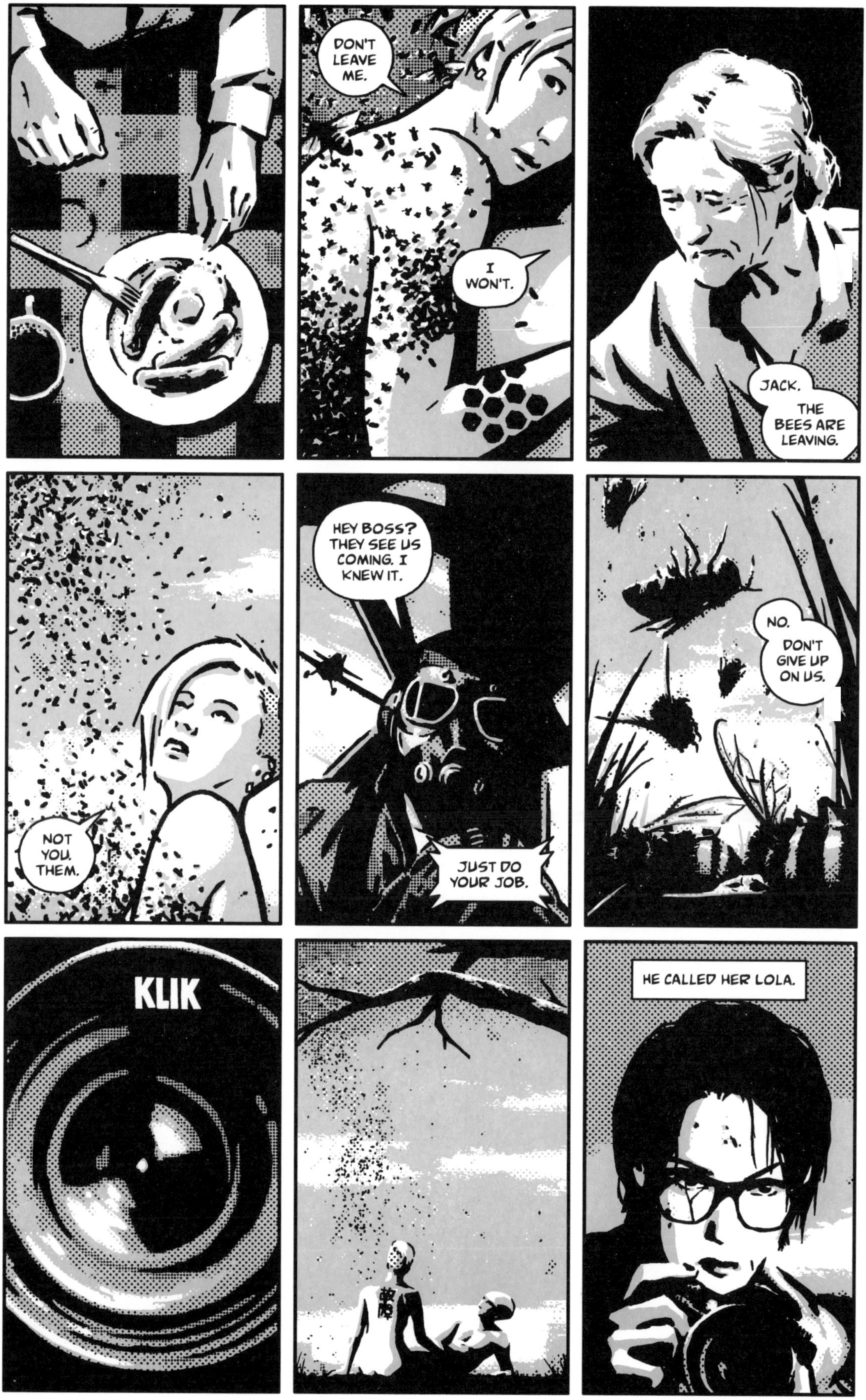
DON'T LEAVE ME.
I WON'T.
JACK.
THE BEES ARE LEAVING.
NOT YOU, THEM.
HEY BOSS? THEY SEE US COMING. I KNEW IT.
JUST DO YOUR JOB.
NO.
DON'T GIVE UP ON US.
KLIK
HE CALLED HER LOLA.

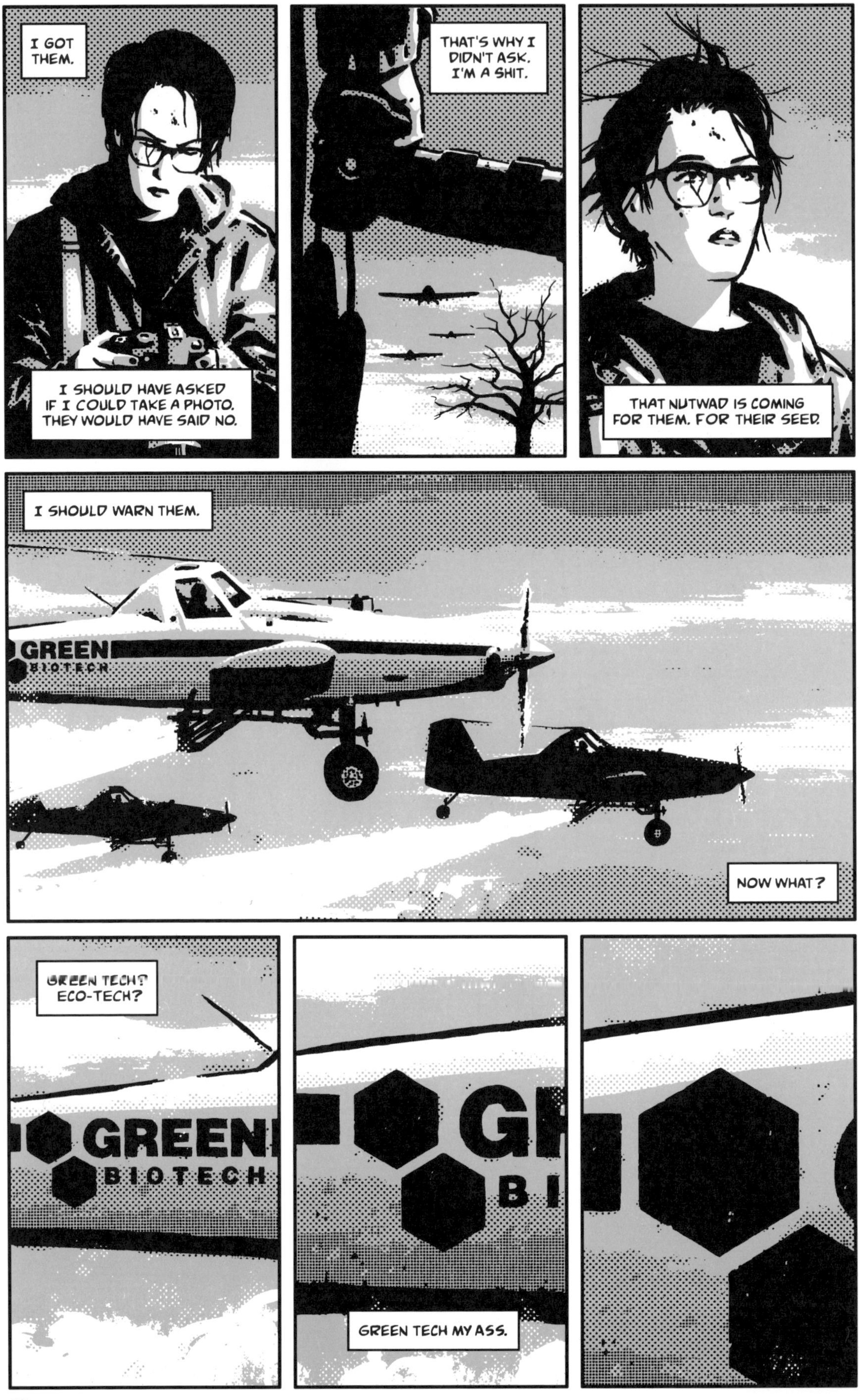
I GOT THEM.
I SHOULD HAVE ASKED IF I COULD TAKE A PHOTO. THEY WOULD HAVE SAID NO.
THAT'S WHY I DIDN'T ASK. I'M A SHIT.
THAT NUTWAD IS COMING FOR THEM. FOR THEIR SEED.
I SHOULD WARN THEM.
GREEN BIOTECH
NOW WHAT?
GREEN TECH? ECO-TECH?
GREEN BIOTECH
GREEN TECH MY ASS.

[3. Invitation to a Shooting.]

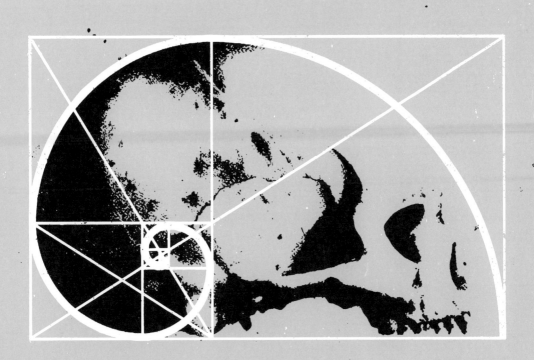

Fig.3

"There is nothing as
eloquent as a
rattlesnake's tail."

- Navajo proverb

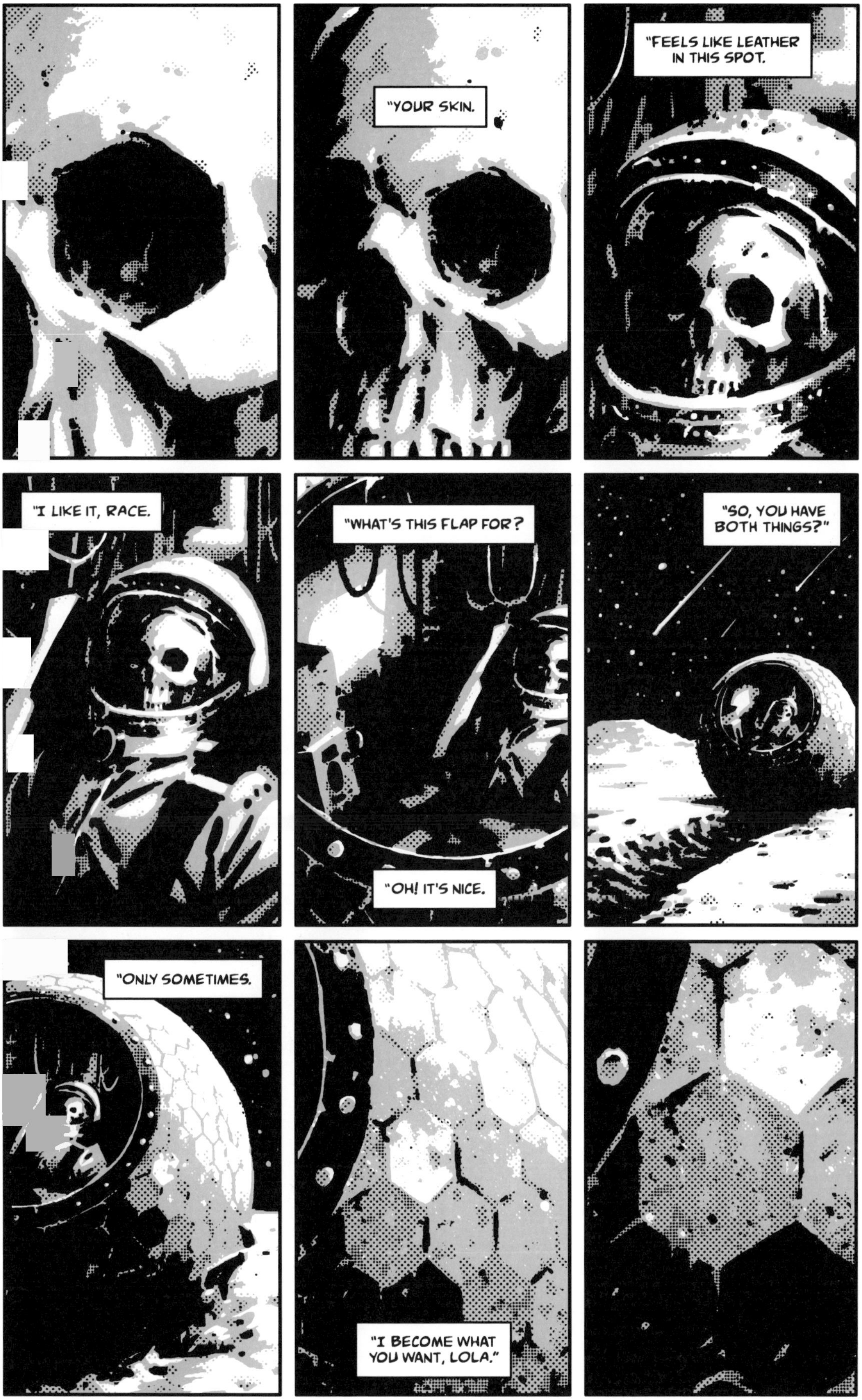
"YOUR SKIN.
"FEELS LIKE LEATHER IN THIS SPOT.
"I LIKE IT, RACE.
"WHAT'S THIS FLAP FOR?
"OH! IT'S NICE.
"SO, YOU HAVE BOTH THINGS?"
"ONLY SOMETIMES.
"I BECOME WHAT YOU WANT, LOLA."

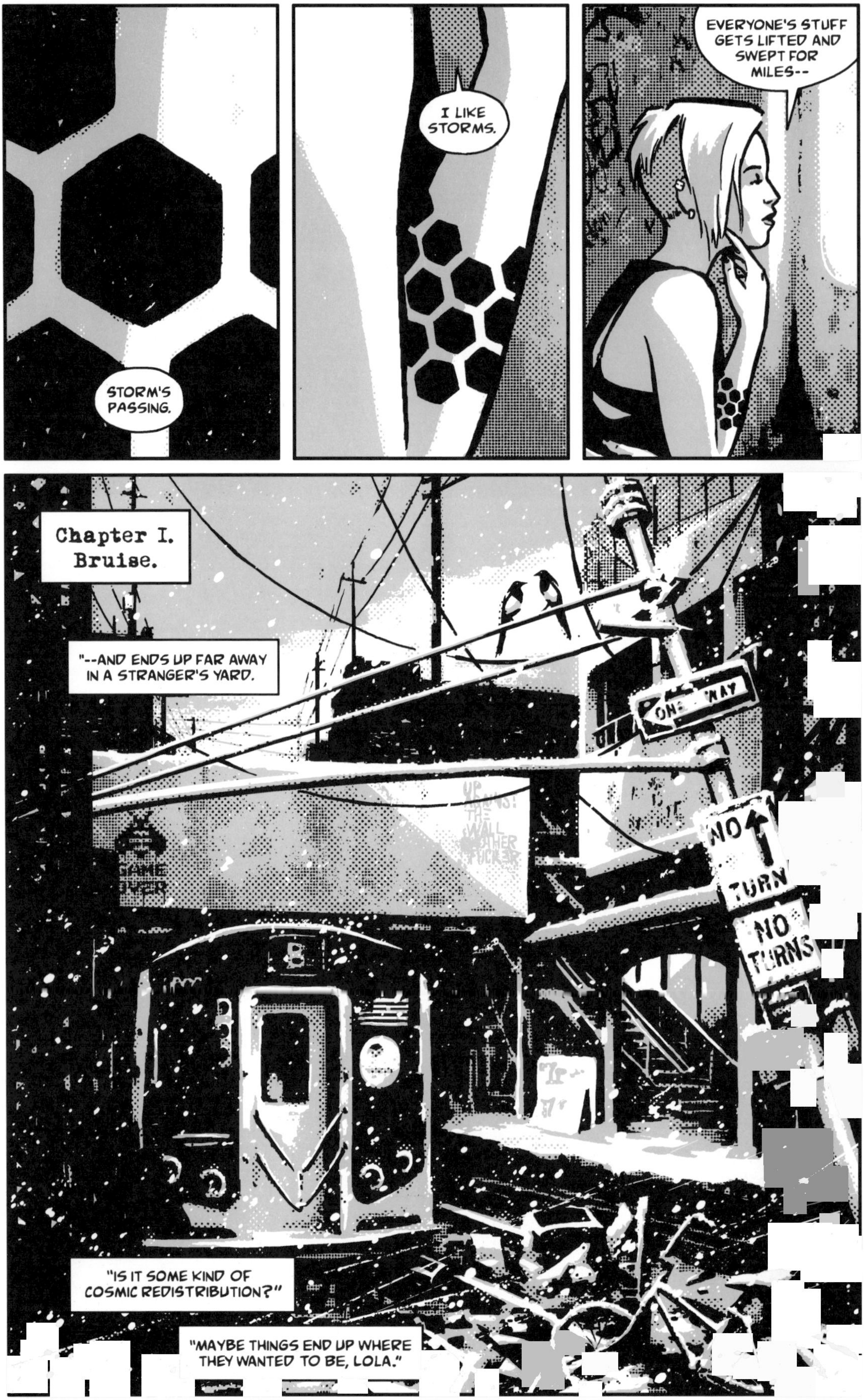
STORM'S PASSING.
I LIKE STORMS.
EVERYONE'S STUFF GETS LIFTED AND SWEPT FOR MILES--
Chapter I. Bruise.
"--AND ENDS UP FAR AWAY IN A STRANGER'S YARD.
ONE WAY
NO TURN
NO TURNS
GAME OVER
"IS IT SOME KIND OF COSMIC REDISTRIBUTION?"
"MAYBE THINGS END UP WHERE THEY WANTED TO BE, LOLA."

THAT SPRAY FROM THE PLANES MESSED WITH THE BEES.

DIDN'T HURT US.

IT HURT ME WHEN THE BEES DIED.

DIDN'T YOU FEEL IT?

I DON'T FEEL MUCH.

WE'RE NOT USED TO TALKING.

MOST PLACES WE'RE SENT, THE LIFE FORMS CAN'T TALK.

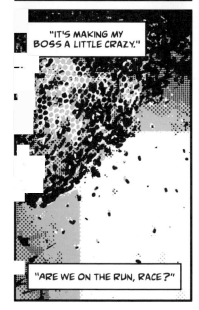

"IT'S MAKING MY BOSS A LITTLE CRAZY."

"ARE WE ON THE RUN, RACE?"

IT'S TOO LATE. THEY'RE HERE.

"DON'T LET THEM TOUCH ME."

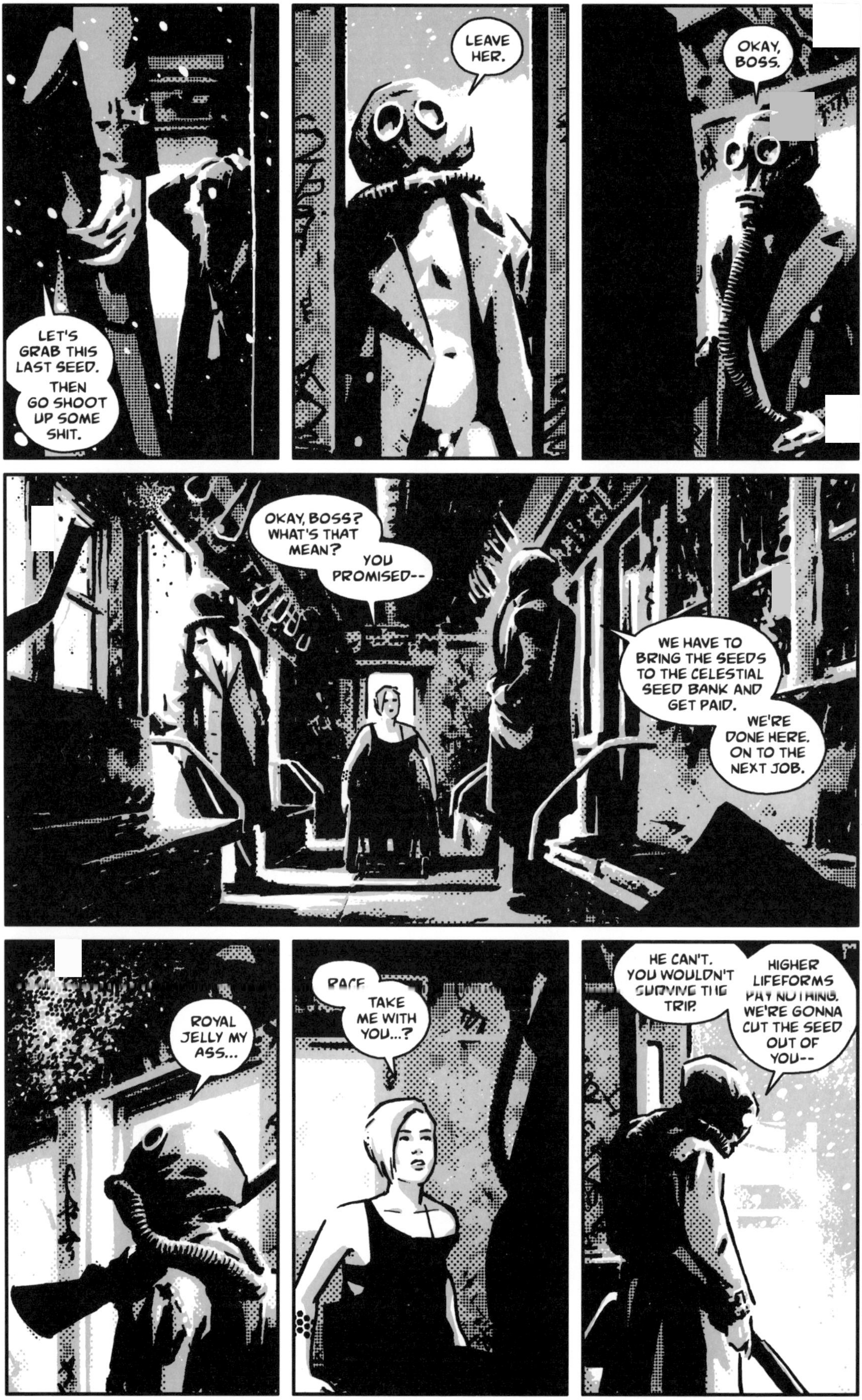

LET'S GRAB THIS LAST SEED.
THEN GO SHOOT UP SOME SHIT.
LEAVE HER.
OKAY, BOSS.
OKAY, BOSS? WHAT'S THAT MEAN?
YOU PROMISED--
WE HAVE TO BRING THE SEEDS TO THE CELESTIAL SEED BANK AND GET PAID.
WE'RE DONE HERE. ON TO THE NEXT JOB.
ROYAL JELLY MY ASS...
RACE
TAKE ME WITH YOU...?
HE CAN'T. YOU WOULDN'T SURVIVE THE TRIP.
HIGHER LIFEFORMS PAY NOTHING. WE'RE GONNA CUT THE SEED OUT OF YOU--

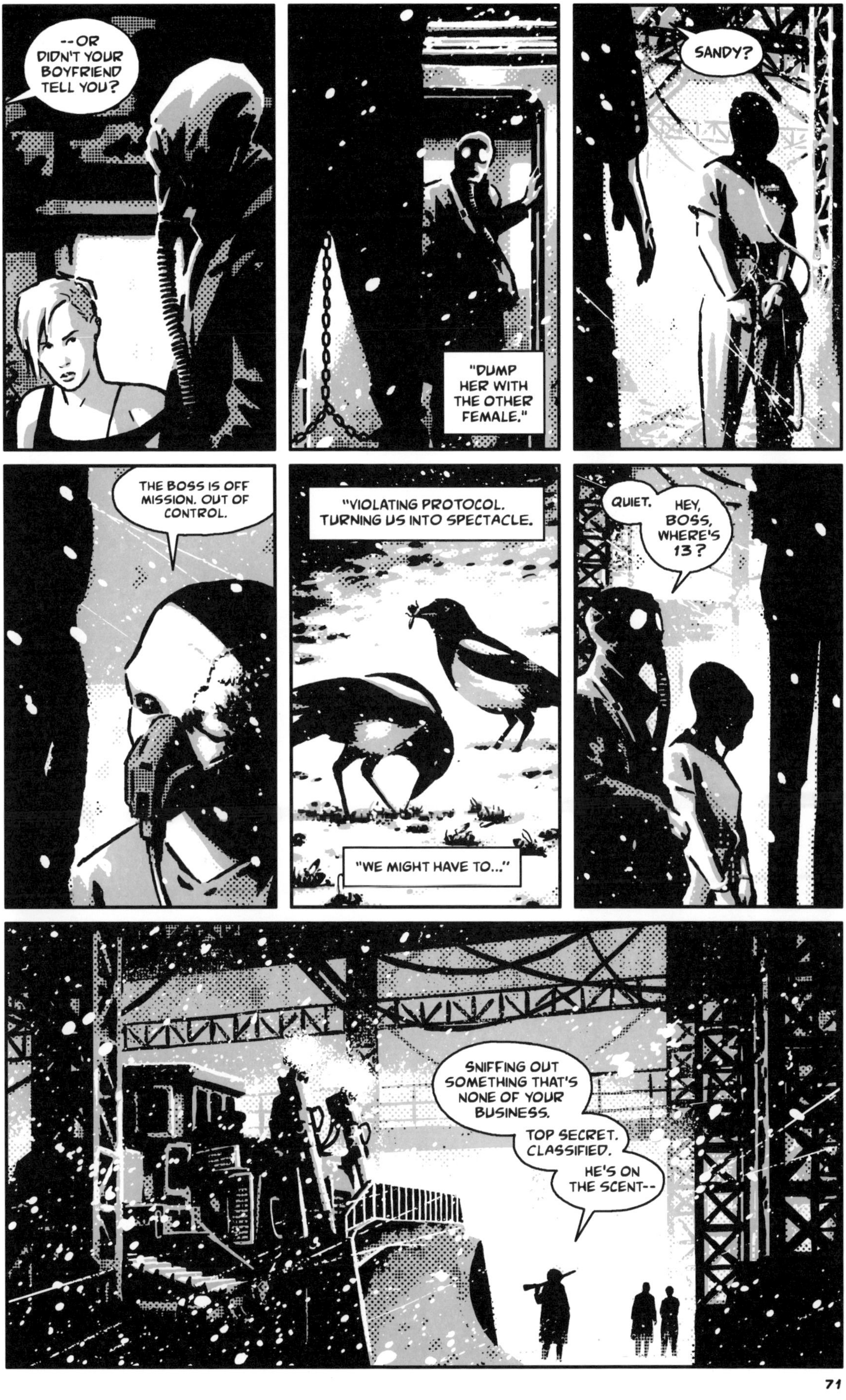

--OR DIDN'T YOUR BOYFRIEND TELL YOU?
"DUMP HER WITH THE OTHER FEMALE."
SANDY?
THE BOSS IS OFF MISSION. OUT OF CONTROL.
"VIOLATING PROTOCOL. TURNING US INTO SPECTACLE.
"WE MIGHT HAVE TO..."
QUIET.
HEY, BOSS, WHERE'S 13?
SNIFFING OUT SOMETHING THAT'S NONE OF YOUR BUSINESS.
TOP SECRET. CLASSIFIED.
HE'S ON THE SCENT--

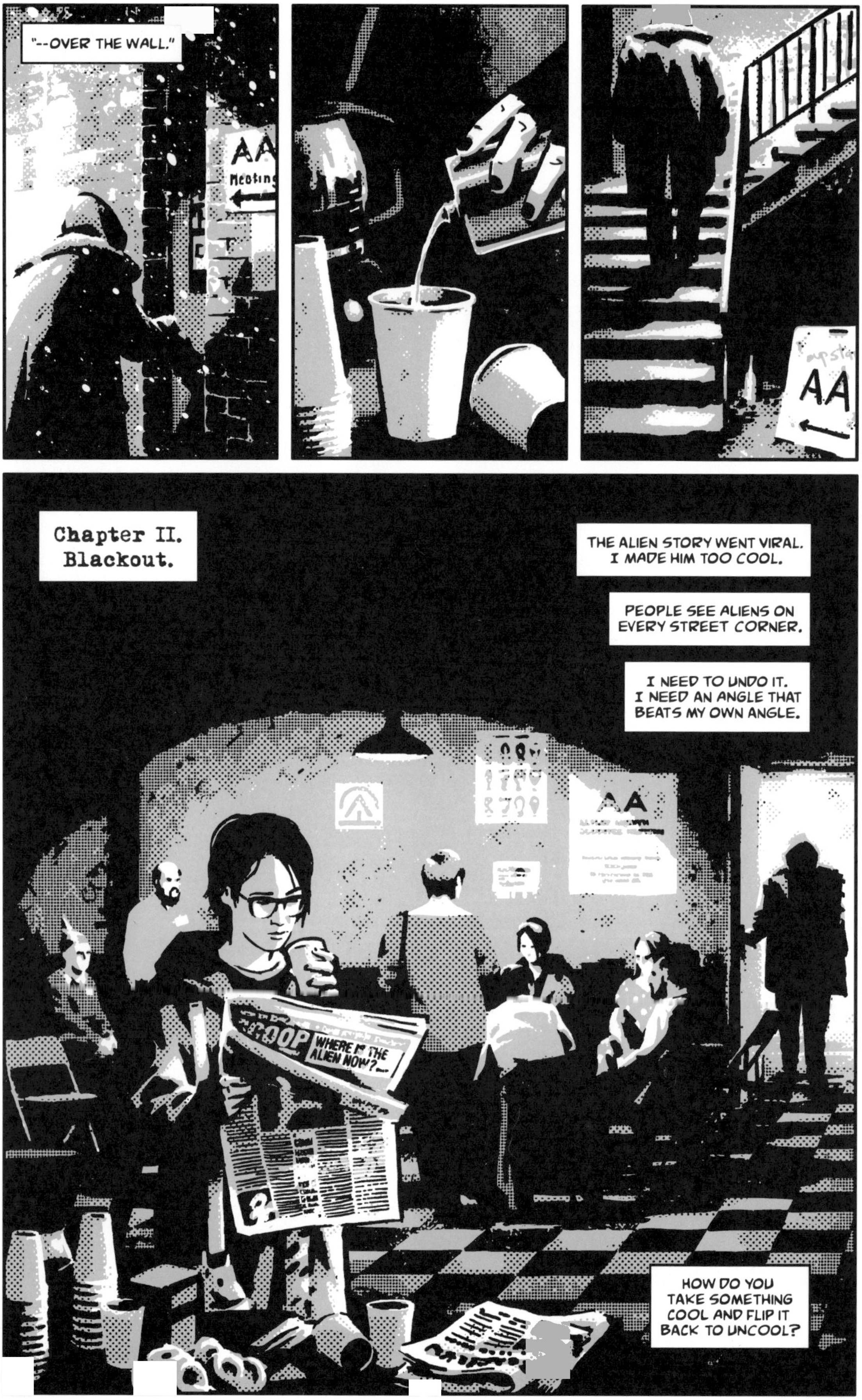
"--OVER THE WALL."
AA
AA
Chapter II.
Blackout.
THE ALIEN STORY WENT VIRAL.
I MADE HIM TOO COOL.
PEOPLE SEE ALIENS ON
EVERY STREET CORNER.
I NEED TO UNDO IT.
I NEED AN ANGLE THAT
BEATS MY OWN ANGLE.
AA
HOW DO YOU
TAKE SOMETHING
COOL AND FLIP IT
BACK TO UNCOOL?

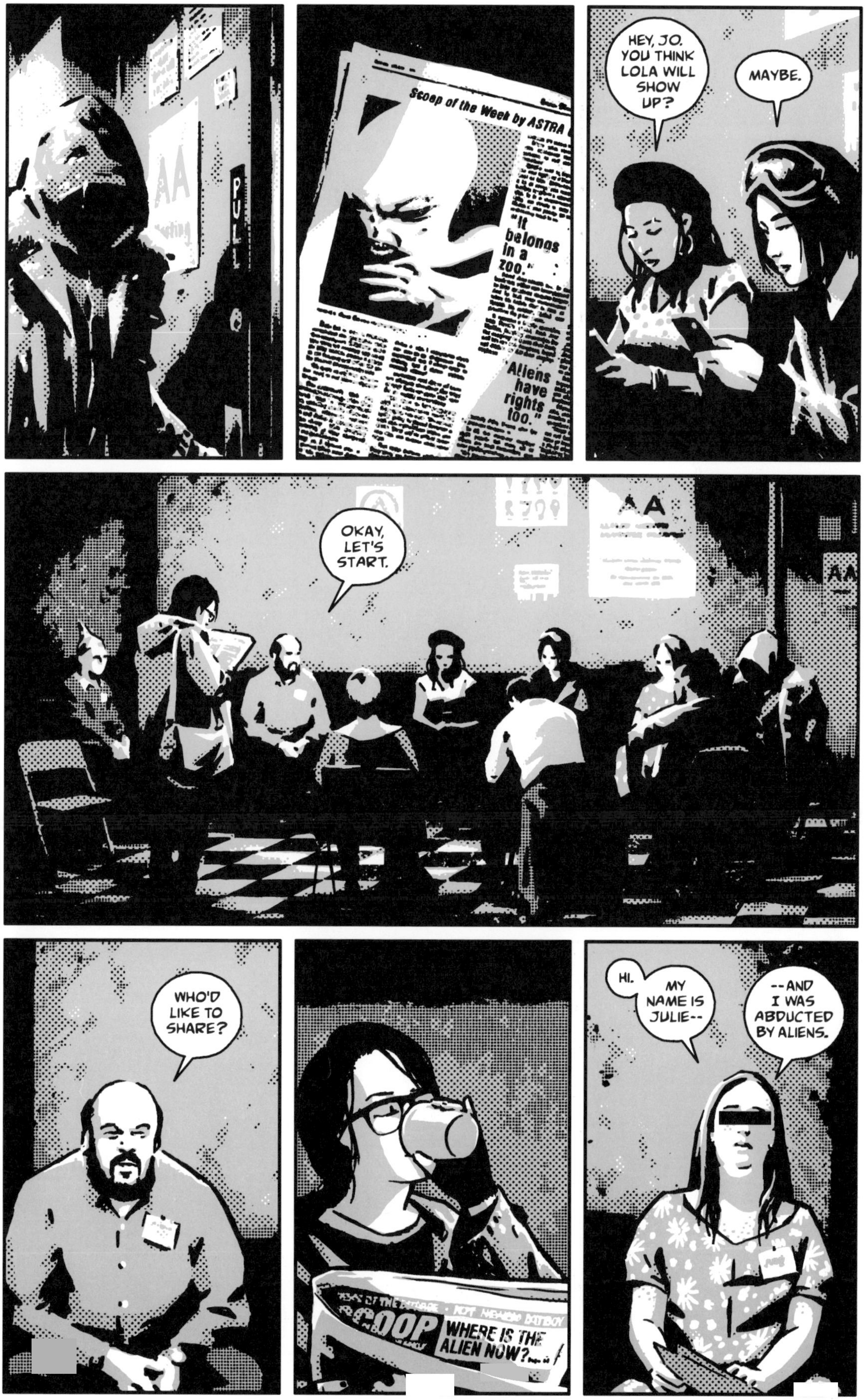
Scoop of the Week by ASTRA
"It belongs in a zoo."
"Aliens have rights too."
HEY, JO. YOU THINK LOLA WILL SHOW UP?
MAYBE.
AA
OKAY, LET'S START.
WHO'D LIKE TO SHARE?
SCOOP
WHERE IS THE ALIEN NOW?...
HI.
MY NAME IS JULIE--
--AND I WAS ABDUCTED BY ALIENS.

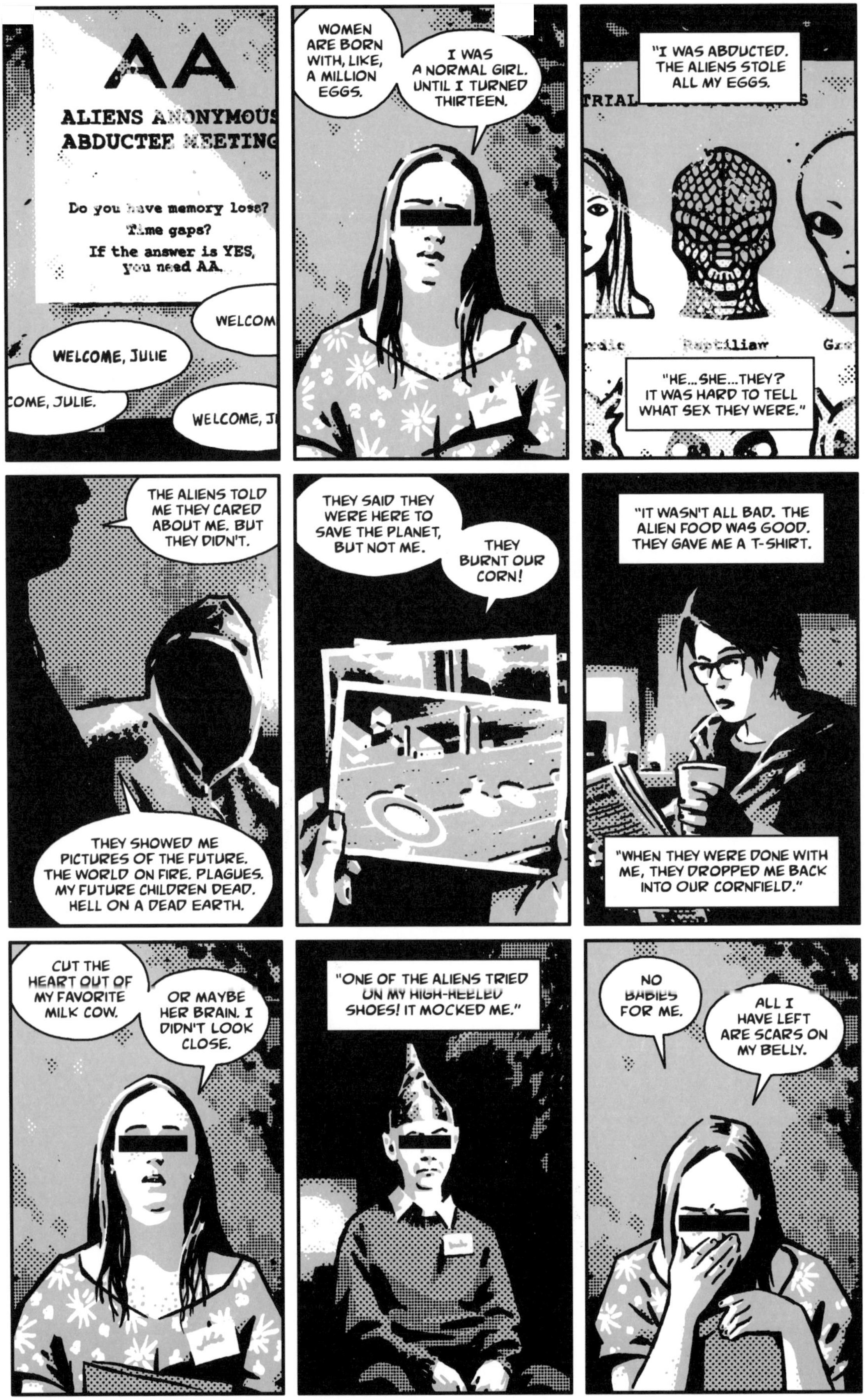
AA
ALIENS ANONYMOUS
ABDUCTEE MEETING
Do you have memory loss?
Time gaps?
If the answer is YES, you need AA.
WELCOM
WELCOME, JULIE
COME, JULIE.
WELCOME, J
WOMEN ARE BORN WITH, LIKE, A MILLION EGGS.
I WAS A NORMAL GIRL. UNTIL I TURNED THIRTEEN.
"I WAS ABDUCTED. THE ALIENS STOLE ALL MY EGGS.
"HE...SHE...THEY? IT WAS HARD TO TELL WHAT SEX THEY WERE."
THE ALIENS TOLD ME THEY CARED ABOUT ME. BUT THEY DIDN'T.
THEY SHOWED ME PICTURES OF THE FUTURE. THE WORLD ON FIRE. PLAGUES. MY FUTURE CHILDREN DEAD. HELL ON A DEAD EARTH.
THEY SAID THEY WERE HERE TO SAVE THE PLANET, BUT NOT ME.
THEY BURNT OUR CORN!
"IT WASN'T ALL BAD. THE ALIEN FOOD WAS GOOD. THEY GAVE ME A T-SHIRT.
"WHEN THEY WERE DONE WITH ME, THEY DROPPED ME BACK INTO OUR CORNFIELD."
CUT THE HEART OUT OF MY FAVORITE MILK COW.
OR MAYBE HER BRAIN. I DIDN'T LOOK CLOSE.
"ONE OF THE ALIENS TRIED ON MY HIGH-HEELED SHOES! IT MOCKED ME."
NO BABIES FOR ME.
ALL I HAVE LEFT ARE SCARS ON MY BELLY.

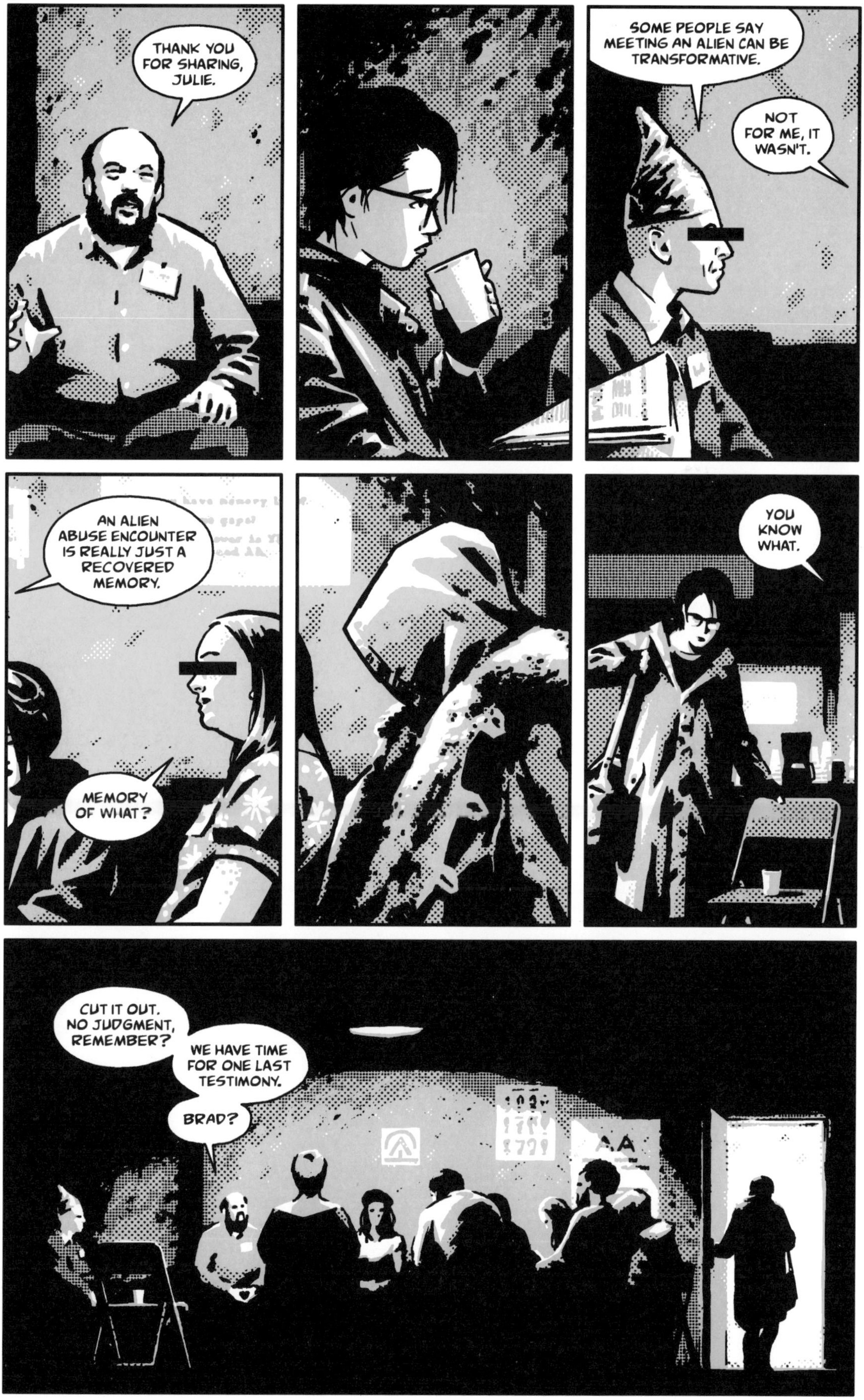
THANK YOU FOR SHARING, JULIE.
SOME PEOPLE SAY MEETING AN ALIEN CAN BE TRANSFORMATIVE.
NOT FOR ME, IT WASN'T.
AN ALIEN ABUSE ENCOUNTER IS REALLY JUST A RECOVERED MEMORY.
MEMORY OF WHAT?
YOU KNOW WHAT.
CUT IT OUT. NO JUDGMENT, REMEMBER?
WE HAVE TIME FOR ONE LAST TESTIMONY.
BRAD?
AA

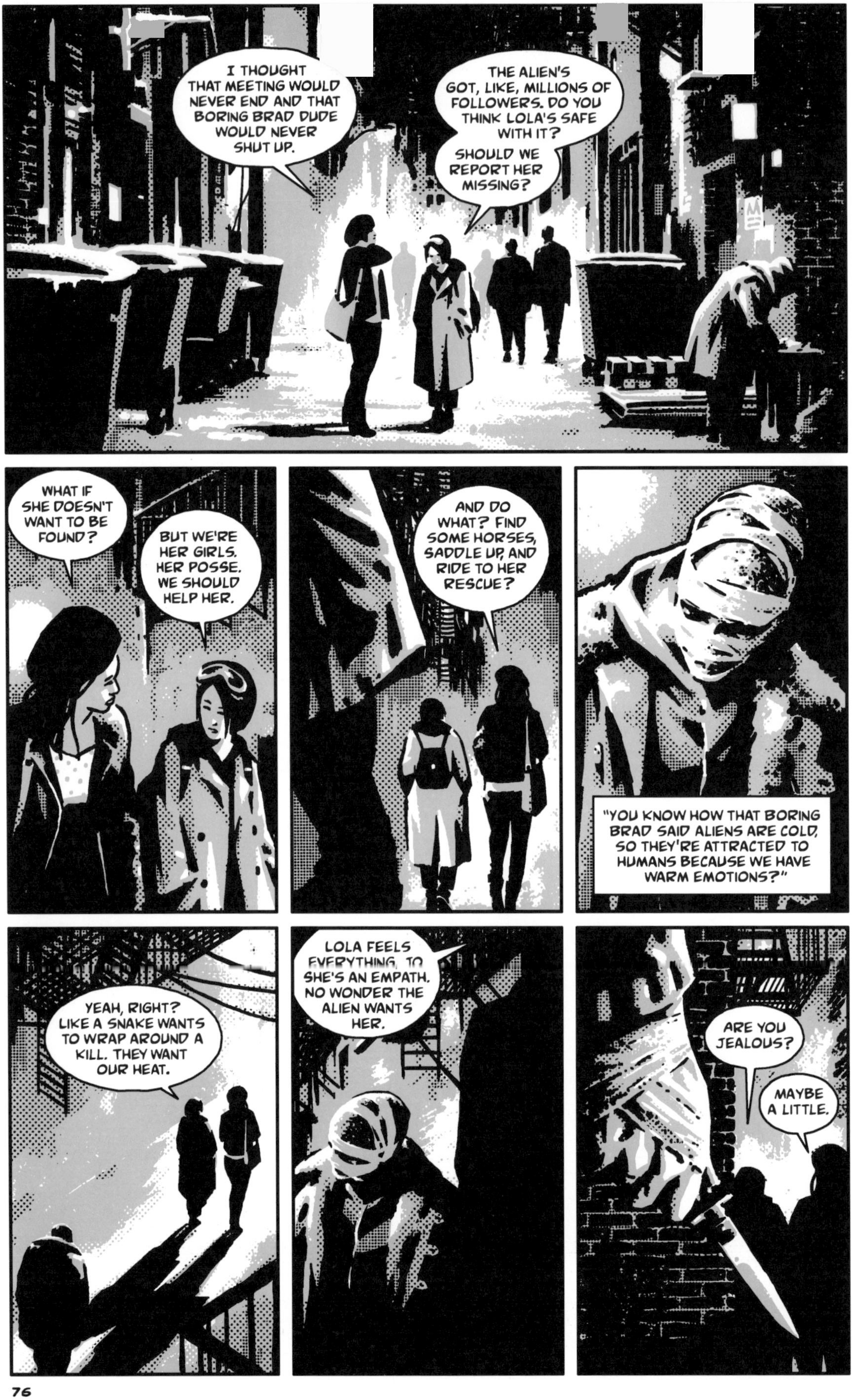
I THOUGHT THAT MEETING WOULD NEVER END AND THAT BORING BRAD DUDE WOULD NEVER SHUT UP.
THE ALIEN'S GOT, LIKE, MILLIONS OF FOLLOWERS. DO YOU THINK LOLA'S SAFE WITH IT?
SHOULD WE REPORT HER MISSING?
WHAT IF SHE DOESN'T WANT TO BE FOUND?
BUT WE'RE HER GIRLS. HER POSSE. WE SHOULD HELP HER.
AND DO WHAT? FIND SOME HORSES, SADDLE UP, AND RIDE TO HER RESCUE?
"YOU KNOW HOW THAT BORING BRAD SAID ALIENS ARE COLD, SO THEY'RE ATTRACTED TO HUMANS BECAUSE WE HAVE WARM EMOTIONS?"
YEAH, RIGHT? LIKE A SNAKE WANTS TO WRAP AROUND A KILL. THEY WANT OUR HEAT.
LOLA FEELS EVERYTHING, TO SHE'S AN EMPATH. NO WONDER THE ALIEN WANTS HER.
ARE YOU JEALOUS?
MAYBE A LITTLE.

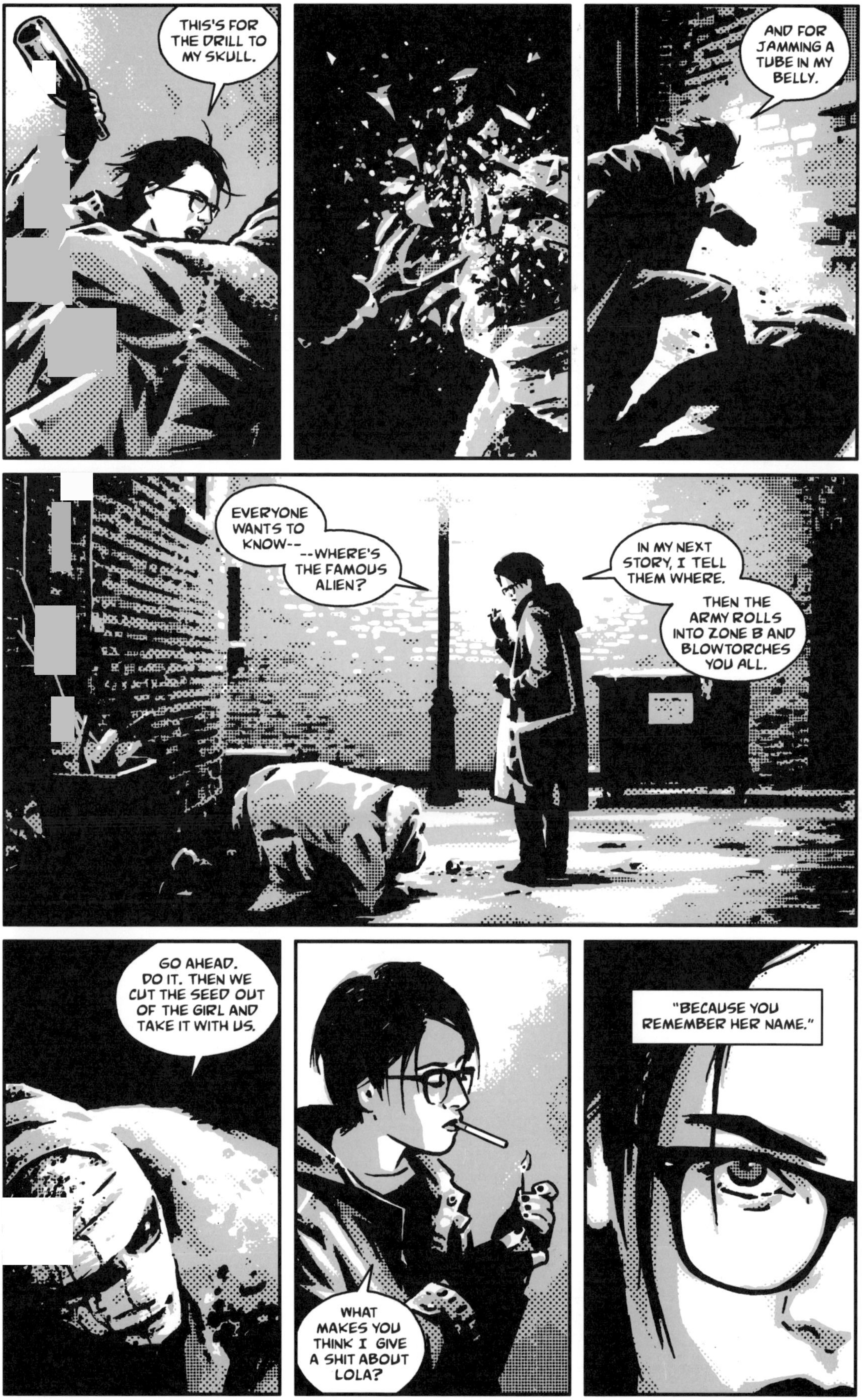
THIS'S FOR THE DRILL TO MY SKULL.
AND FOR JAMMING A TUBE IN MY BELLY.
EVERYONE WANTS TO KNOW--
--WHERE'S THE FAMOUS ALIEN?
IN MY NEXT STORY, I TELL THEM WHERE.
THEN THE ARMY ROLLS INTO ZONE B AND BLOWTORCHES YOU ALL.
GO AHEAD. DO IT. THEN WE CUT THE SEED OUT OF THE GIRL AND TAKE IT WITH US.
WHAT MAKES YOU THINK I GIVE A SHIT ABOUT LOLA?
"BECAUSE YOU REMEMBER HER NAME."

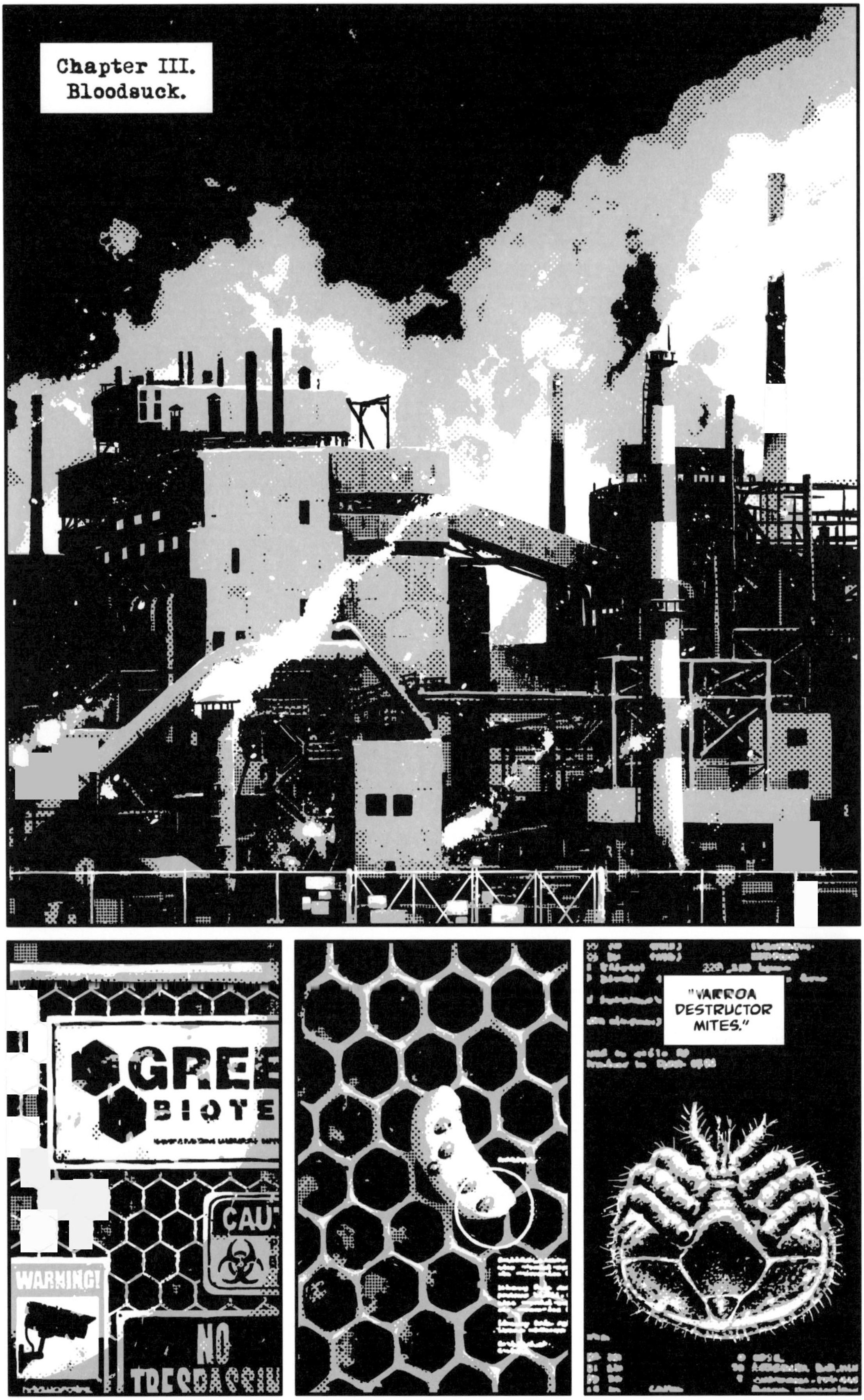
Chapter III.
Bloodsuck.
GREE
BIOTE
CAU
WARNING!
NO
"VARROA DESTRUCTOR MITES."

THE BEES CAN'T BEAT THE BLOODSUCKERS.
NOT WITHOUT MY HELP, BUDDY.
VIRAL INFECTIONS. PESTICIDES. PARASITES.
"SNEAK THIEVES INFILTRATE THE HIVE AND TAKE IT OVER."
ALICE, JUST PLANT MORE WILDFLOWERS FOR THE BEES--
"--RE-CREATE THEIR WORLD."
RE-CREATE THE WORLD, BUDDY?
"AND REST ON THE SEVENTH DAY, I ASSUME?"

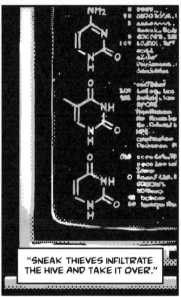

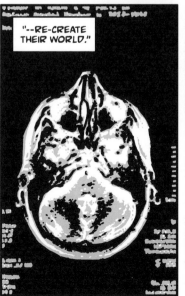

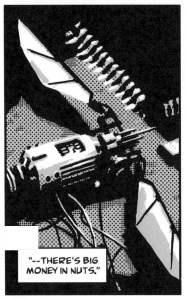

FEEDING BEES SUGAR AND ANTIBIOTICS IS A FAST-FOOD ROAD TO HELL.
THEY HAVE TO SURVIVE THE LONG TRUCKER ROADTRIPS TO POLLINATE ALMOND FIELDS--
"--THERE'S BIG MONEY IN NUTS."
ANYWAY, WE WON'T NEED REAL BEES MUCH LONGER.
"MORE TECHNOLOGY IS NOT THE ANSWER, ALICE."
WHAT'S RE-FREEZING THE ARCTIC ICE, HUH, BUDDY? MY SUBTERRANEAN PUMPS AND SOLAR-DEFLECTION TECH. MY CARBON-DIOXIDE SPACE VACUUMS.
"YOU RUSHED IN THERE.
"I WOULD HAVE FOUND A NATURAL FIX--"
--WHO SENT MYCELIUM TO EAT THE OIL SPILLS AND DECONTAMINATE RADIOACTIVE CHERNOBYL?
I DID.

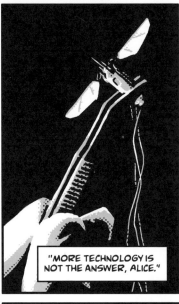

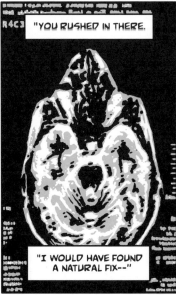

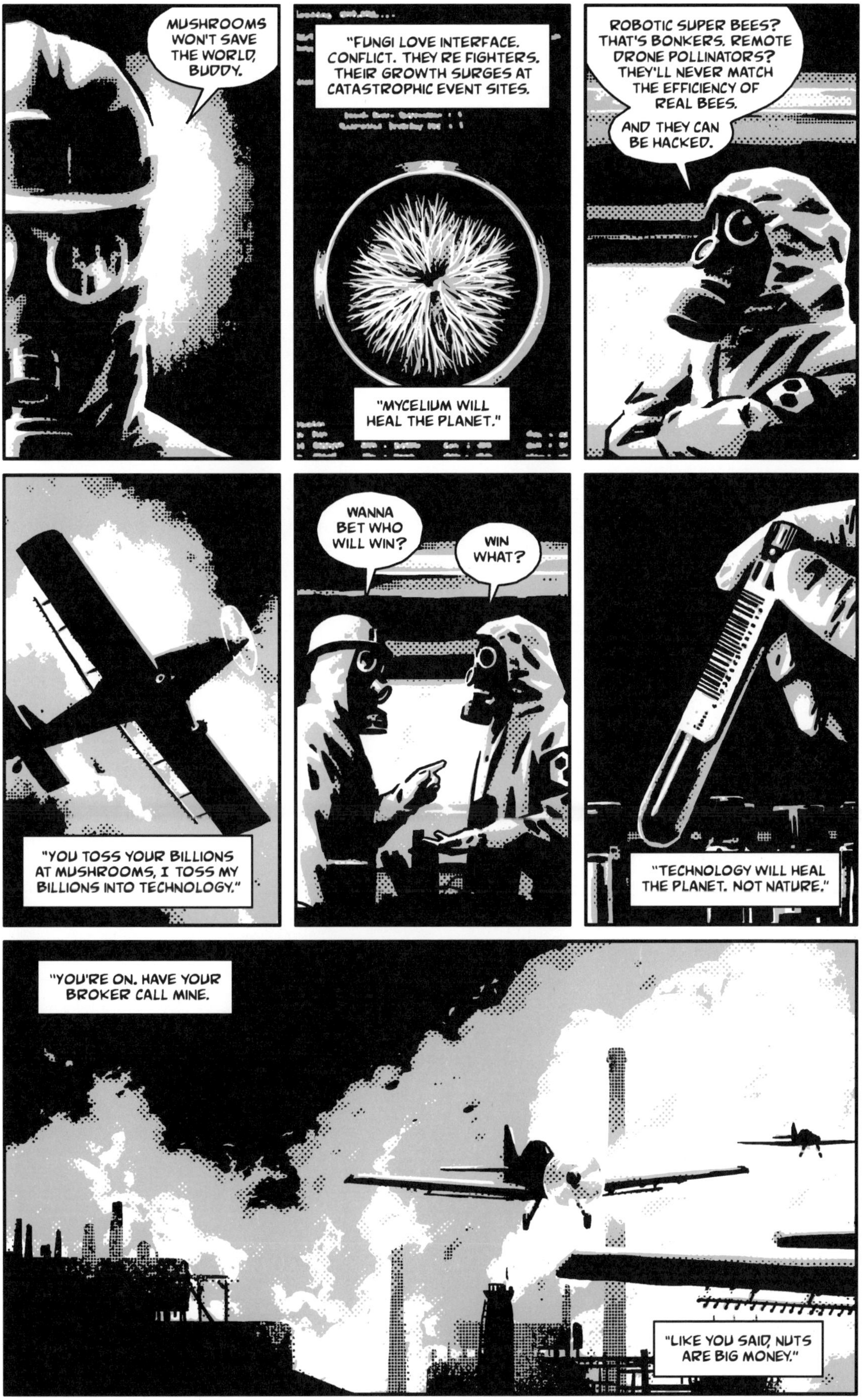
MUSHROOMS WON'T SAVE THE WORLD, BUDDY.
"FUNGI LOVE INTERFACE. CONFLICT. THEY RE FIGHTERS. THEIR GROWTH SURGES AT CATASTROPHIC EVENT SITES.
"MYCELIUM WILL HEAL THE PLANET."
ROBOTIC SUPER BEES? THAT'S BONKERS. REMOTE DRONE POLLINATORS? THEY'LL NEVER MATCH THE EFFICIENCY OF REAL BEES.
AND THEY CAN BE HACKED.
"YOU TOSS YOUR BILLIONS AT MUSHROOMS, I TOSS MY BILLIONS INTO TECHNOLOGY."
WANNA BET WHO WILL WIN?
WIN WHAT?
"TECHNOLOGY WILL HEAL THE PLANET. NOT NATURE."
"YOU'RE ON. HAVE YOUR BROKER CALL MINE.
"LIKE YOU SAID, NUTS ARE BIG MONEY."

THE ICARUS OVERSHOT ITS MARK.

TAKING THE BILLIONAIRE INSIDE WITH IT.

ENDED UP LIGHT AS A SPORE IN THE WIND.

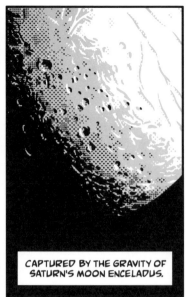

CAPTURED BY THE GRAVITY OF SATURN'S MOON ENCELADUS.

Chapter IV.
Brains.

LOOKS LIKE THE RICH BASTARD HAD A CLOSE ENCOUNTER WITH A FIRE BALL.

FLESH BURNT TO BONE.

SPACE AGENCY SHARED IMAGES CAPTURED BY THE CAPSULE'S CAM.

DIGITAL FILE IS DENSE WITH INFORMATION.

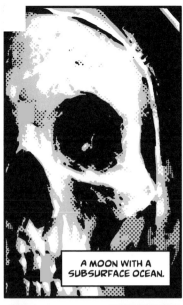

A MOON WITH A SUBSURFACE OCEAN.

COMPLEX ORGANIC MOLECULES. LIQUID AND HYDROGEN--

--A MOON WITH THE KEYS TO LIFE.

POOR GUY SURE WENT TO SEED.

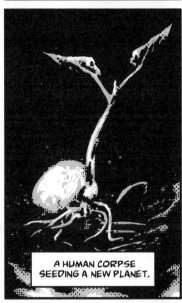

A HUMAN CORPSE SEEDING A NEW PLANET.

BUT WITH WHAT?

IS THAT A BELLY BUMP, LOLA? ANOTHER SEED?

THE MONEY SHOT. THE CLICK-BAIT.

DIGITAL CATNIP MONEY MONEY MONEY SHOT.

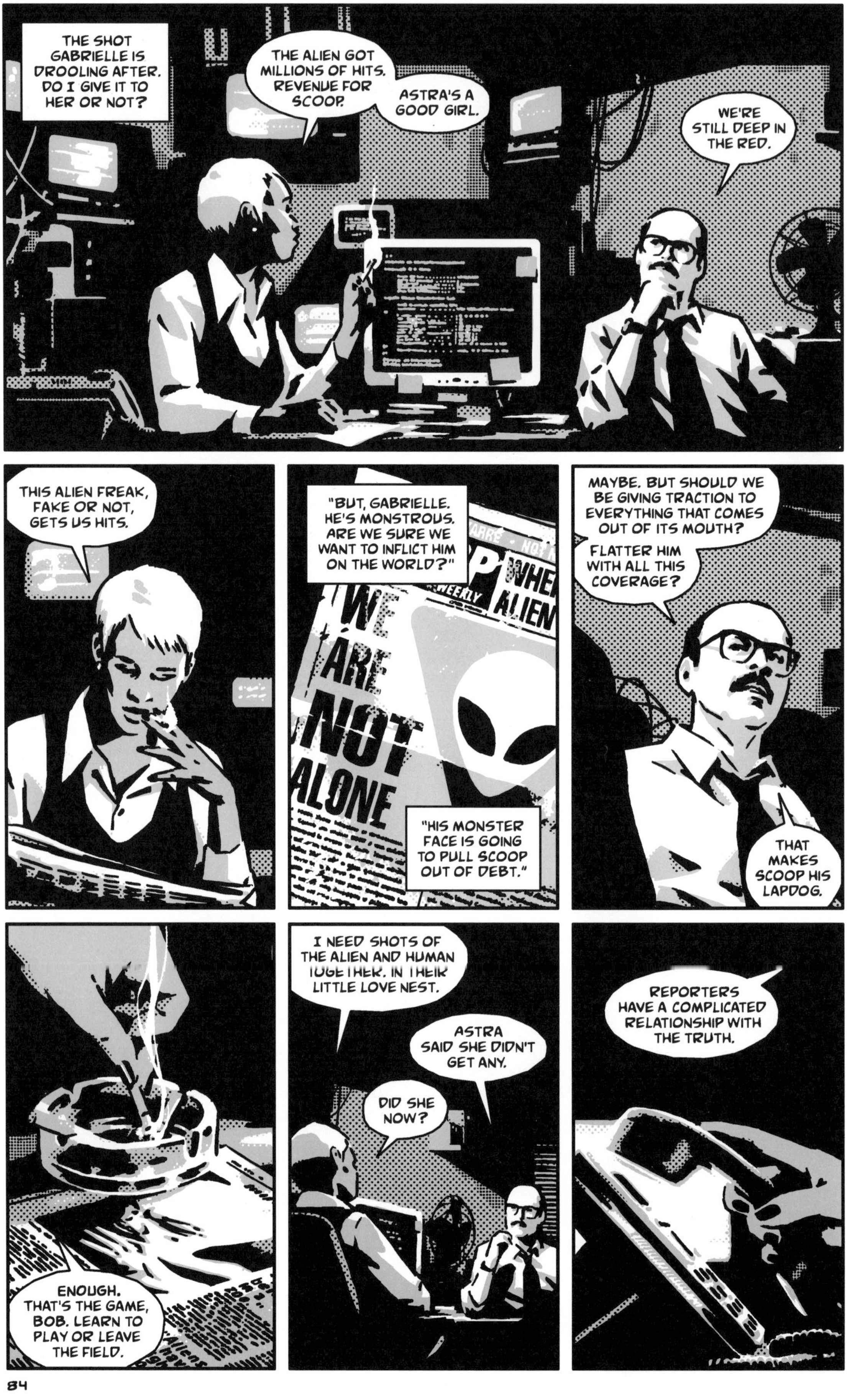
THE SHOT GABRIELLE IS DROOLING AFTER. DO I GIVE IT TO HER OR NOT?
THE ALIEN GOT MILLIONS OF HITS. REVENUE FOR SCOOP.
ASTRA'S A GOOD GIRL.
WE'RE STILL DEEP IN THE RED.
THIS ALIEN FREAK, FAKE OR NOT, GETS US HITS.
"BUT, GABRIELLE. HE'S MONSTROUS. ARE WE SURE WE WANT TO INFLICT HIM ON THE WORLD?"
WE ARE NOT ALONE
"HIS MONSTER FACE IS GOING TO PULL SCOOP OUT OF DEBT."
MAYBE. BUT SHOULD WE BE GIVING TRACTION TO EVERYTHING THAT COMES OUT OF ITS MOUTH?
FLATTER HIM WITH ALL THIS COVERAGE?
THAT MAKES SCOOP HIS LAPDOG.
ENOUGH. THAT'S THE GAME, BOB. LEARN TO PLAY OR LEAVE THE FIELD.
I NEED SHOTS OF THE ALIEN AND HUMAN TOGETHER. IN THEIR LITTLE LOVE NEST.
ASTRA SAID SHE DIDN'T GET ANY.
DID SHE NOW?
REPORTERS HAVE A COMPLICATED RELATIONSHIP WITH THE TRUTH.

Incoming Call ...
> From: Gabrielle
(00.55.76.788...)
[options]
> Dismiss...<X>
> Answer....<V>

HONEY

HEY, GABRIELLE. THINKING OF YOU RIGHT NOW, CHECK YOUR MAIL.

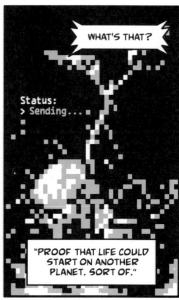

WHAT'S THAT?

Status:
> Sending...

"PROOF THAT LIFE COULD START ON ANOTHER PLANET. SORT OF."

SMART GIRL. OKAY. THAT'S GOOD FOR PAGE TWO. WRITE IT UP.

BUT I NEED A COVER STORY.

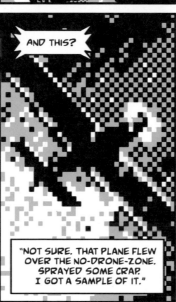

AND THIS?

"NOT SURE. THAT PLANE FLEW OVER THE NO-DRONE-ZONE. SPRAYED SOME CRAP. I GOT A SAMPLE OF IT."

AGRO-CHEMICAL PRETENDING TO BE ECO-TECH?

DIG INTO IT. LET'S SEE HOW GREEN THEY REALLY ARE.

I STILL NEED TO FILL THE SWEET SPOT ON PAGE ONE. I WANT TO SEE THE ALIEN BODIES UP CLOSE.

I WANT THE ALIEN HUMAN LOVE NEST. I WANT ALIEN SEX. YOU'VE GOT TO GO BACK.

AND DO WHAT? ASK THEM TO STRIP? OR JUST RIP THEIR CLOTHES OFF?

WHATEVER GETS THE STORY.

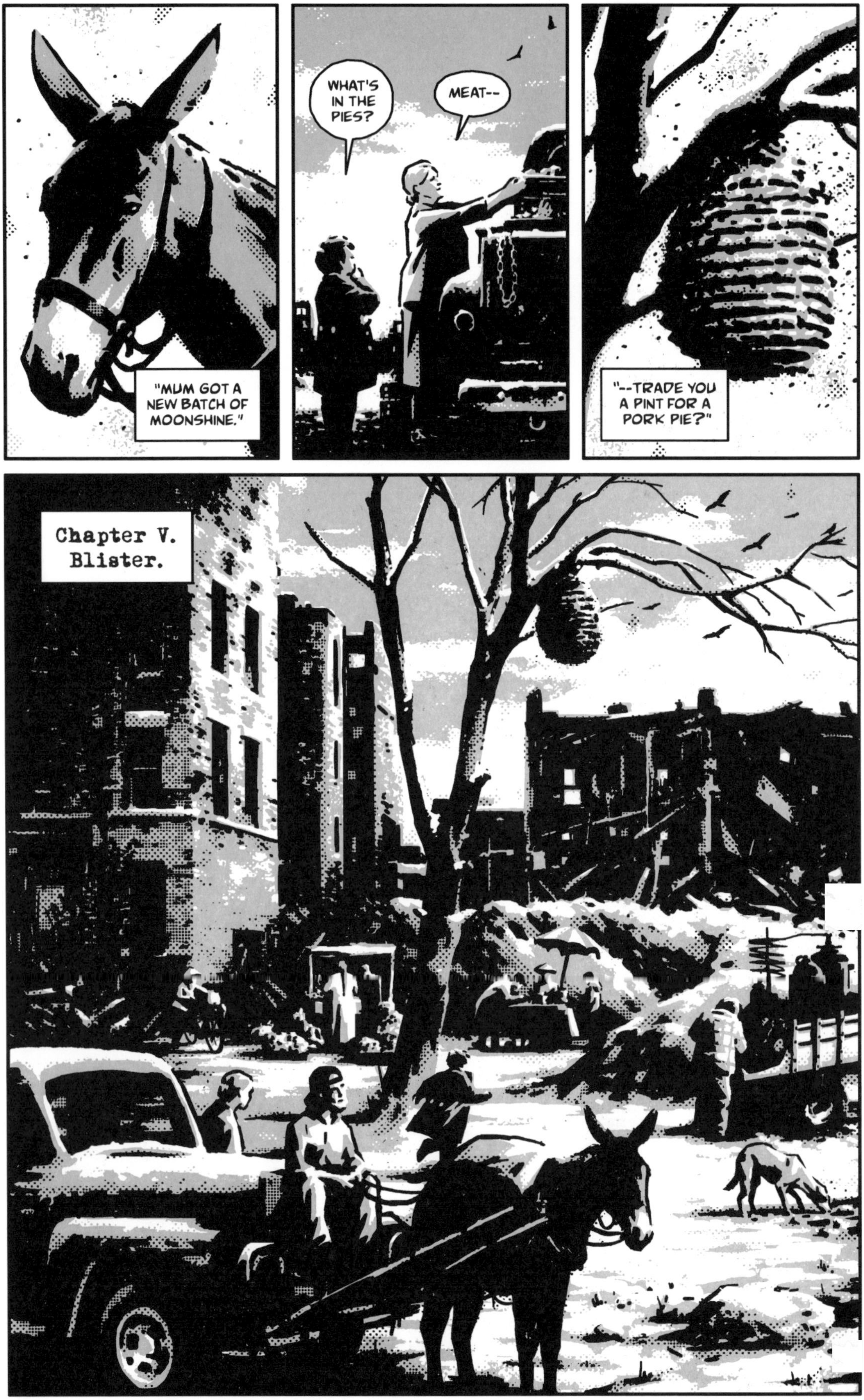
"MUM GOT A NEW BATCH OF MOONSHINE."
WHAT'S IN THE PIES?
MEAT--
"--TRADE YOU A PINT FOR A PORK PIE?"
Chapter V.
Blister.

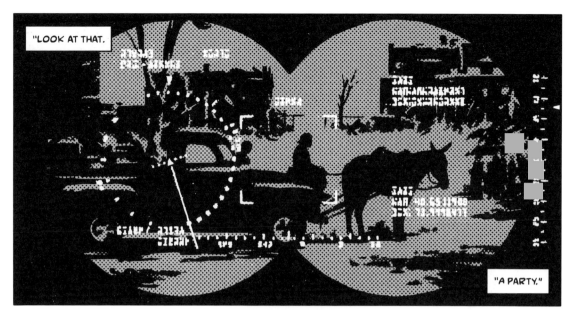

"LOOK AT THAT.

"A PARTY."

WE WEREN'T INVITED.

SO THE FEMALE KICKED YOUR ASS? HEH, A SHAME WE DIDN'T GET TO SEE HER BRAIN.

"BUT, BUT... I GOT SOMETHING BETTER. IT SAYS YOU'RE FAMOUS.

ALIEN NOW? Page 54

"SHE MADE YOU FAMOUS."

SHE'S GOT POWER, HUH?

RACE--

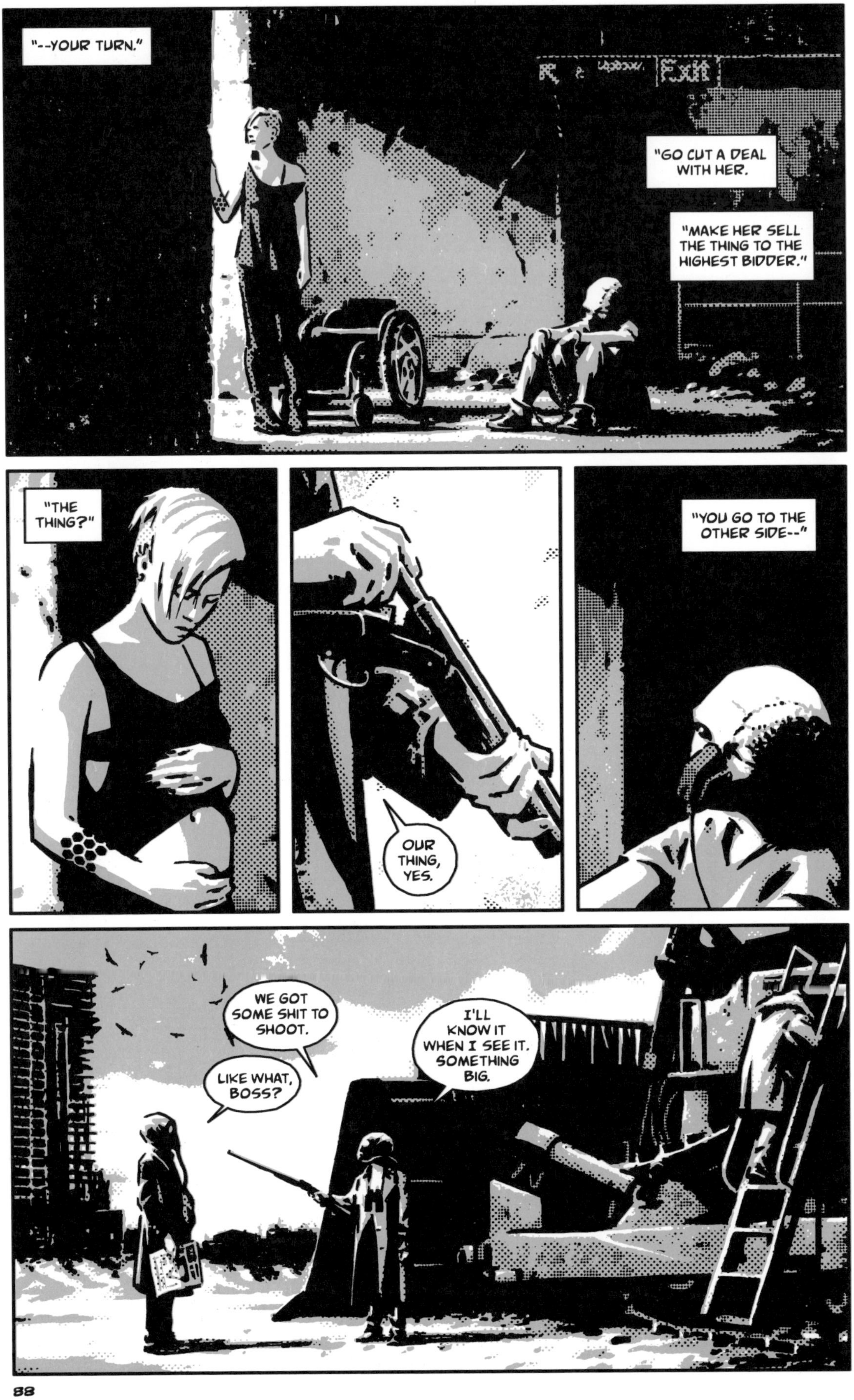
"--YOUR TURN."
"GO CUT A DEAL WITH HER.
"MAKE HER SELL THE THING TO THE HIGHEST BIDDER."
"THE THING?"
OUR THING, YES.
"YOU GO TO THE OTHER SIDE--"
WE GOT SOME SHIT TO SHOOT.
LIKE WHAT, BOSS?
I'LL KNOW IT WHEN I SEE IT. SOMETHING BIG.

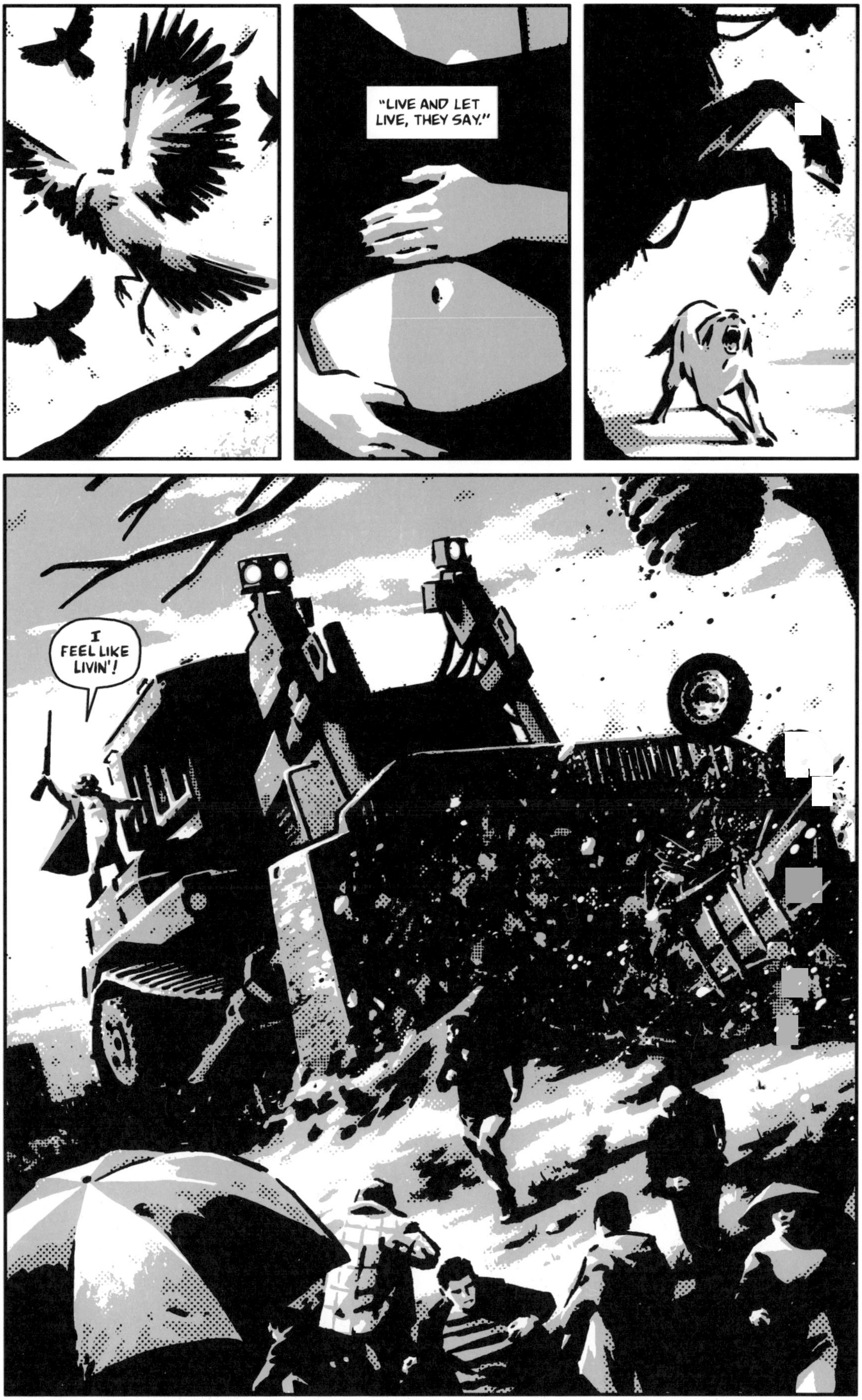
"LIVE AND LET LIVE, THEY SAY."
I FEEL LIKE LIVIN'!

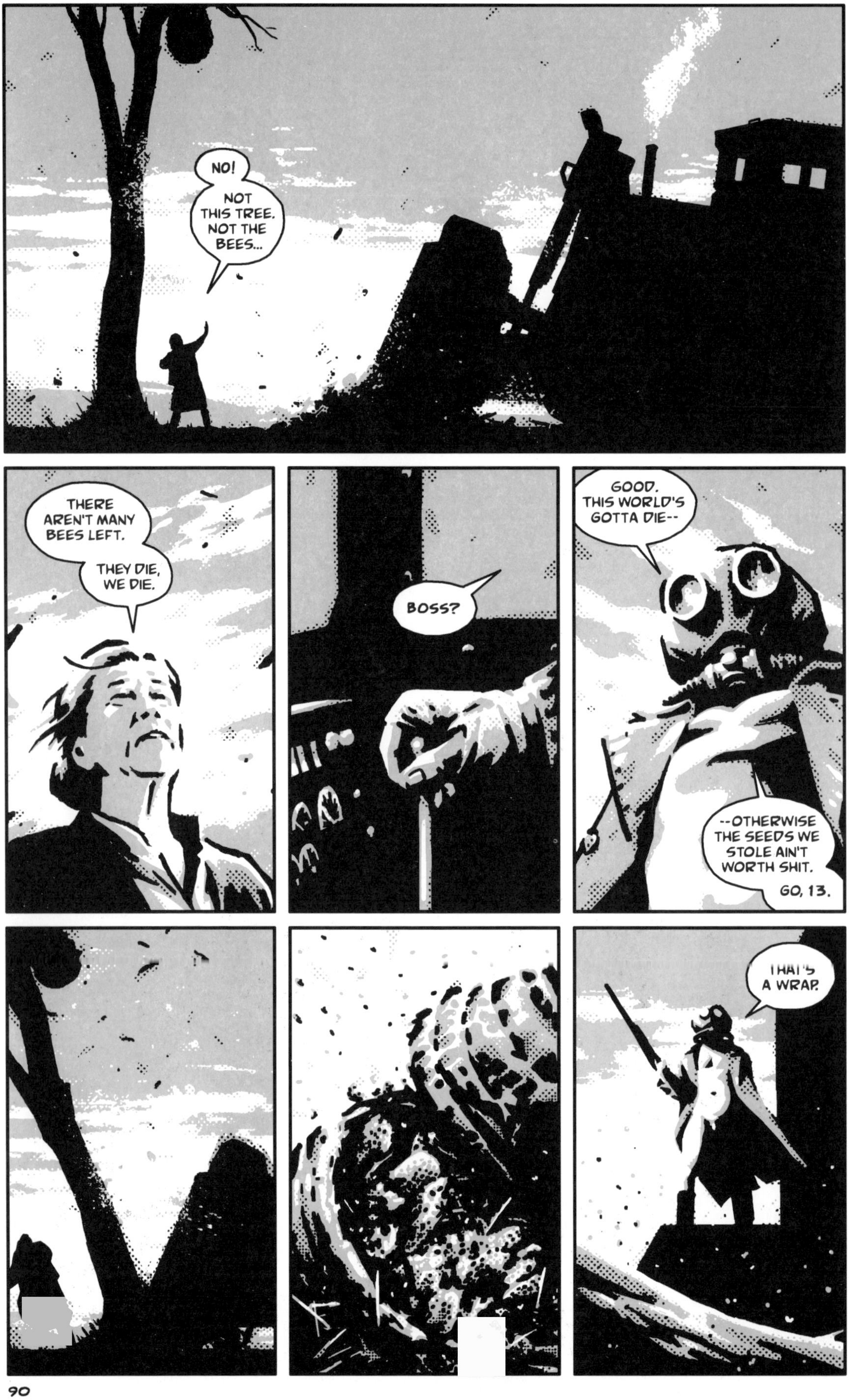
NO!
NOT THIS TREE. NOT THE BEES...
THERE AREN'T MANY BEES LEFT.
THEY DIE, WE DIE.
BOSS?
GOOD. THIS WORLD'S GOTTA DIE--
--OTHERWISE THE SEEDS WE STOLE AIN'T WORTH SHIT.
GO, 13.
THAT'S A WRAP.

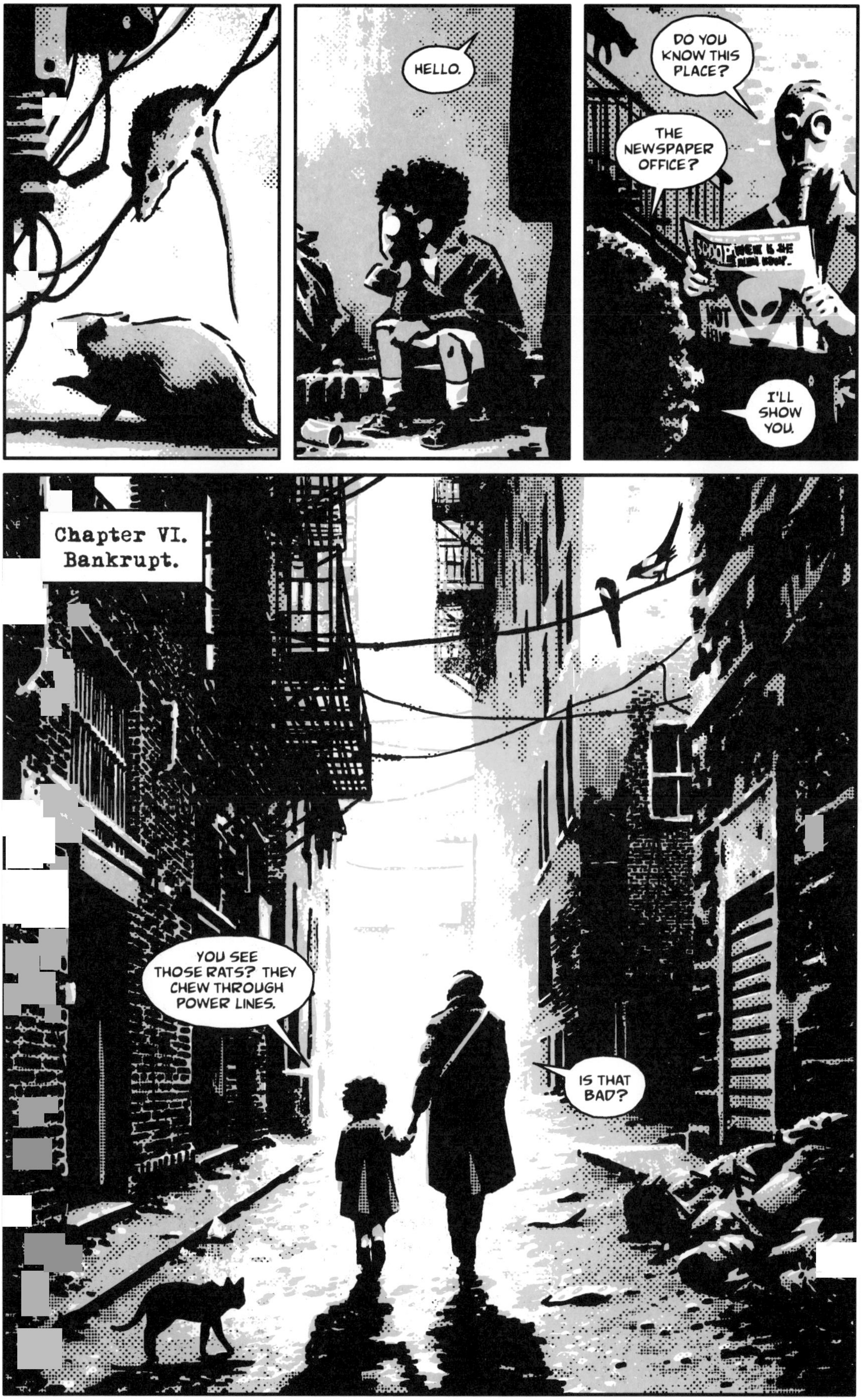
HELLO.
DO YOU KNOW THIS PLACE?
THE NEWSPAPER OFFICE?
I'LL SHOW YOU.
Chapter VI. Bankrupt.
YOU SEE THOSE RATS? THEY CHEW THROUGH POWER LINES.
IS THAT BAD?

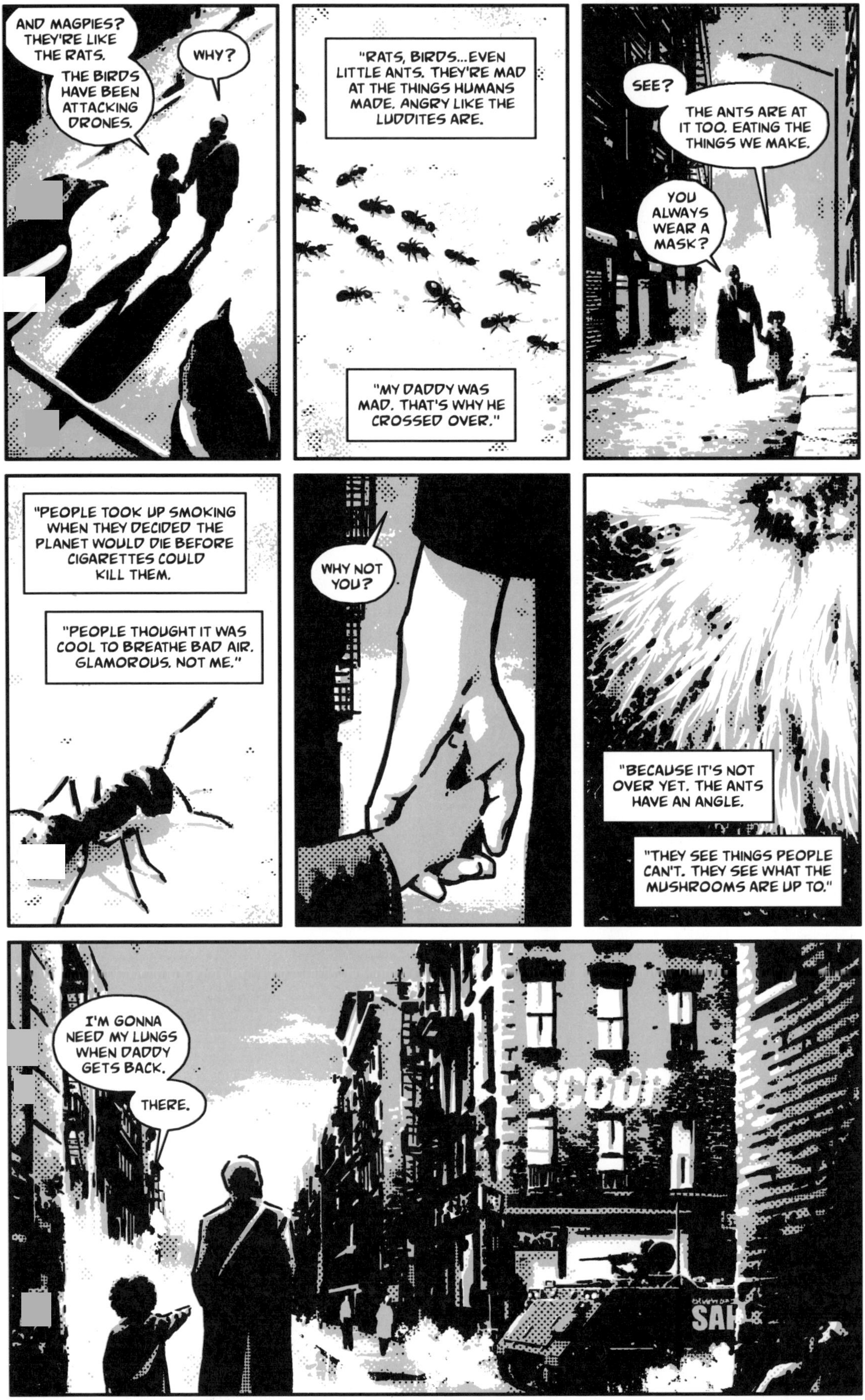
AND MAGPIES? THEY'RE LIKE THE RATS.
WHY?
THE BIRDS HAVE BEEN ATTACKING DRONES.
"RATS, BIRDS...EVEN LITTLE ANTS. THEY'RE MAD AT THE THINGS HUMANS MADE. ANGRY LIKE THE LUDDITES ARE.
"MY DADDY WAS MAD. THAT'S WHY HE CROSSED OVER."
SEE?
THE ANTS ARE AT IT TOO. EATING THE THINGS WE MAKE.
YOU ALWAYS WEAR A MASK?
"PEOPLE TOOK UP SMOKING WHEN THEY DECIDED THE PLANET WOULD DIE BEFORE CIGARETTES COULD KILL THEM.
"PEOPLE THOUGHT IT WAS COOL TO BREATHE BAD AIR. GLAMOROUS. NOT ME."
WHY NOT YOU?
"BECAUSE IT'S NOT OVER YET. THE ANTS HAVE AN ANGLE.
"THEY SEE THINGS PEOPLE CAN'T. THEY SEE WHAT THE MUSHROOMS ARE UP TO."
I'M GONNA NEED MY LUNGS WHEN DADDY GETS BACK.
THERE.
SCOOP

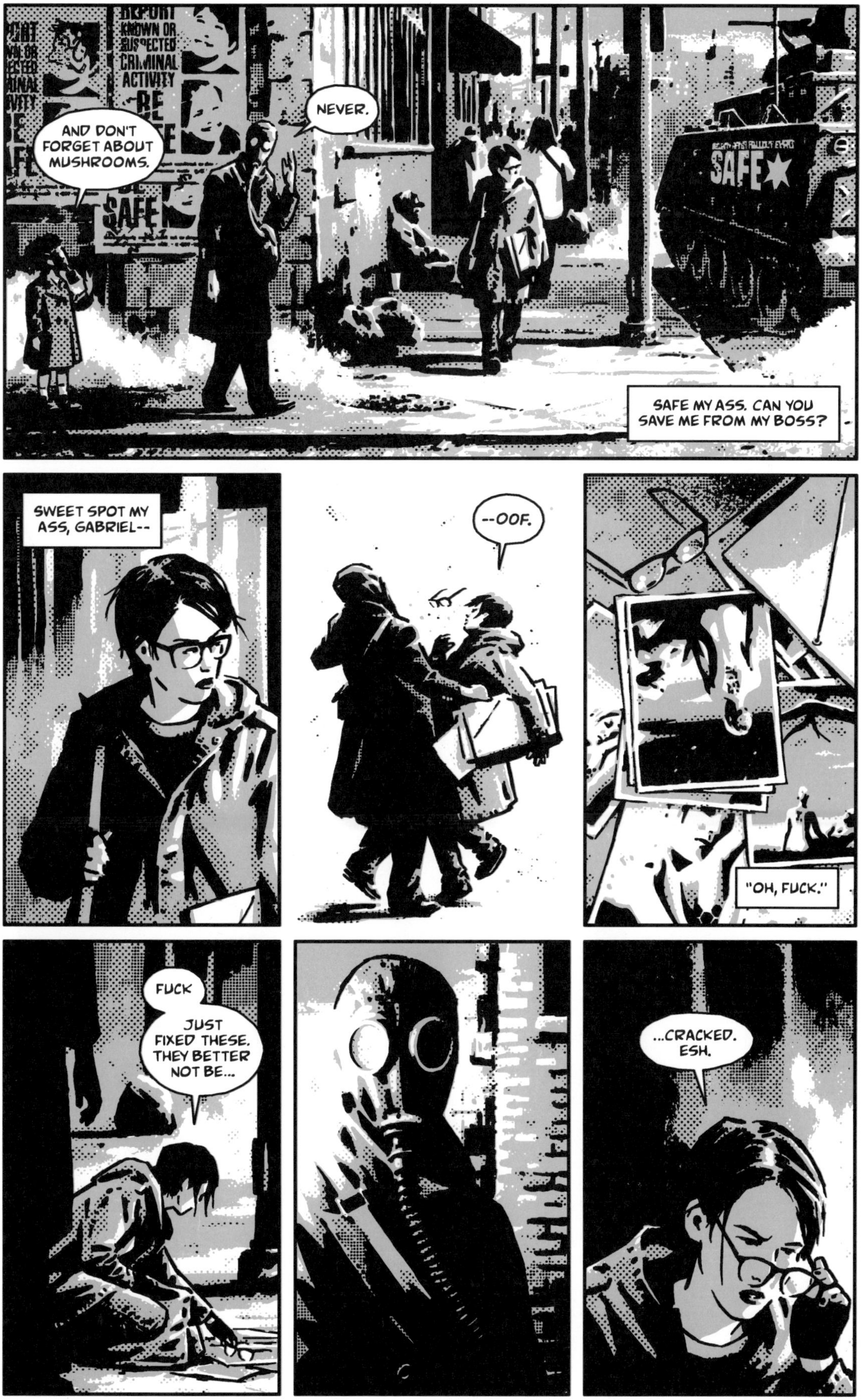
KNOWN OR
SUSPECTED
CRIMINAL
ACTIVITY
SAFE
AND DON'T FORGET ABOUT MUSHROOMS.
NEVER.
SAFE
SAFE MY ASS. CAN YOU SAVE ME FROM MY BOSS?
SWEET SPOT MY ASS, GABRIEL--
--OOF.
"OH, FUCK."
FUCK
JUST FIXED THESE. THEY BETTER NOT BE...
...CRACKED. ESH.

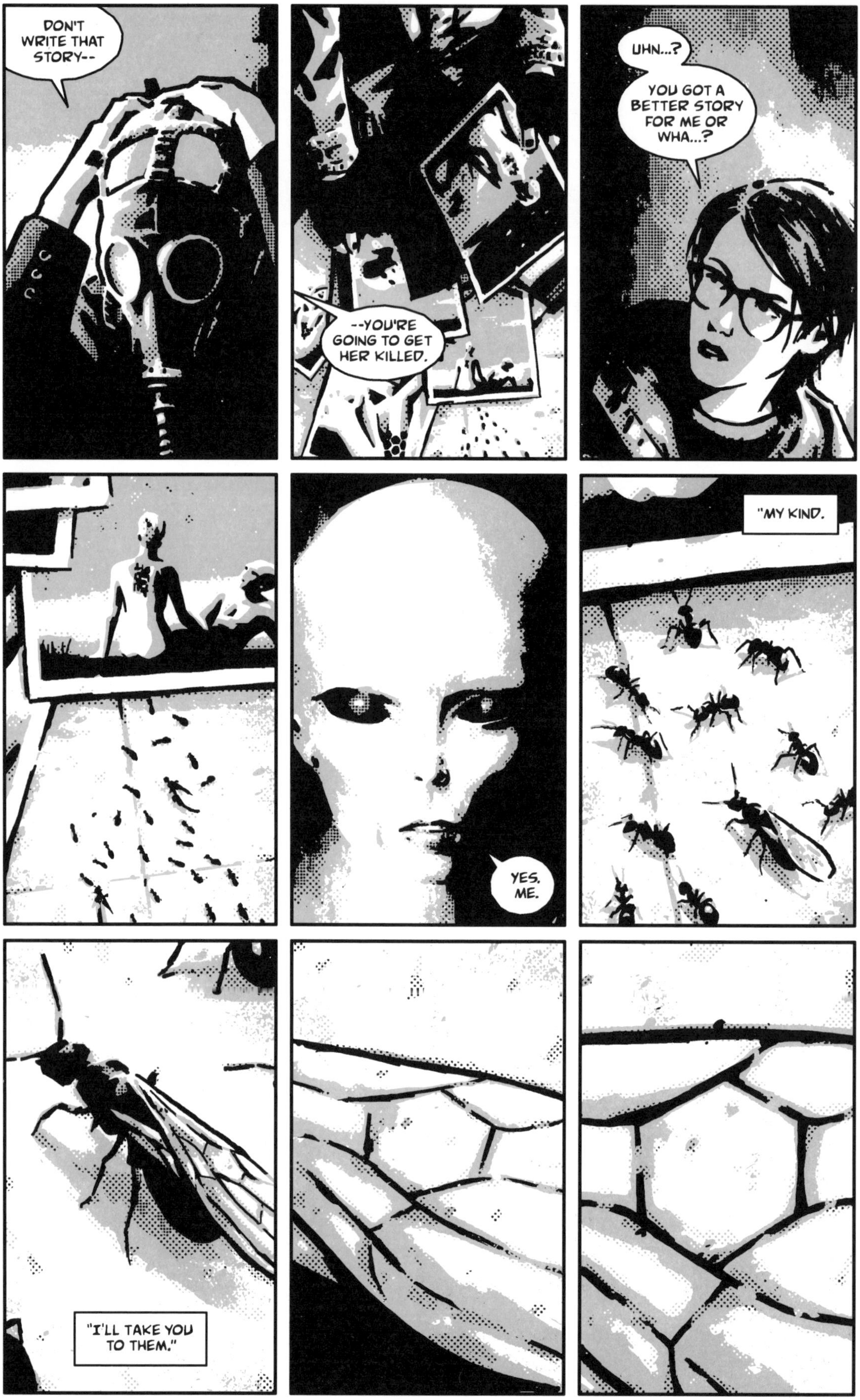
DON'T WRITE THAT STORY--
--YOU'RE GOING TO GET HER KILLED.
UHN...?
YOU GOT A BETTER STORY FOR ME OR WHA...?
YES. ME.
"MY KIND.
"I'LL TAKE YOU TO THEM."
!!

[4. Undertow.]

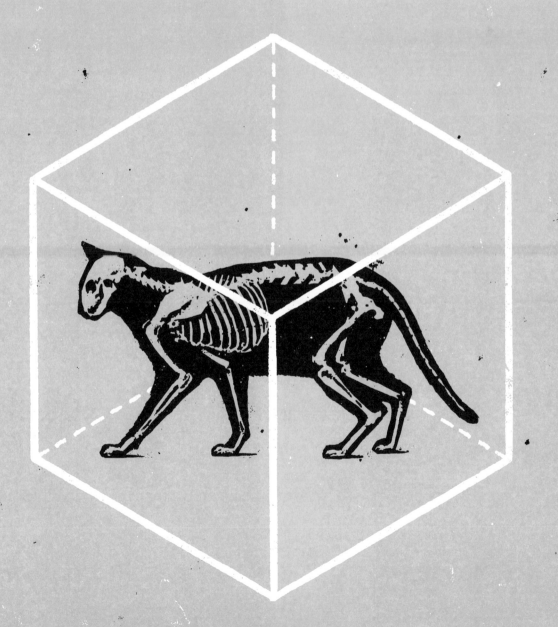

Fig.4

"Hell is truth seen
too late."

-Thomas Hobbes

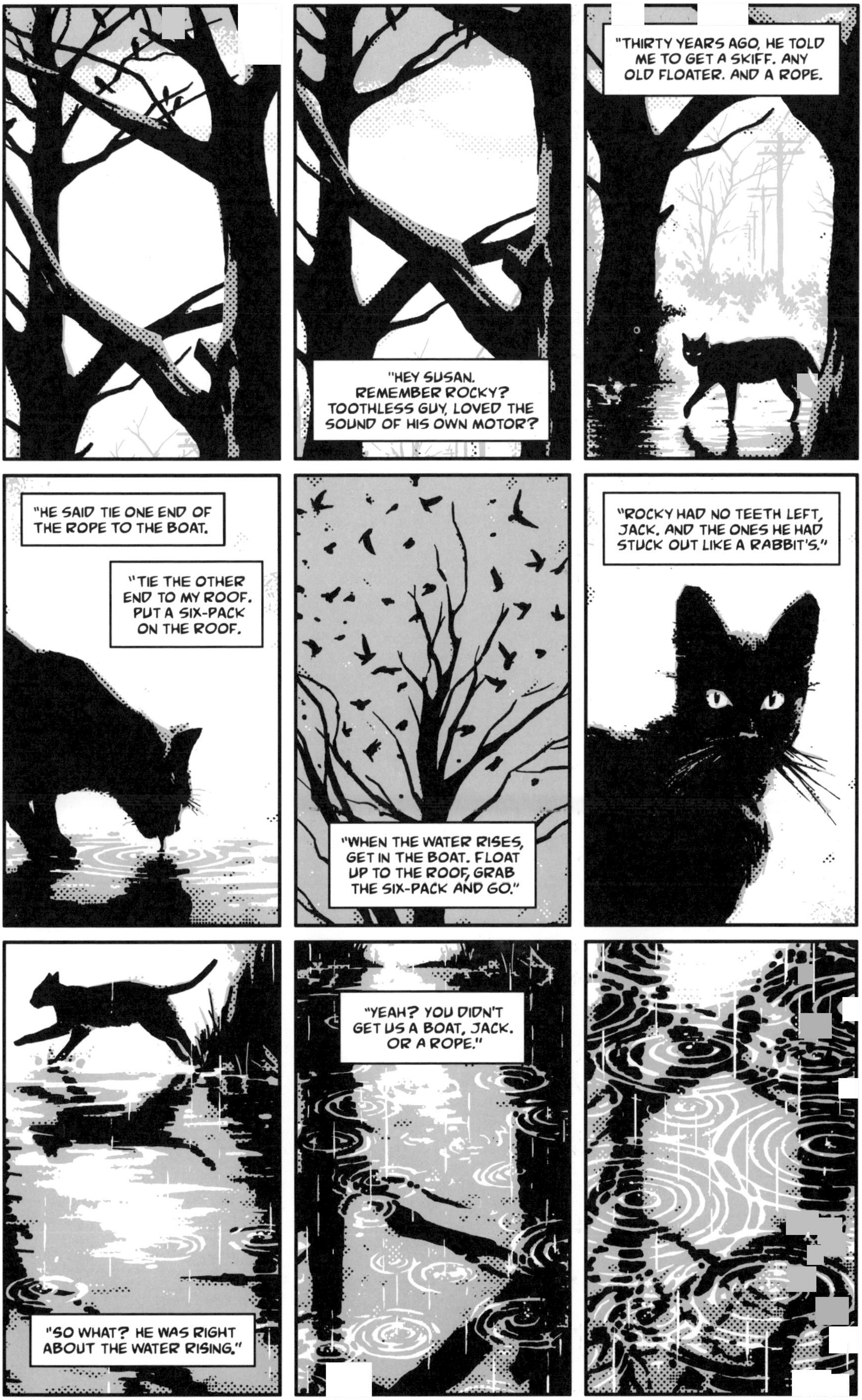
"HEY SUSAN.
REMEMBER ROCKY?
TOOTHLESS GUY, LOVED THE
SOUND OF HIS OWN MOTOR?
"THIRTY YEARS AGO, HE TOLD
ME TO GET A SKIFF. ANY
OLD FLOATER. AND A ROPE.
"HE SAID TIE ONE END OF
THE ROPE TO THE BOAT.
"TIE THE OTHER
END TO MY ROOF.
PUT A SIX-PACK
ON THE ROOF.
"WHEN THE WATER RISES,
GET IN THE BOAT. FLOAT
UP TO THE ROOF, GRAB
THE SIX-PACK AND GO."
"ROCKY HAD NO TEETH LEFT,
JACK. AND THE ONES HE HAD
STUCK OUT LIKE A RABBIT'S."
"SO WHAT? HE WAS RIGHT
ABOUT THE WATER RISING."
"YEAH? YOU DIDN'T
GET US A BOAT, JACK.
OR A ROPE."

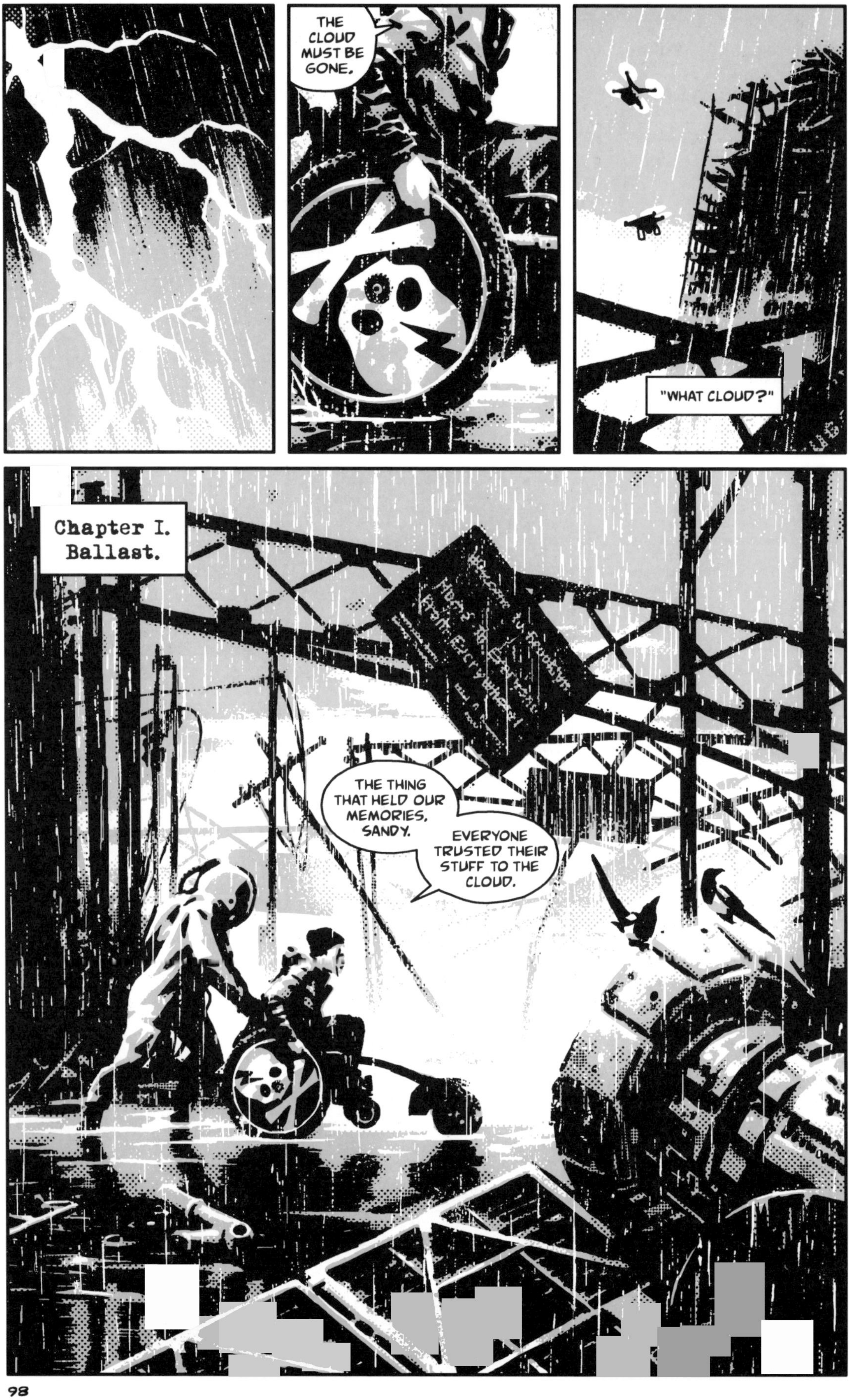
THE CLOUD MUST BE GONE.
"WHAT CLOUD?"
Chapter I. Ballast.
THE THING THAT HELD OUR MEMORIES, SANDY.
EVERYONE TRUSTED THEIR STUFF TO THE CLOUD.

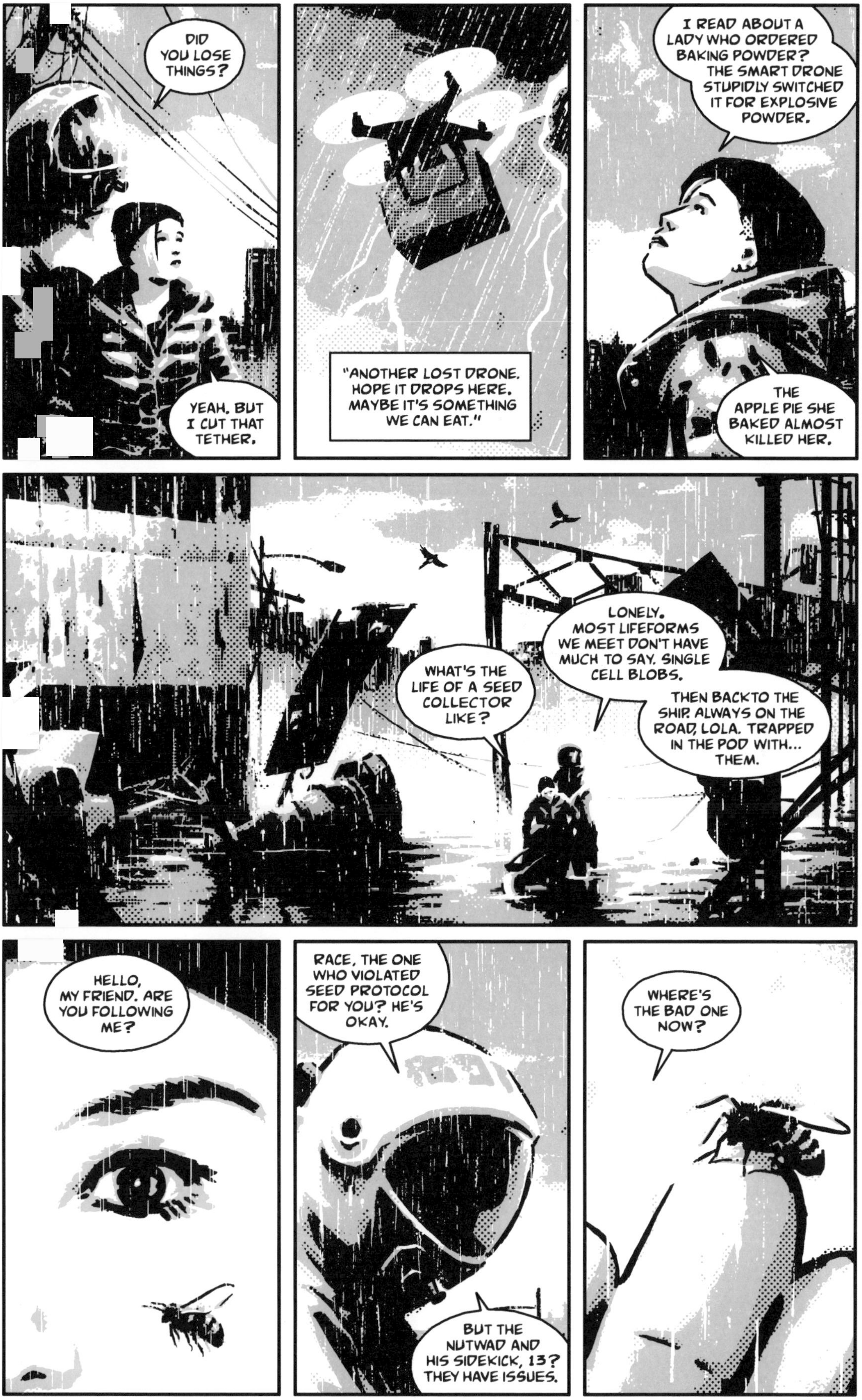
DID YOU LOSE THINGS?
YEAH, BUT I CUT THAT TETHER.
"ANOTHER LOST DRONE. HOPE IT DROPS HERE. MAYBE IT'S SOMETHING WE CAN EAT."
I READ ABOUT A LADY WHO ORDERED BAKING POWDER?
THE SMART DRONE STUPIDLY SWITCHED IT FOR EXPLOSIVE POWDER.
THE APPLE PIE SHE BAKED ALMOST KILLED HER.
WHAT'S THE LIFE OF A SEED COLLECTOR LIKE?
LONELY. MOST LIFEFORMS WE MEET DON'T HAVE MUCH TO SAY. SINGLE CELL BLOBS.
THEN BACK TO THE SHIP. ALWAYS ON THE ROAD, LOLA. TRAPPED IN THE POD WITH... THEM.
HELLO, MY FRIEND. ARE YOU FOLLOWING ME?
RACE, THE ONE WHO VIOLATED SEED PROTOCOL FOR YOU? HE'S OKAY.
BUT THE NUTWAD AND HIS SIDEKICK, 13? THEY HAVE ISSUES.
WHERE'S THE BAD ONE NOW?

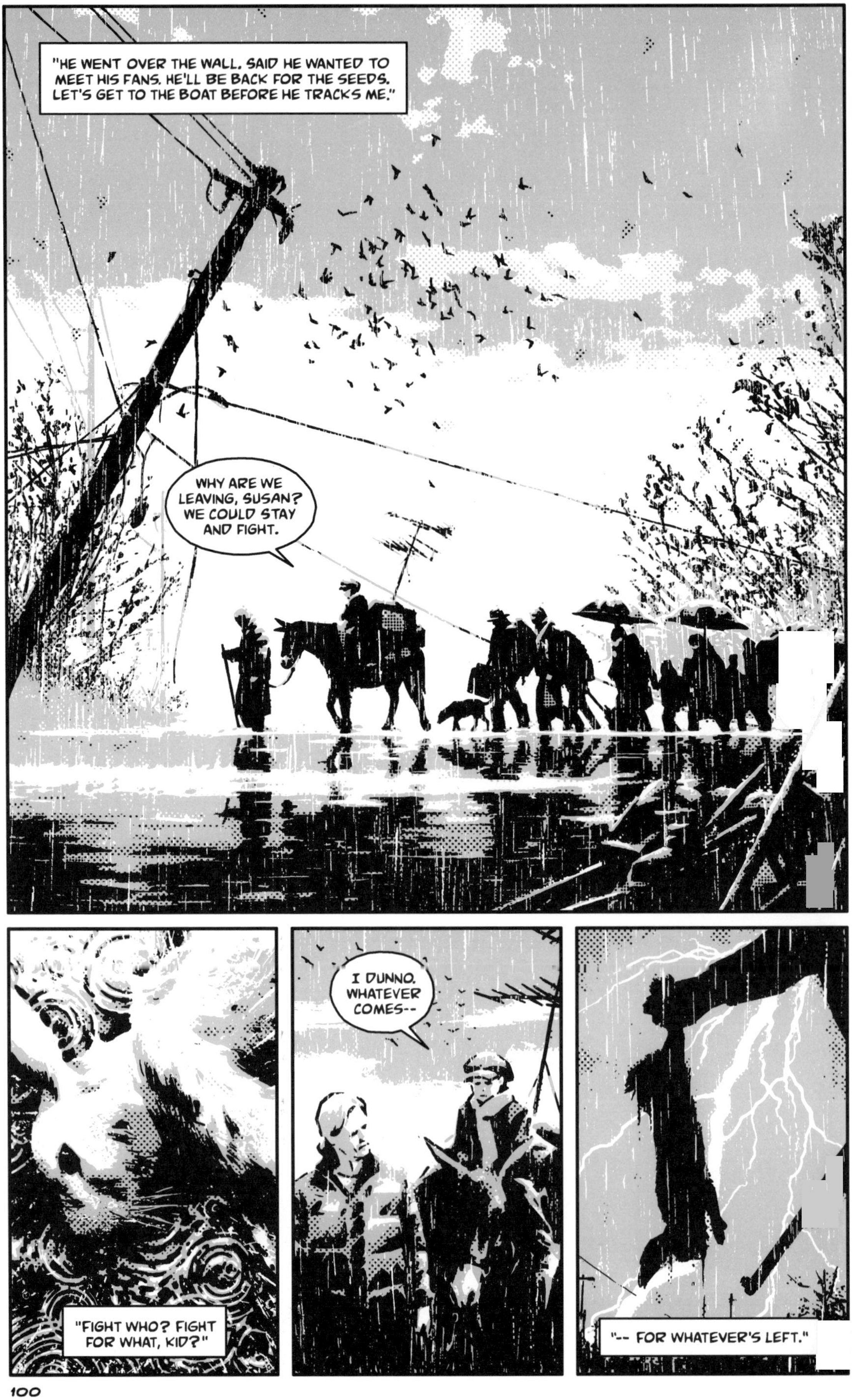
"HE WENT OVER THE WALL. SAID HE WANTED TO MEET HIS FANS. HE'LL BE BACK FOR THE SEEDS. LET'S GET TO THE BOAT BEFORE HE TRACKS ME."
WHY ARE WE LEAVING, SUSAN? WE COULD STAY AND FIGHT.
"FIGHT WHO? FIGHT FOR WHAT, KID?"
I DUNNO. WHATEVER COMES--
"-- FOR WHATEVER'S LEFT."

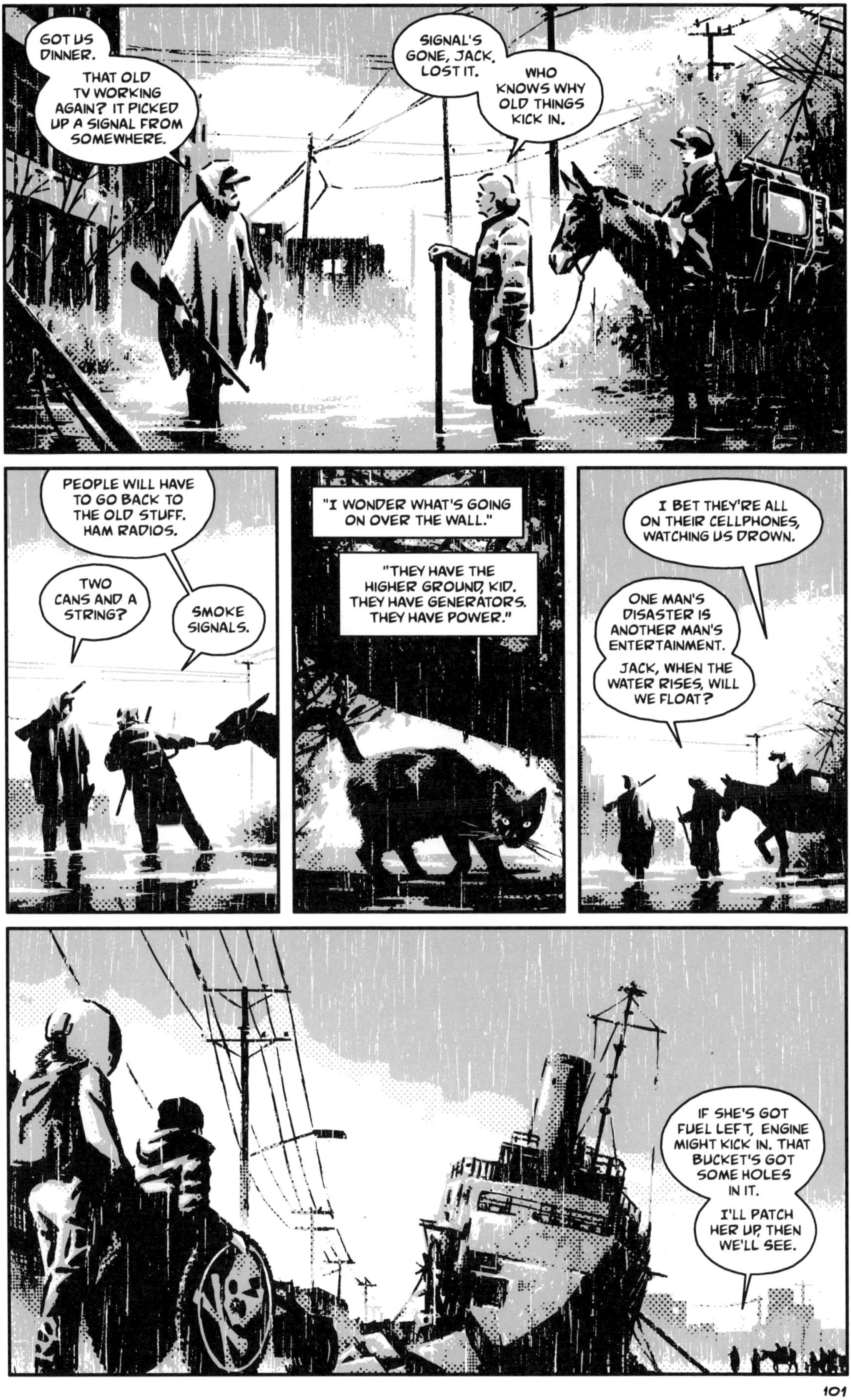
GOT US DINNER.
THAT OLD TV WORKING AGAIN? IT PICKED UP A SIGNAL FROM SOMEWHERE.
SIGNAL'S GONE, JACK. LOST IT.
WHO KNOWS WHY OLD THINGS KICK IN.
PEOPLE WILL HAVE TO GO BACK TO THE OLD STUFF. HAM RADIOS.
TWO CANS AND A STRING?
SMOKE SIGNALS.
"I WONDER WHAT'S GOING ON OVER THE WALL."
"THEY HAVE THE HIGHER GROUND, KID. THEY HAVE GENERATORS. THEY HAVE POWER."
I BET THEY'RE ALL ON THEIR CELLPHONES, WATCHING US DROWN.
ONE MAN'S DISASTER IS ANOTHER MAN'S ENTERTAINMENT.
JACK, WHEN THE WATER RISES, WILL WE FLOAT?
IF SHE'S GOT FUEL LEFT, ENGINE MIGHT KICK IN. THAT BUCKET'S GOT SOME HOLES IN IT.
I'LL PATCH HER UP, THEN WE'LL SEE.

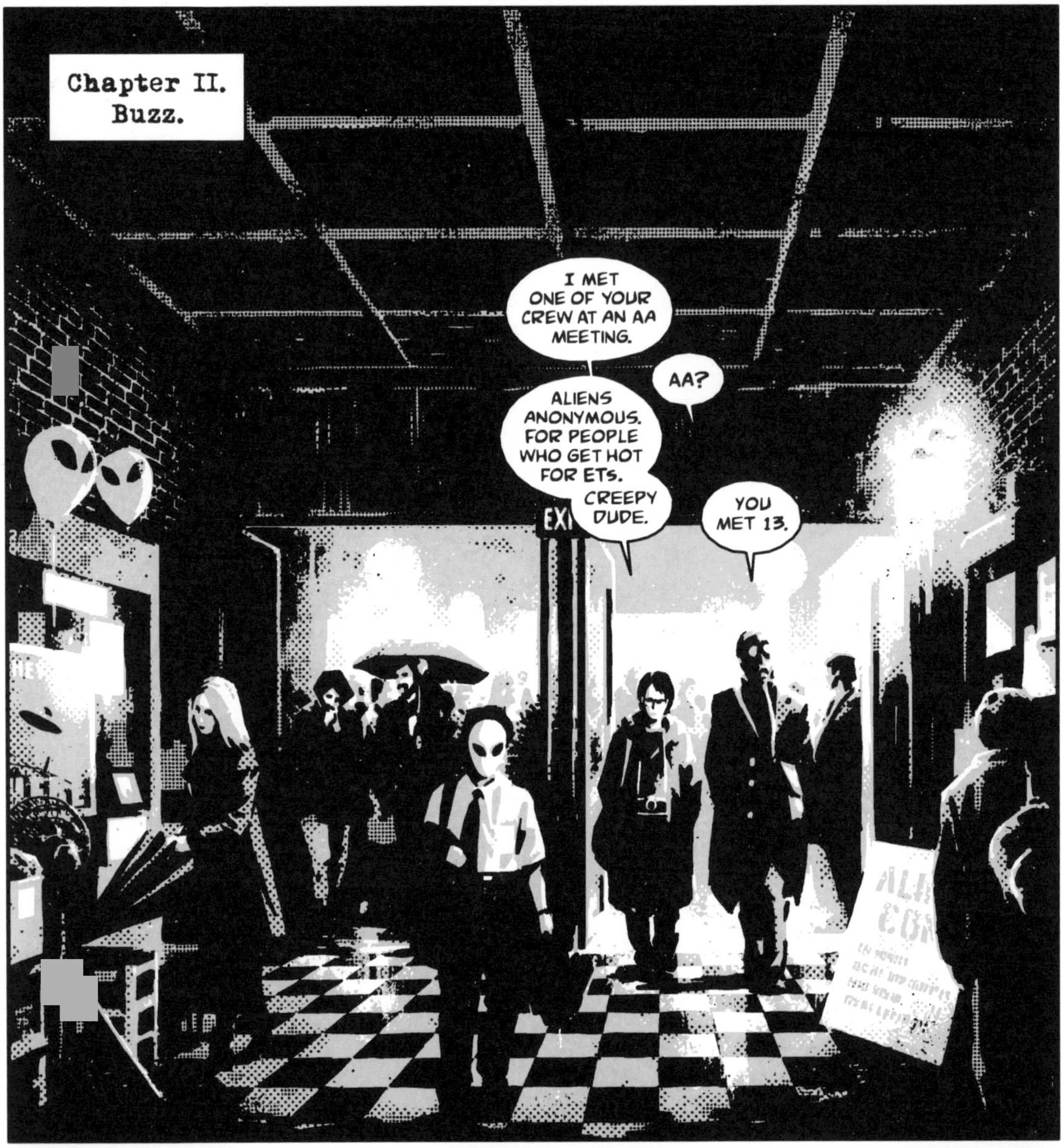
Chapter II.
Buzz.
I MET ONE OF YOUR CREW AT AN AA MEETING.
AA?
ALIENS ANONYMOUS. FOR PEOPLE WHO GET HOT FOR ETs.
CREEPY DUDE.
YOU MET 13.

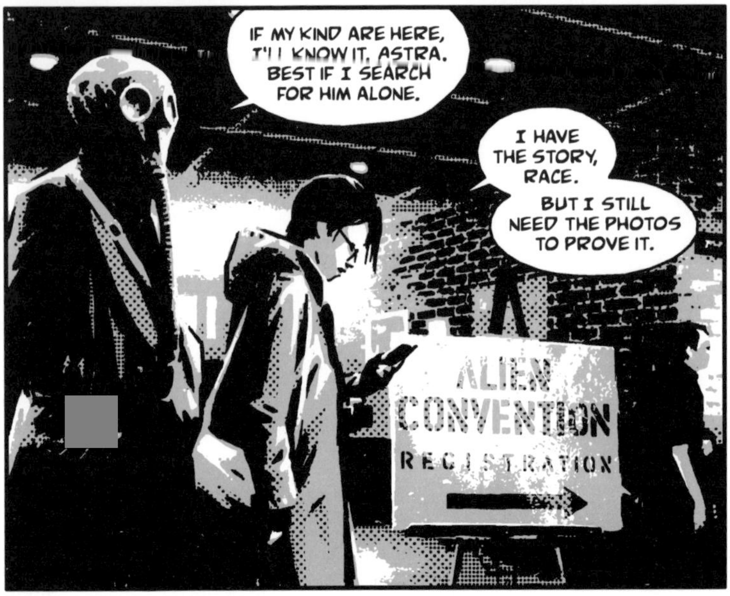
IF MY KIND ARE HERE, I'LL KNOW IT, ASTRA. BEST IF I SEARCH FOR HIM ALONE.
I HAVE THE STORY, RACE.
BUT I STILL NEED THE PHOTOS TO PROVE IT.
ALIEN CONVENTION
REGISTRATION

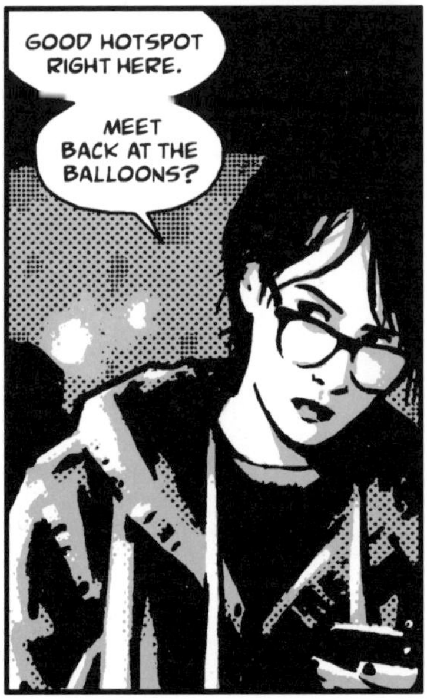
GOOD HOTSPOT RIGHT HERE.
MEET BACK AT THE BALLOONS?

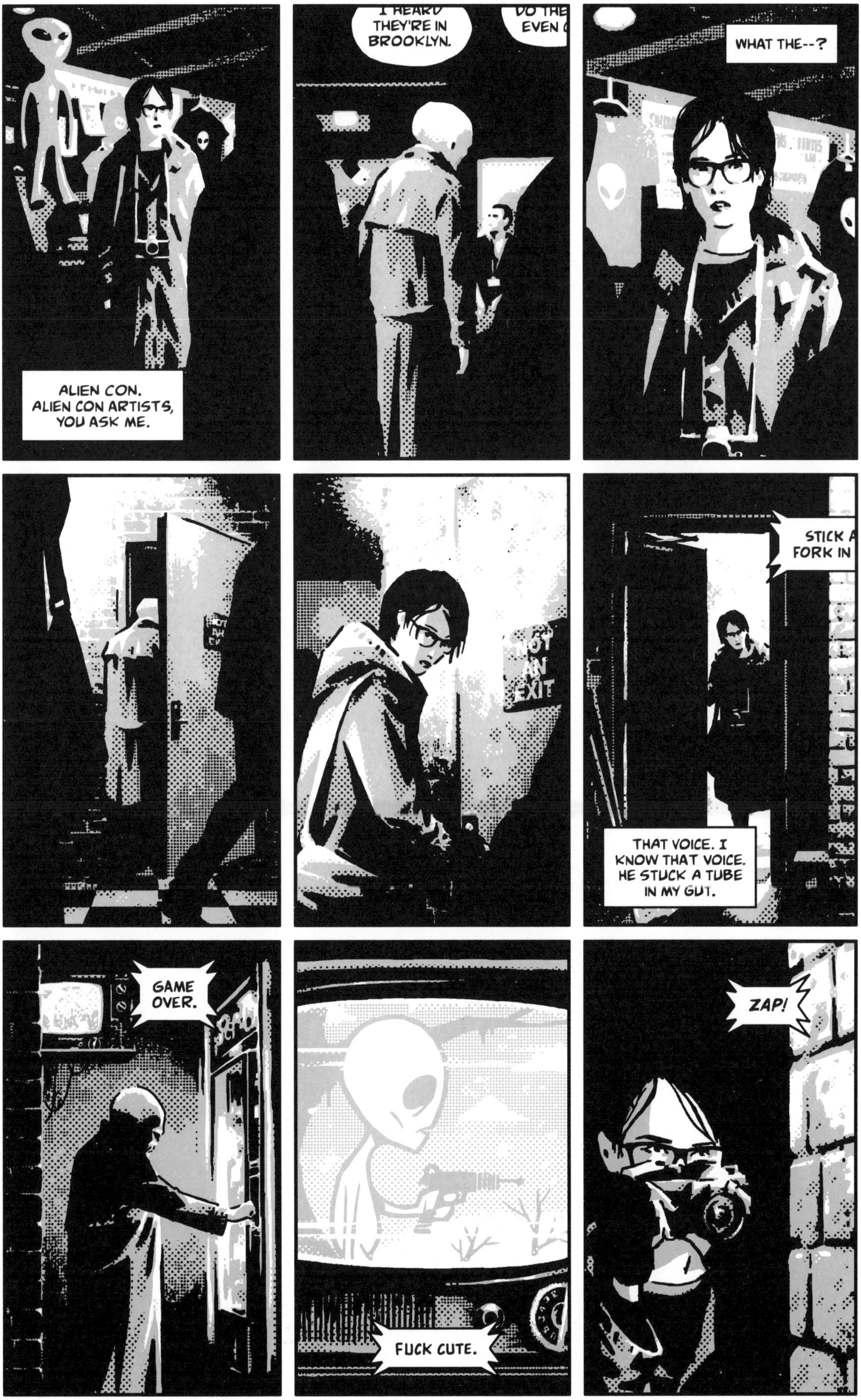

ALIEN CON. ALIEN CON ARTISTS, YOU ASK ME.
I HEARD THEY'RE IN BROOKLYN.
DO THE EVEN
WHAT THE--?
NOT AN EXIT
STICK A FORK IN
THAT VOICE. I KNOW THAT VOICE. HE STUCK A TUBE IN MY GUT.
GAME OVER.
FUCK CUTE.
ZAP!

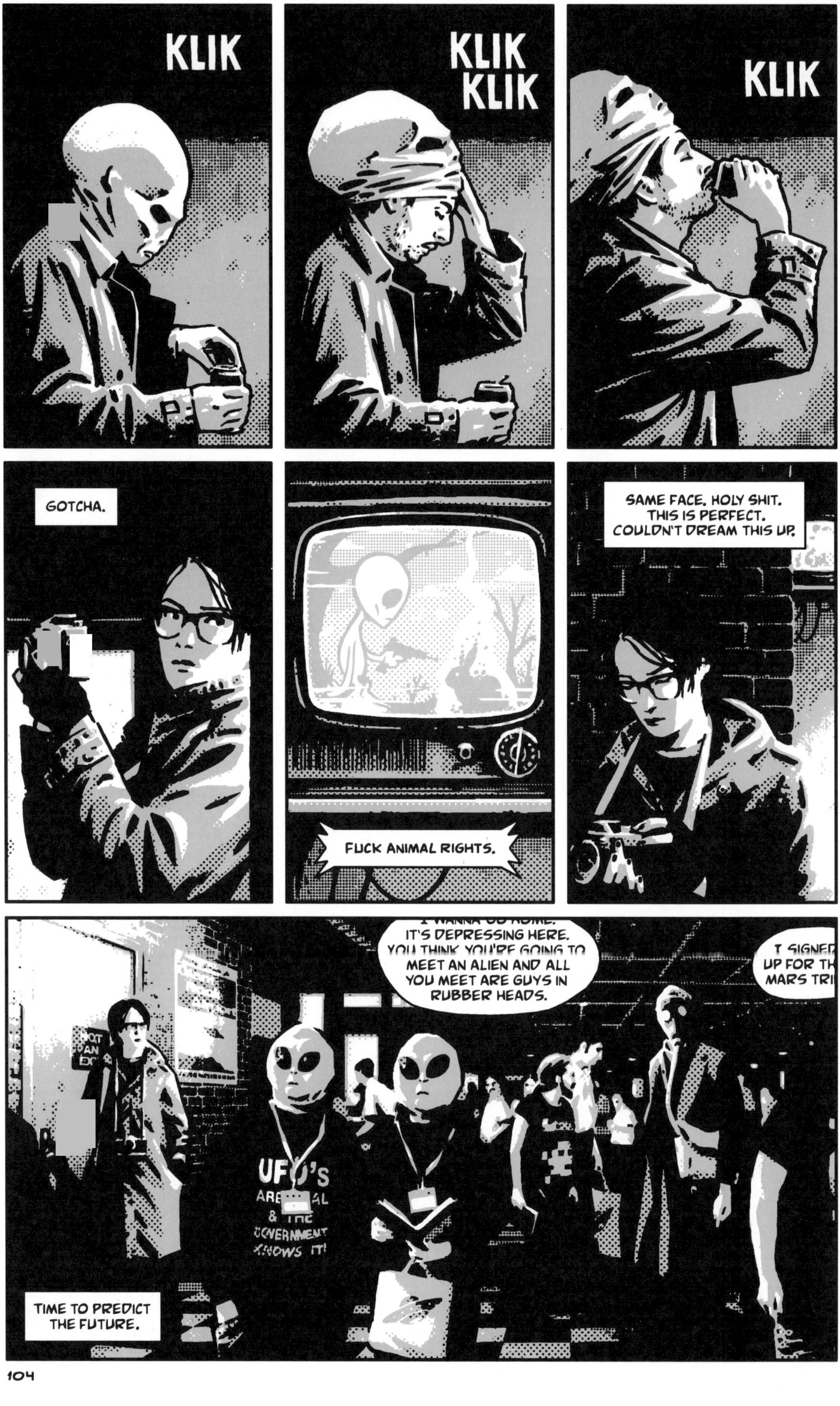
KLIK
KLIK
KLIK
KLIK
GOTCHA.
FUCK ANIMAL RIGHTS.
SAME FACE. HOLY SHIT. THIS IS PERFECT. COULDN'T DREAM THIS UP.
I WANNA GO HOME. IT'S DEPRESSING HERE. YOU THINK YOU'RE GOING TO MEET AN ALIEN AND ALL YOU MEET ARE GUYS IN RUBBER HEADS.
I SIGNED UP FOR TH MARS TRI
TIME TO PREDICT THE FUTURE.

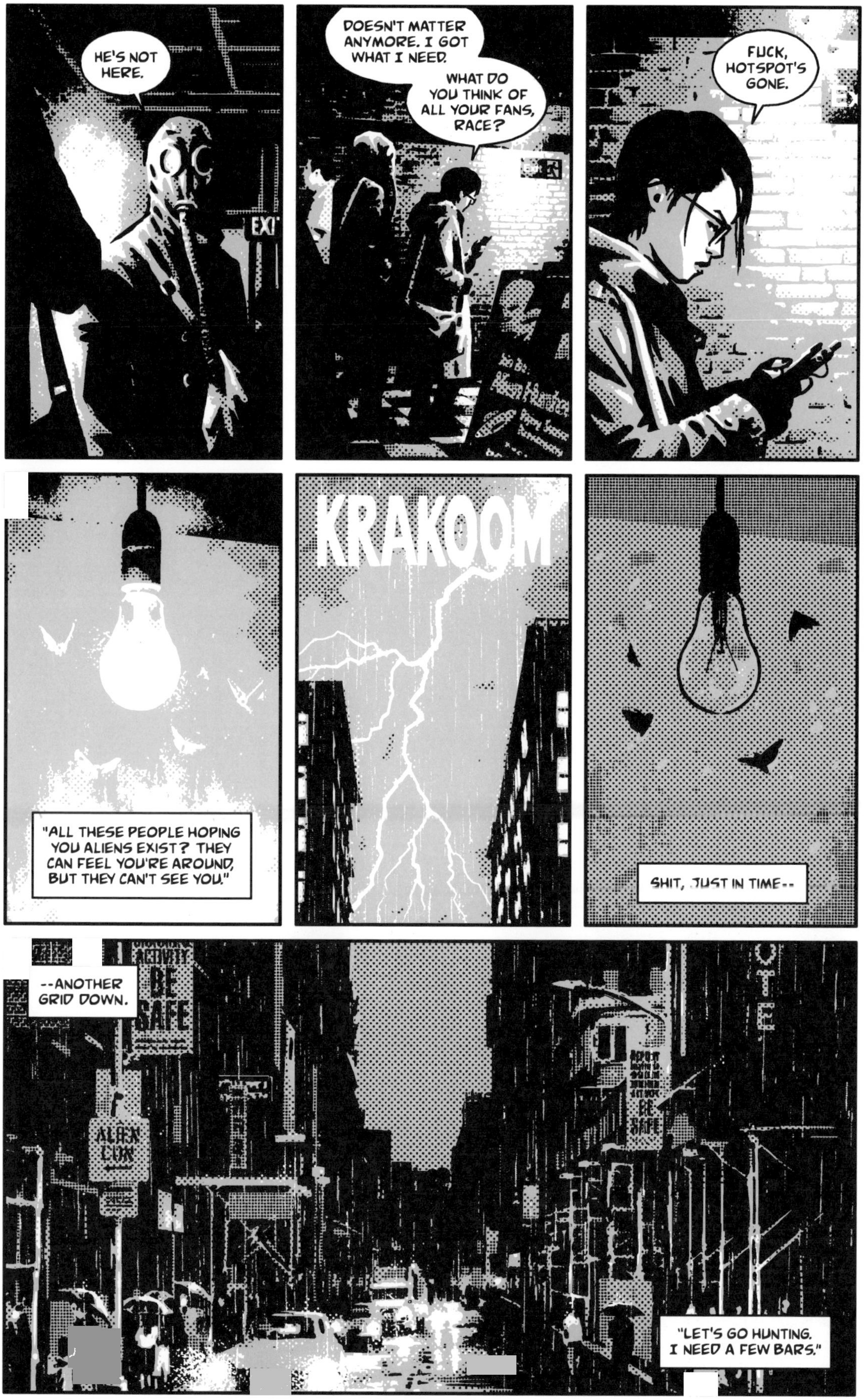
HE'S NOT HERE.
DOESN'T MATTER ANYMORE. I GOT WHAT I NEED.
WHAT DO YOU THINK OF ALL YOUR FANS, RACE?
FUCK, HOTSPOT'S GONE.
"ALL THESE PEOPLE HOPING YOU ALIENS EXIST? THEY CAN FEEL YOU'RE AROUND, BUT THEY CAN'T SEE YOU."
KRAKOOM
SHIT, JUST IN TIME--
--ANOTHER GRID DOWN.
BE SAFE
"LET'S GO HUNTING. I NEED A FEW BARS."

SORRY OUT OF SERVICE

I GUESS WE ALWAYS KNEW THIS DAY WOULD COME.

MONEY STUCK IN BANKS, LAUNDRY STUCK IN DIGITAL MACHINES...

TK TK TK TK

Out of Service

Apologies for any inconvenience

SCREENS BLINKING OUT ACROSS THE GLOBE.

Chapter III. Blitz.

BIKE LANE BIKES ONLY

ONE WAY

POWER FOR SALE

TURNS OUT WE WERE ROWING AGAINST THE TIDE.

PADDLING IN CIRCLES, NO CLUE WHICH WAY THE RIVER FLOWS.

THEY SAY A RISING TIDE LIFTS ALL BOATS.

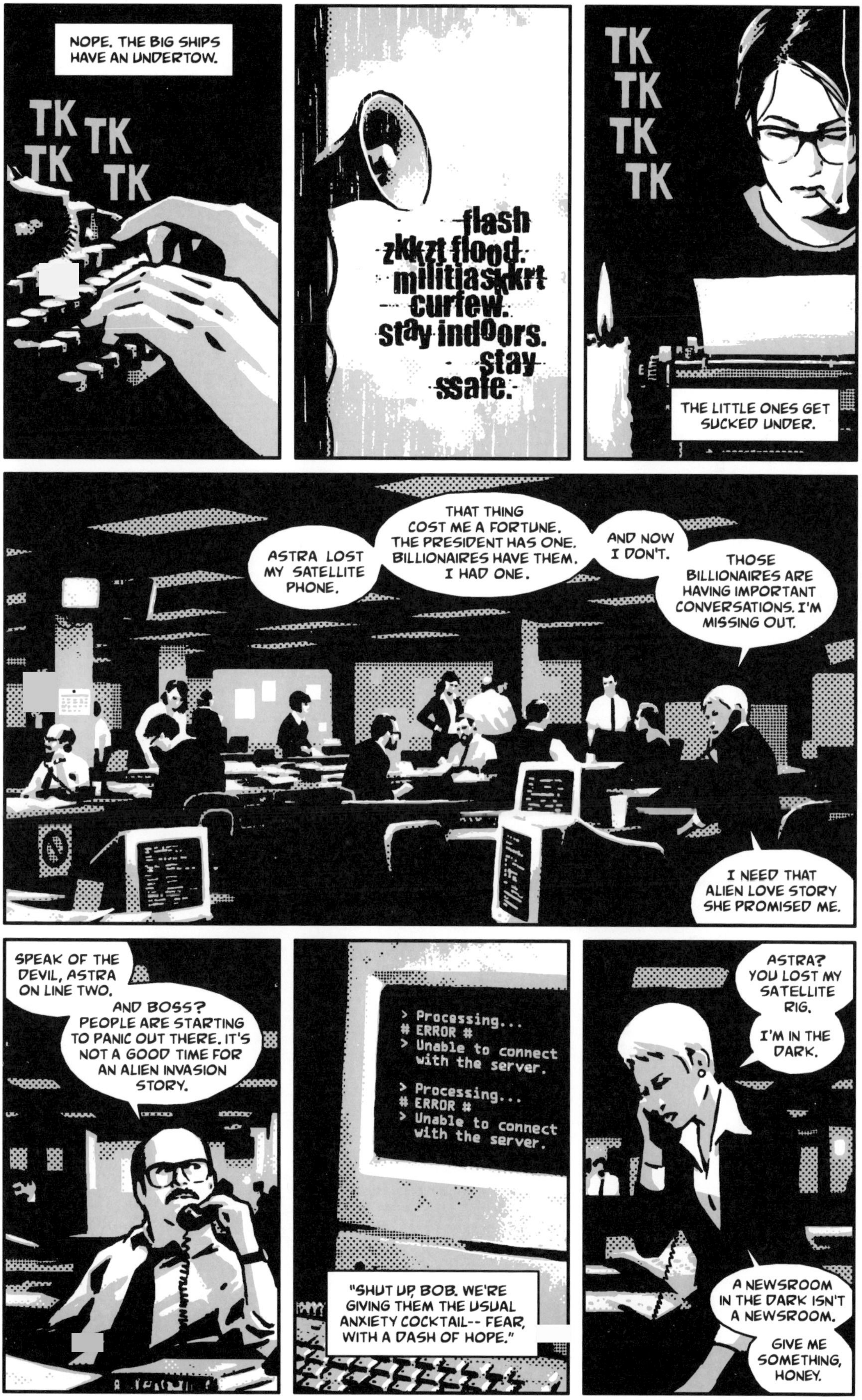
NOPE. THE BIG SHIPS HAVE AN UNDERTOW.
TK TK TK TK
flash zkkzt flood. militiaskkrt curfew. stay indoors. stay ssafe.
TK TK TK TK
THE LITTLE ONES GET SUCKED UNDER.
ASTRA LOST MY SATELLITE PHONE.
THAT THING COST ME A FORTUNE. THE PRESIDENT HAS ONE. BILLIONAIRES HAVE THEM. I HAD ONE.
AND NOW I DON'T.
THOSE BILLIONAIRES ARE HAVING IMPORTANT CONVERSATIONS. I'M MISSING OUT.
I NEED THAT ALIEN LOVE STORY SHE PROMISED ME.
SPEAK OF THE DEVIL, ASTRA ON LINE TWO.
AND BOSS? PEOPLE ARE STARTING TO PANIC OUT THERE. IT'S NOT A GOOD TIME FOR AN ALIEN INVASION STORY.
> Processing... # ERROR # > Unable to connect with the server.
> Processing... # ERROR # > Unable to connect with the server.
"SHUT UP, BOB. WE'RE GIVING THEM THE USUAL ANXIETY COCKTAIL-- FEAR, WITH A DASH OF HOPE."
ASTRA? YOU LOST MY SATELLITE RIG.
I'M IN THE DARK.
A NEWSROOM IN THE DARK ISN'T A NEWSROOM.
GIVE ME SOMETHING, HONEY.

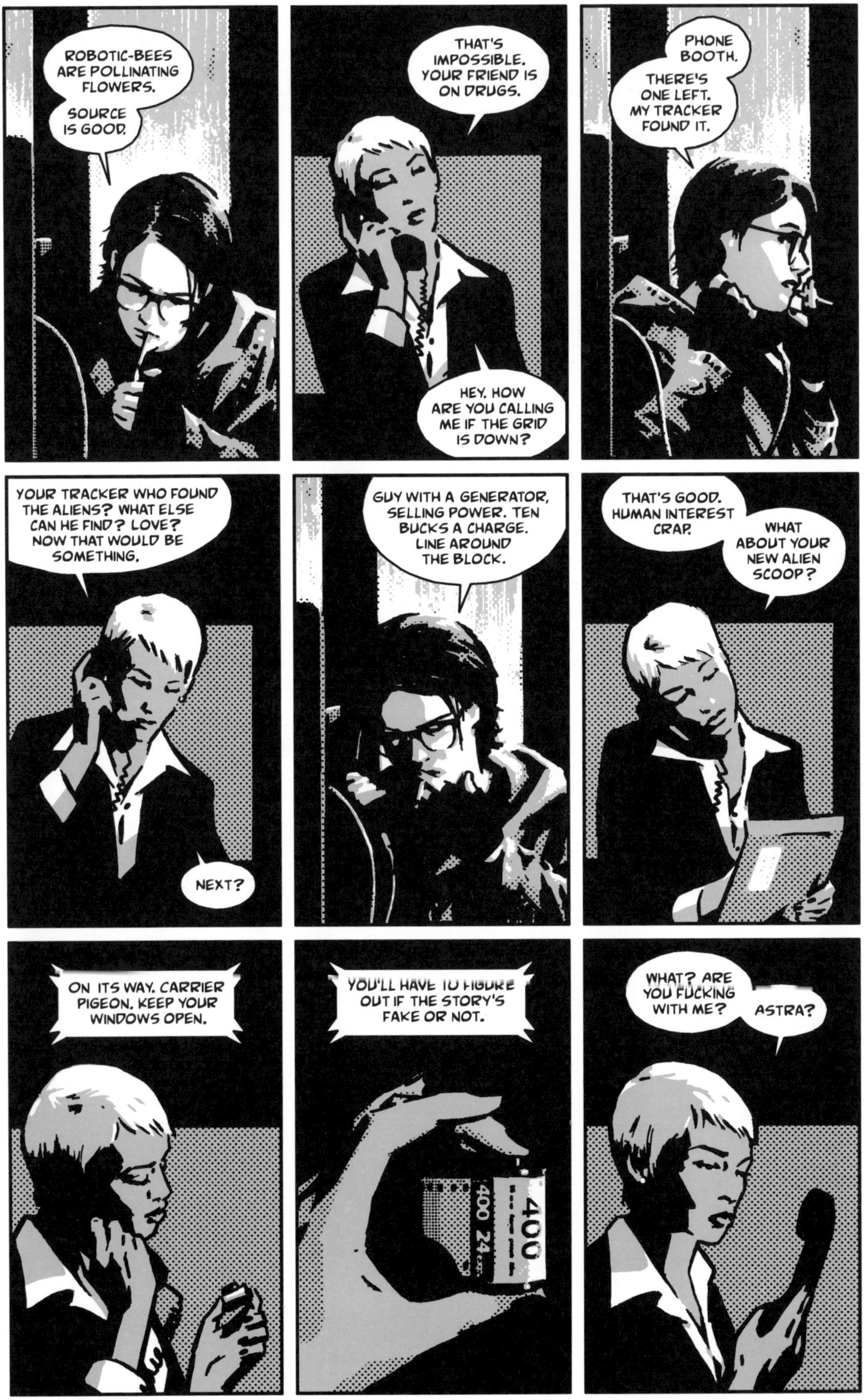
ROBOTIC-BEES ARE POLLINATING FLOWERS.
SOURCE IS GOOD.
THAT'S IMPOSSIBLE. YOUR FRIEND IS ON DRUGS.
HEY. HOW ARE YOU CALLING ME IF THE GRID IS DOWN?
PHONE BOOTH.
THERE'S ONE LEFT. MY TRACKER FOUND IT.
YOUR TRACKER WHO FOUND THE ALIENS? WHAT ELSE CAN HE FIND? LOVE? NOW THAT WOULD BE SOMETHING.
NEXT?
GUY WITH A GENERATOR, SELLING POWER. TEN BUCKS A CHARGE. LINE AROUND THE BLOCK.
THAT'S GOOD. HUMAN INTEREST CRAP.
WHAT ABOUT YOUR NEW ALIEN SCOOP?
ON ITS WAY. CARRIER PIGEON. KEEP YOUR WINDOWS OPEN.
YOU'LL HAVE TO FIGURE OUT IF THE STORY'S FAKE OR NOT.
400
400 24
WHAT? ARE YOU FUCKING WITH ME?
ASTRA?

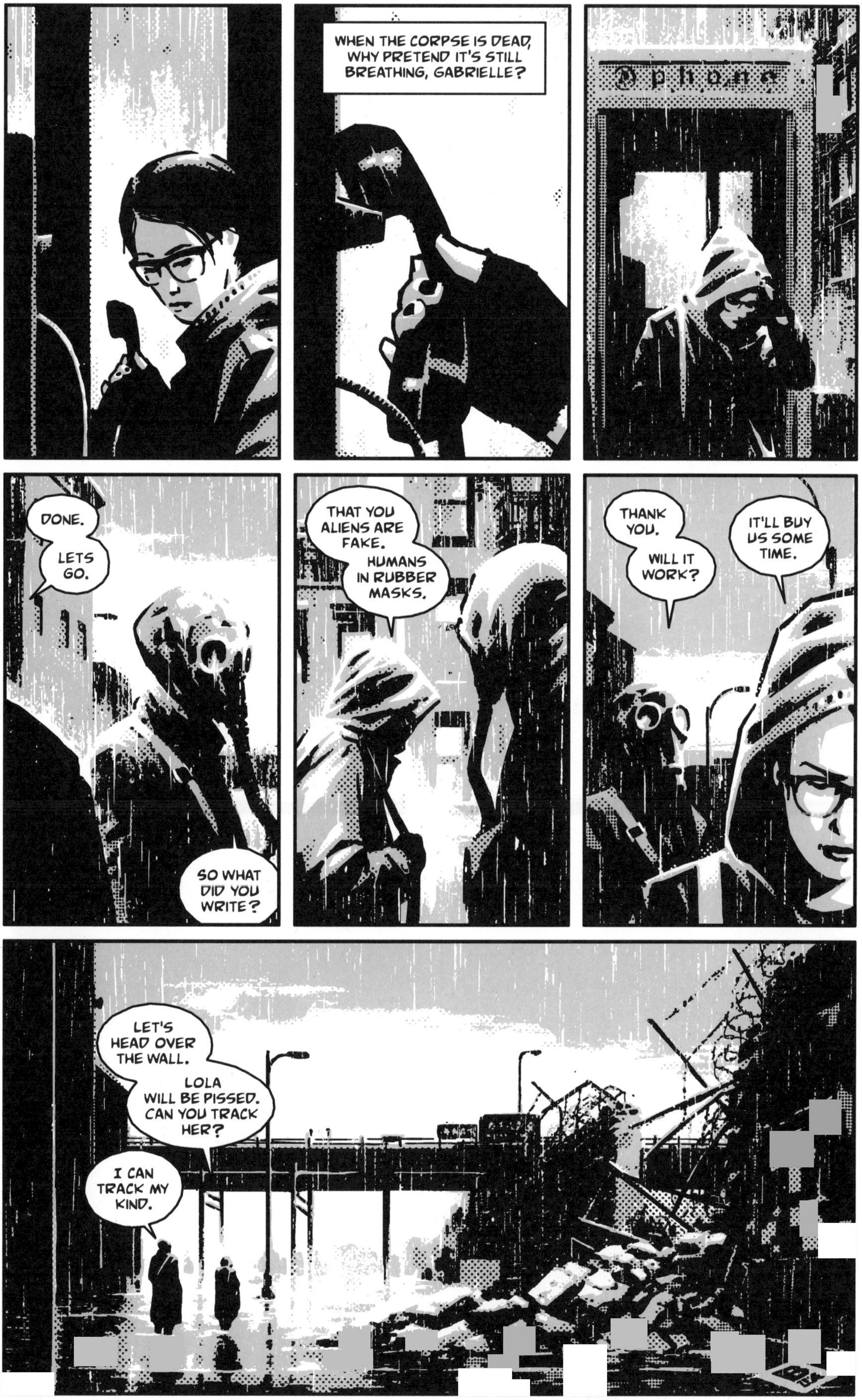
WHEN THE CORPSE IS DEAD, WHY PRETEND IT'S STILL BREATHING, GABRIELLE?
phone
DONE.
LETS GO.
SO WHAT DID YOU WRITE?
THAT YOU ALIENS ARE FAKE.
HUMANS IN RUBBER MASKS.
THANK YOU.
WILL IT WORK?
IT'LL BUY US SOME TIME.
LET'S HEAD OVER THE WALL.
LOLA WILL BE PISSED. CAN YOU TRACK HER?
I CAN TRACK MY KIND.

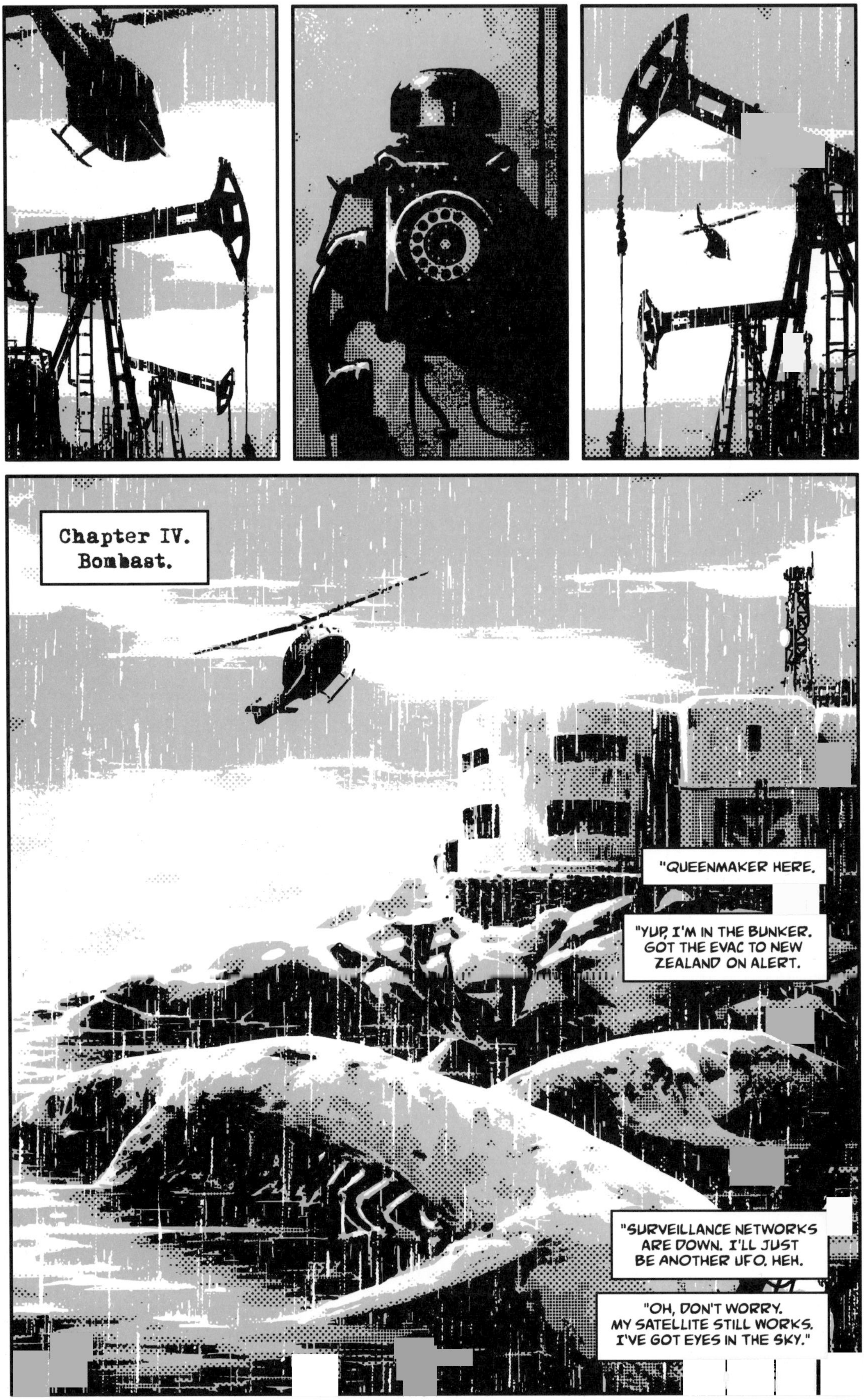
Chapter IV.
Bombast.
"QUEENMAKER HERE.
"YUP, I'M IN THE BUNKER. GOT THE EVAC TO NEW ZEALAND ON ALERT.
"SURVEILLANCE NETWORKS ARE DOWN. I'LL JUST BE ANOTHER UFO. HEH.
"OH, DON'T WORRY. MY SATELLITE STILL WORKS. I'VE GOT EYES IN THE SKY."

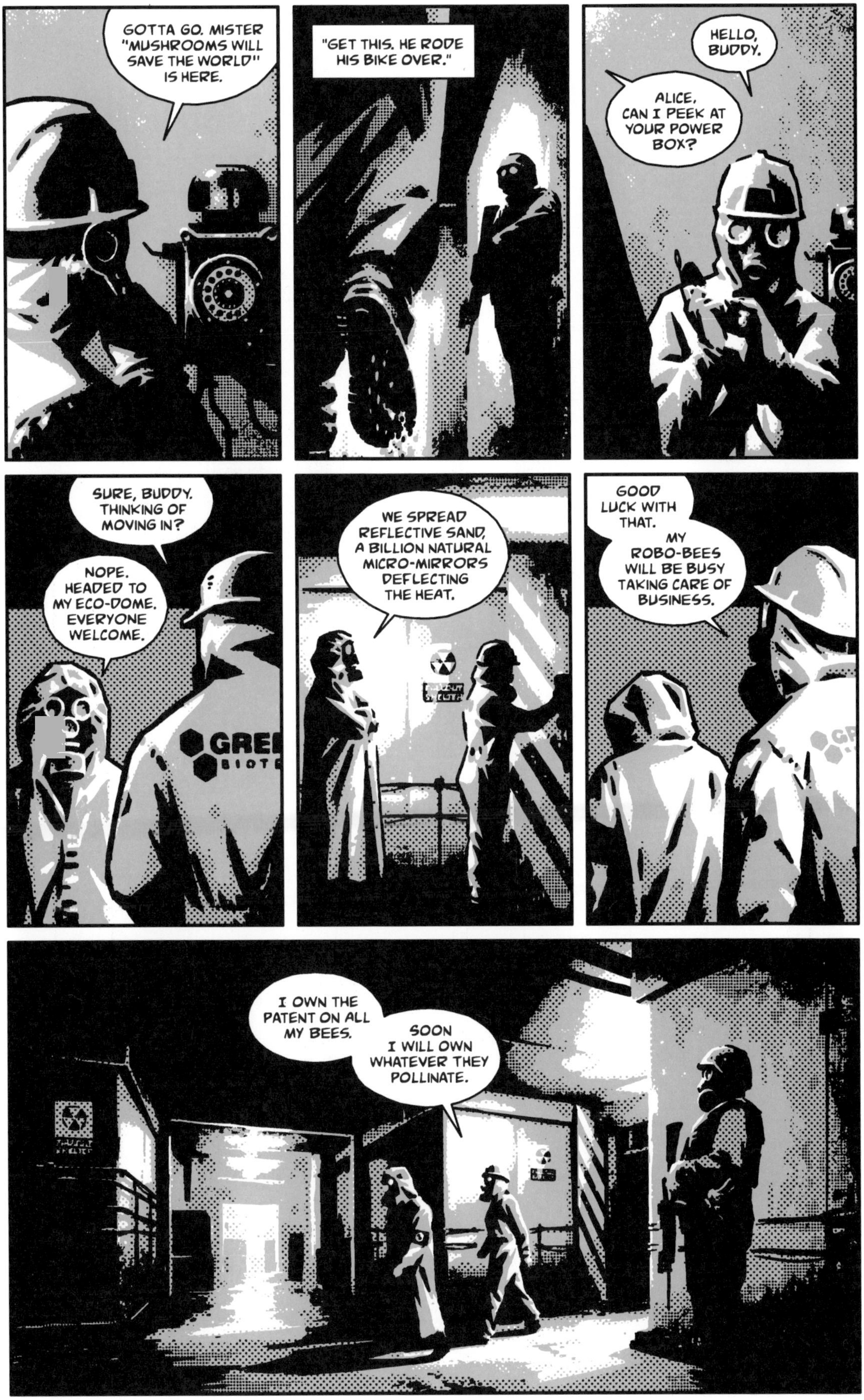
GOTTA GO. MISTER "MUSHROOMS WILL SAVE THE WORLD" IS HERE.
"GET THIS. HE RODE HIS BIKE OVER."
HELLO, BUDDY.
ALICE, CAN I PEEK AT YOUR POWER BOX?
SURE, BUDDY. THINKING OF MOVING IN?
NOPE. HEADED TO MY ECO-DOME. EVERYONE WELCOME.
WE SPREAD REFLECTIVE SAND, A BILLION NATURAL MICRO-MIRRORS DEFLECTING THE HEAT.
GOOD LUCK WITH THAT.
MY ROBO-BEES WILL BE BUSY TAKING CARE OF BUSINESS.
I OWN THE PATENT ON ALL MY BEES.
SOON I WILL OWN WHATEVER THEY POLLINATE.

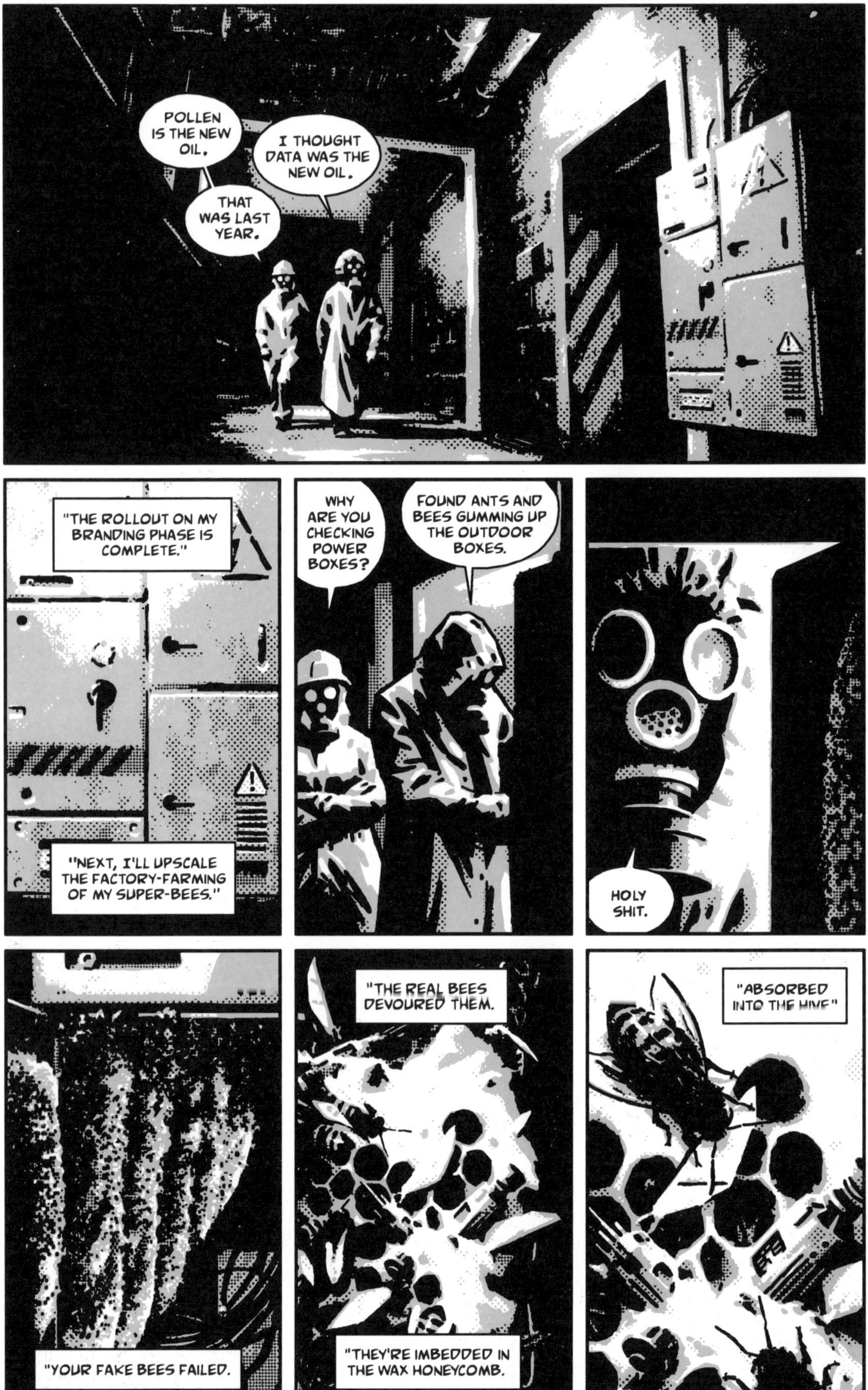
POLLEN IS THE NEW OIL.
I THOUGHT DATA WAS THE NEW OIL.
THAT WAS LAST YEAR.
"THE ROLLOUT ON MY BRANDING PHASE IS COMPLETE."
"NEXT, I'LL UPSCALE THE FACTORY-FARMING OF MY SUPER-BEES."
WHY ARE YOU CHECKING POWER BOXES?
FOUND ANTS AND BEES GUMMING UP THE OUTDOOR BOXES.
HOLY SHIT.
"YOUR FAKE BEES FAILED.
"THE REAL BEES DEVOURED THEM.
"THEY'RE IMBEDDED IN THE WAX HONEYCOMB.
"ABSORBED INTO THE HIVE"

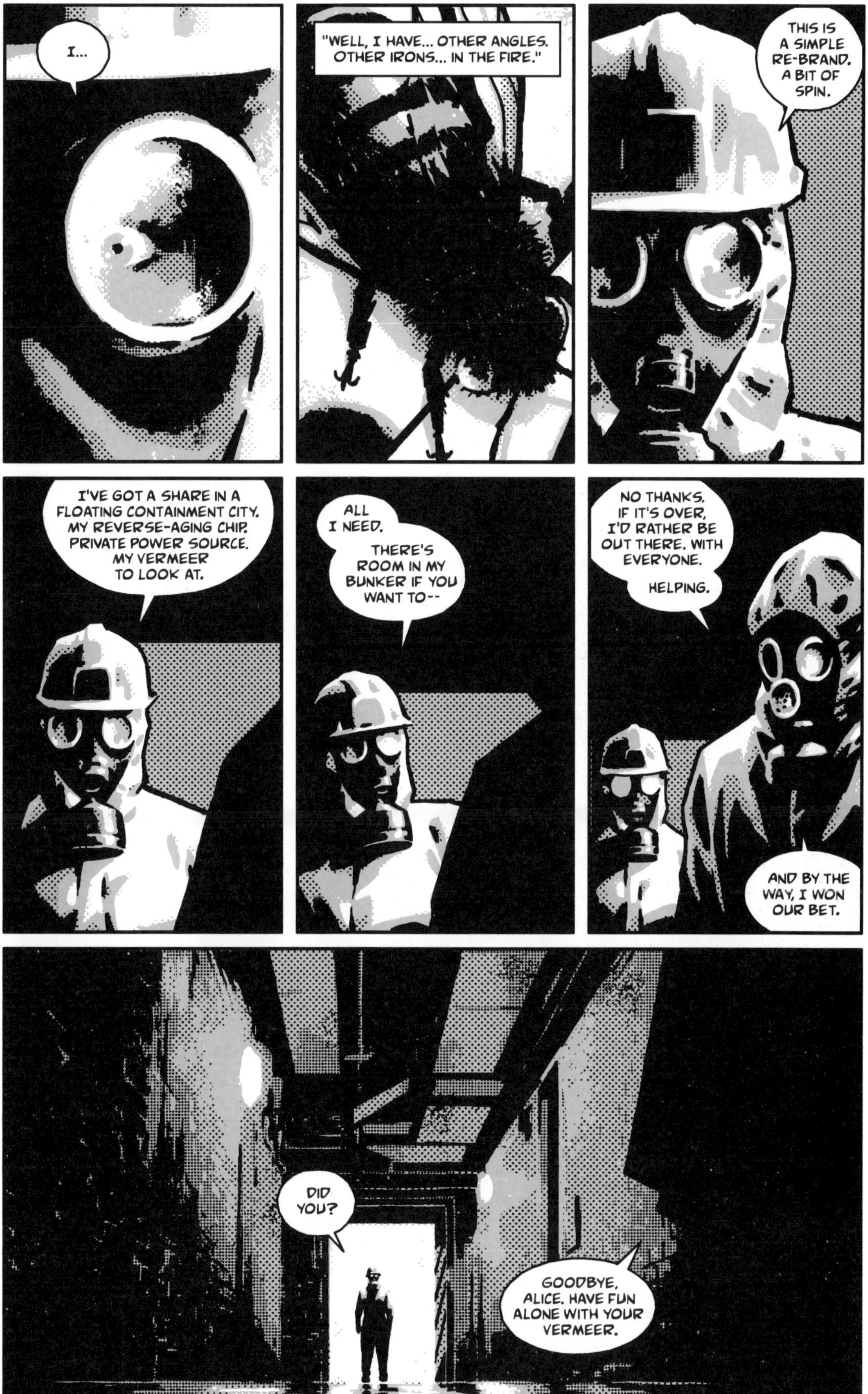
I...
"WELL, I HAVE... OTHER ANGLES. OTHER IRONS... IN THE FIRE."
THIS IS A SIMPLE RE-BRAND. A BIT OF SPIN.
I'VE GOT A SHARE IN A FLOATING CONTAINMENT CITY. MY REVERSE-AGING CHIP. PRIVATE POWER SOURCE. MY VERMEER TO LOOK AT.
ALL I NEED.
THERE'S ROOM IN MY BUNKER IF YOU WANT TO--
NO THANKS. IF IT'S OVER, I'D RATHER BE OUT THERE. WITH EVERYONE.
HELPING.
AND BY THE WAY, I WON OUR BET.
DID YOU?
GOODBYE, ALICE. HAVE FUN ALONE WITH YOUR VERMEER.

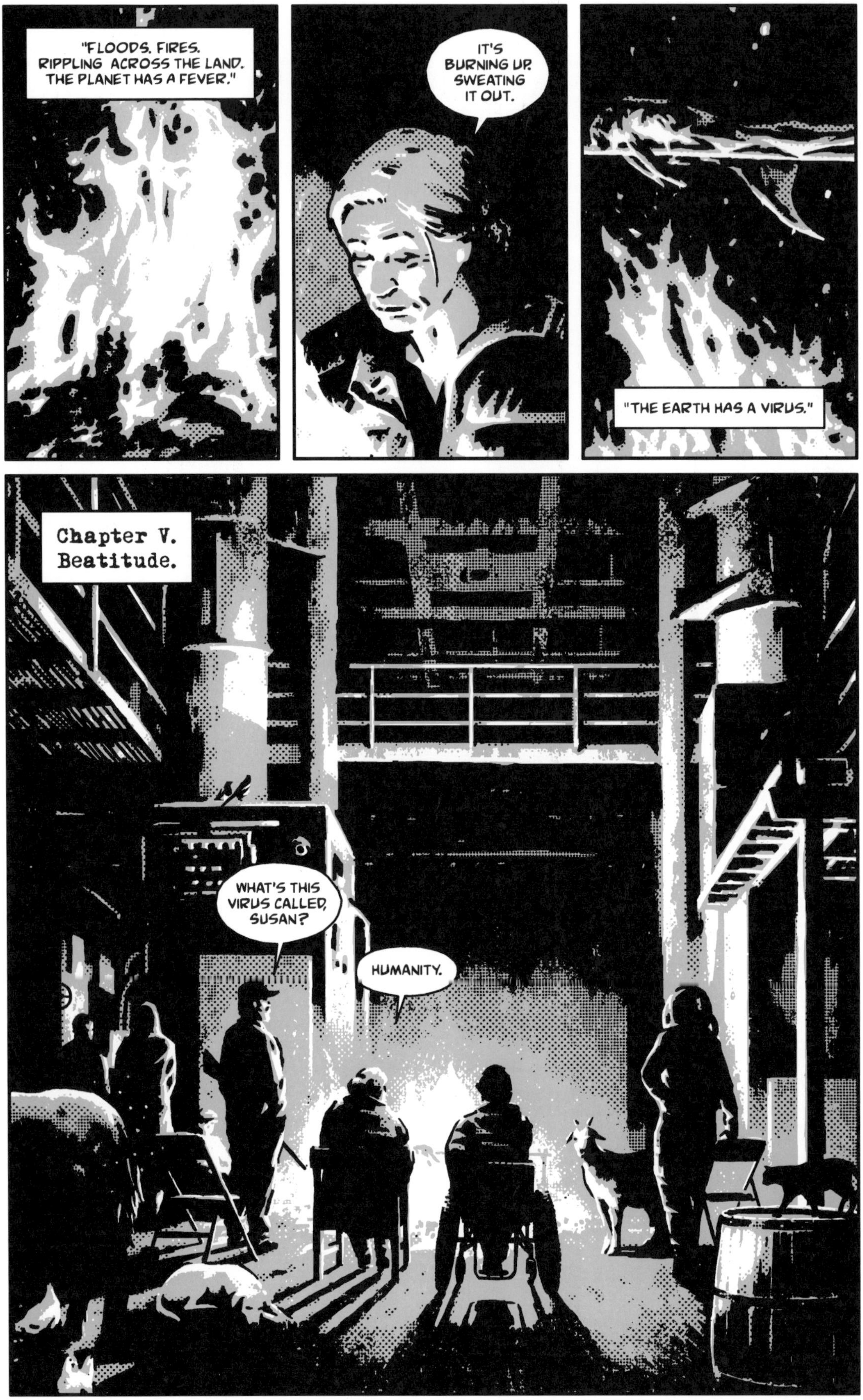
"FLOODS. FIRES. RIPPLING ACROSS THE LAND. THE PLANET HAS A FEVER."
IT'S BURNING UP. SWEATING IT OUT.
"THE EARTH HAS A VIRUS."
Chapter V. Beatitude.
WHAT'S THIS VIRUS CALLED, SUSAN?
HUMANITY.

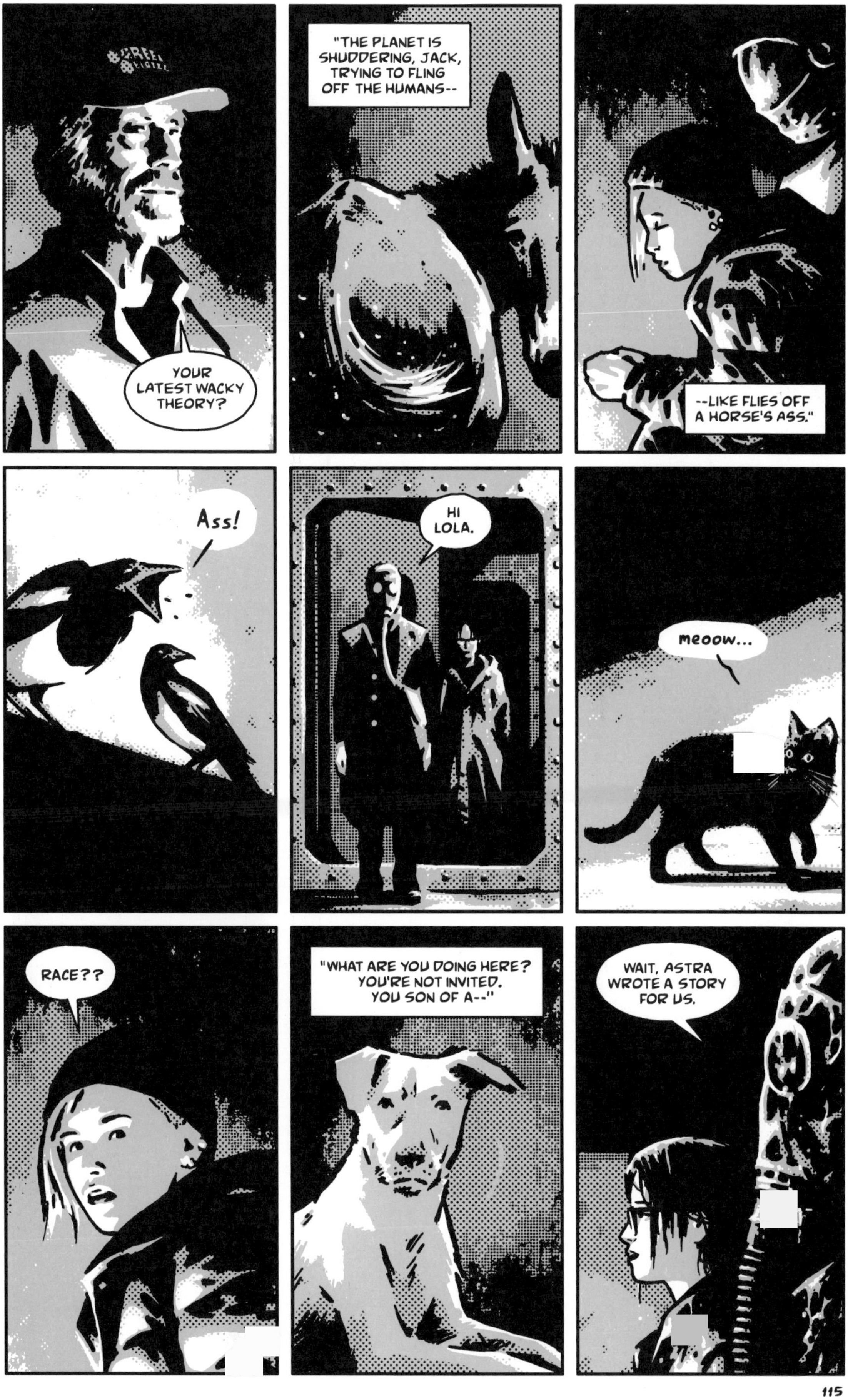
YOUR LATEST WACKY THEORY?
"THE PLANET IS SHUDDERING, JACK, TRYING TO FLING OFF THE HUMANS--
--LIKE FLIES OFF A HORSE'S ASS."
Ass!
HI LOLA.
meoow...
RACE??
"WHAT ARE YOU DOING HERE? YOU'RE NOT INVITED. YOU SON OF A--"
WAIT, ASTRA WROTE A STORY FOR US.

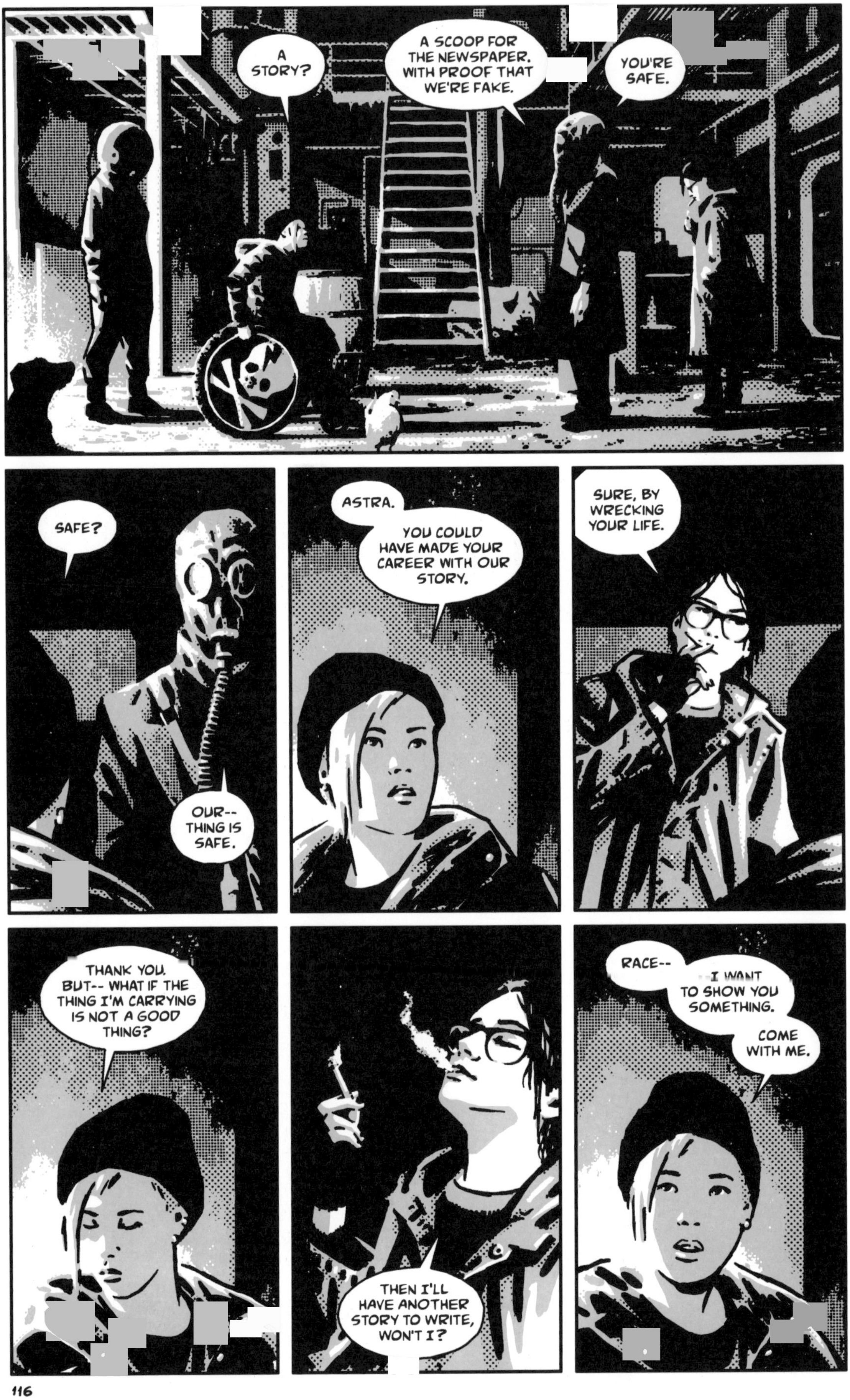
A STORY?
A SCOOP FOR THE NEWSPAPER. WITH PROOF THAT WE'RE FAKE.
YOU'RE SAFE.
SAFE?
OUR-- THING IS SAFE.
ASTRA.
YOU COULD HAVE MADE YOUR CAREER WITH OUR STORY.
SURE, BY WRECKING YOUR LIFE.
THANK YOU. BUT-- WHAT IF THE THING I'M CARRYING IS NOT A GOOD THING?
THEN I'LL HAVE ANOTHER STORY TO WRITE, WON'T I?
RACE--
I WANT TO SHOW YOU SOMETHING.
COME WITH ME.

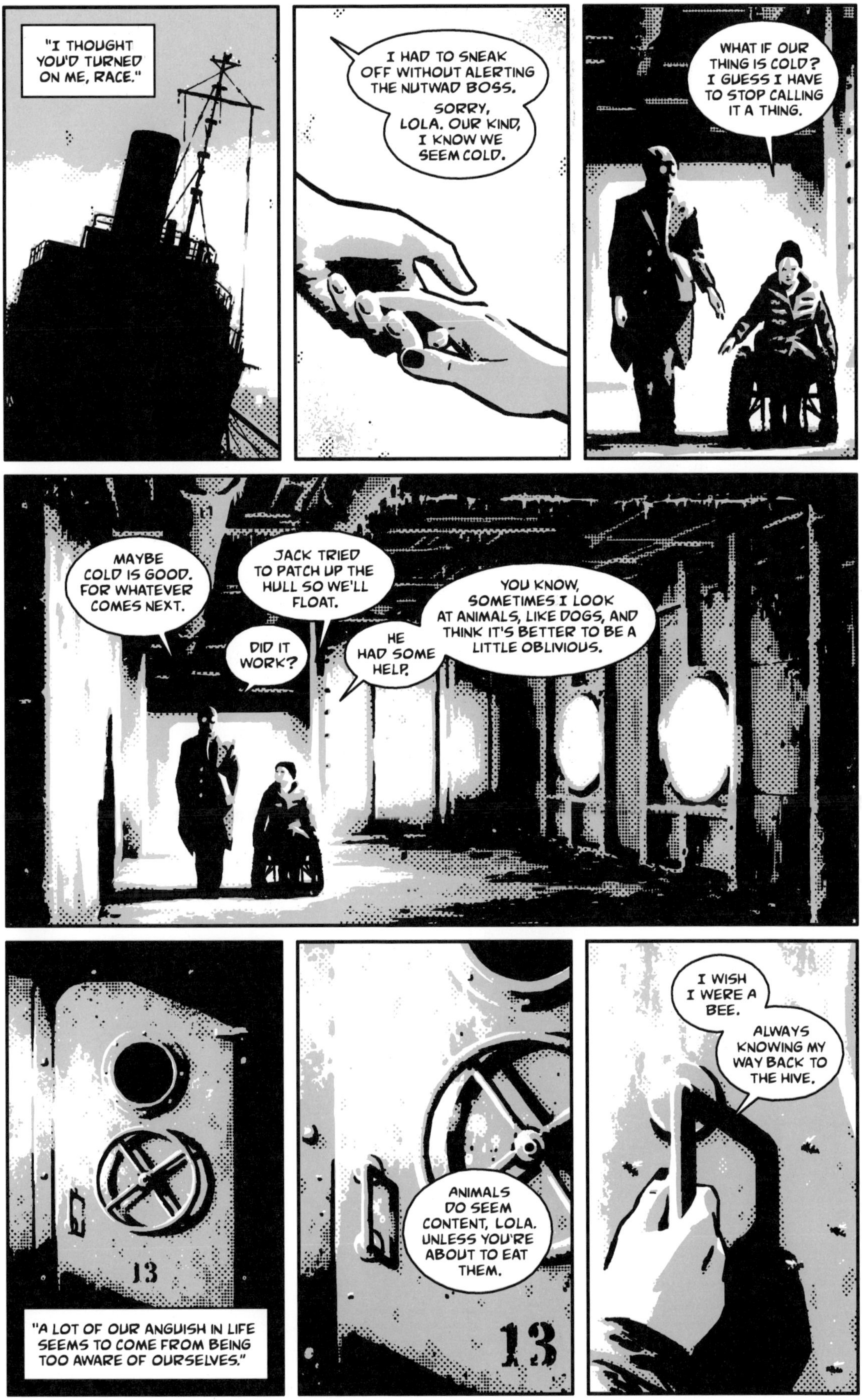
"I THOUGHT YOU'D TURNED ON ME, RACE."
I HAD TO SNEAK OFF WITHOUT ALERTING THE NUTWAD BOSS.
SORRY, LOLA. OUR KIND, I KNOW WE SEEM COLD.
WHAT IF OUR THING IS COLD? I GUESS I HAVE TO STOP CALLING IT A THING.
MAYBE COLD IS GOOD. FOR WHATEVER COMES NEXT.
JACK TRIED TO PATCH UP THE HULL SO WE'LL FLOAT.
DID IT WORK?
HE HAD SOME HELP.
YOU KNOW, SOMETIMES I LOOK AT ANIMALS, LIKE DOGS, AND THINK IT'S BETTER TO BE A LITTLE OBLIVIOUS.
13
"A LOT OF OUR ANGUISH IN LIFE SEEMS TO COME FROM BEING TOO AWARE OF OURSELVES."
ANIMALS DO SEEM CONTENT, LOLA. UNLESS YOU'RE ABOUT TO EAT THEM.
13
I WISH I WERE A BEE.
ALWAYS KNOWING MY WAY BACK TO THE HIVE.

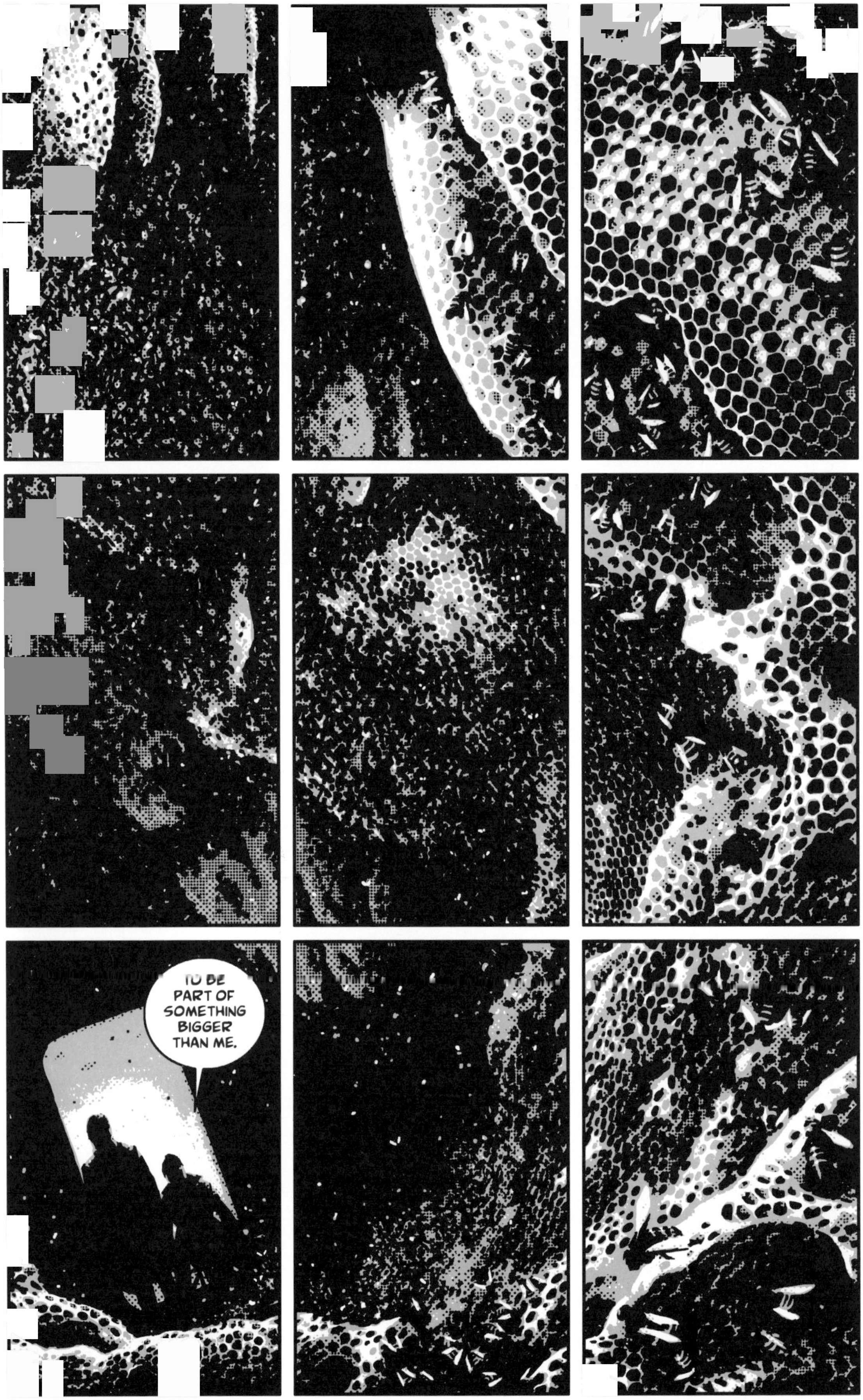
TO BE PART OF SOMETHING BIGGER THAN ME.

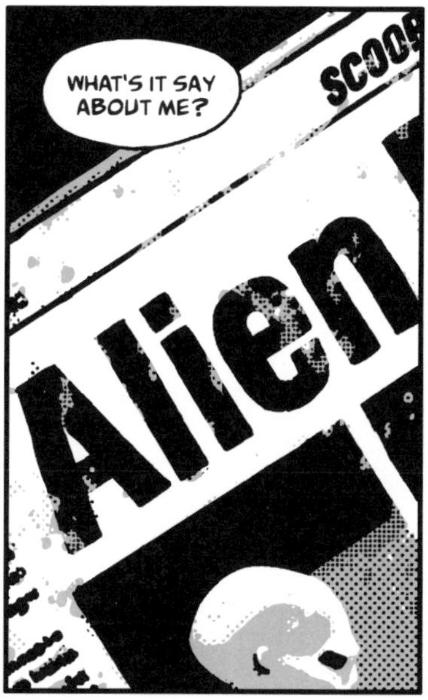
WHAT'S IT SAY ABOUT ME?
SCOOP
Alien

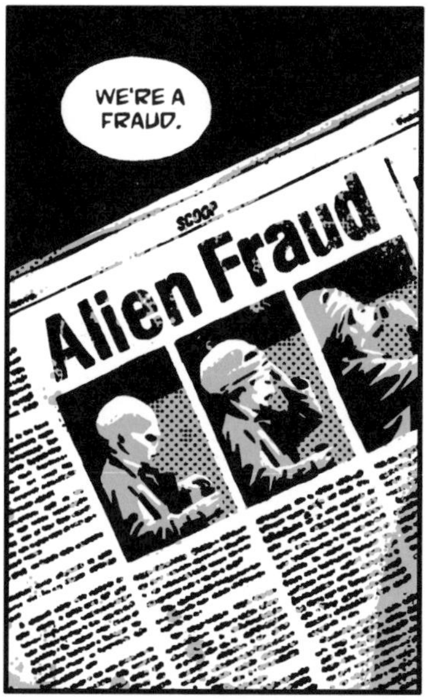
WE'RE A FRAUD.
SCOOP
Alien Fraud

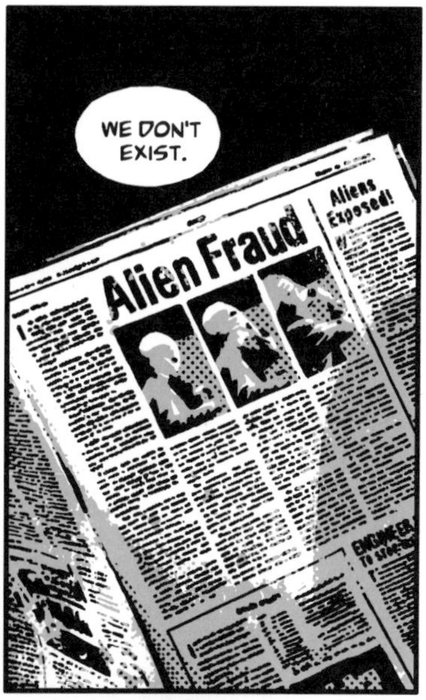
WE DON'T EXIST.
Alien Fraud
Aliens Exposed!

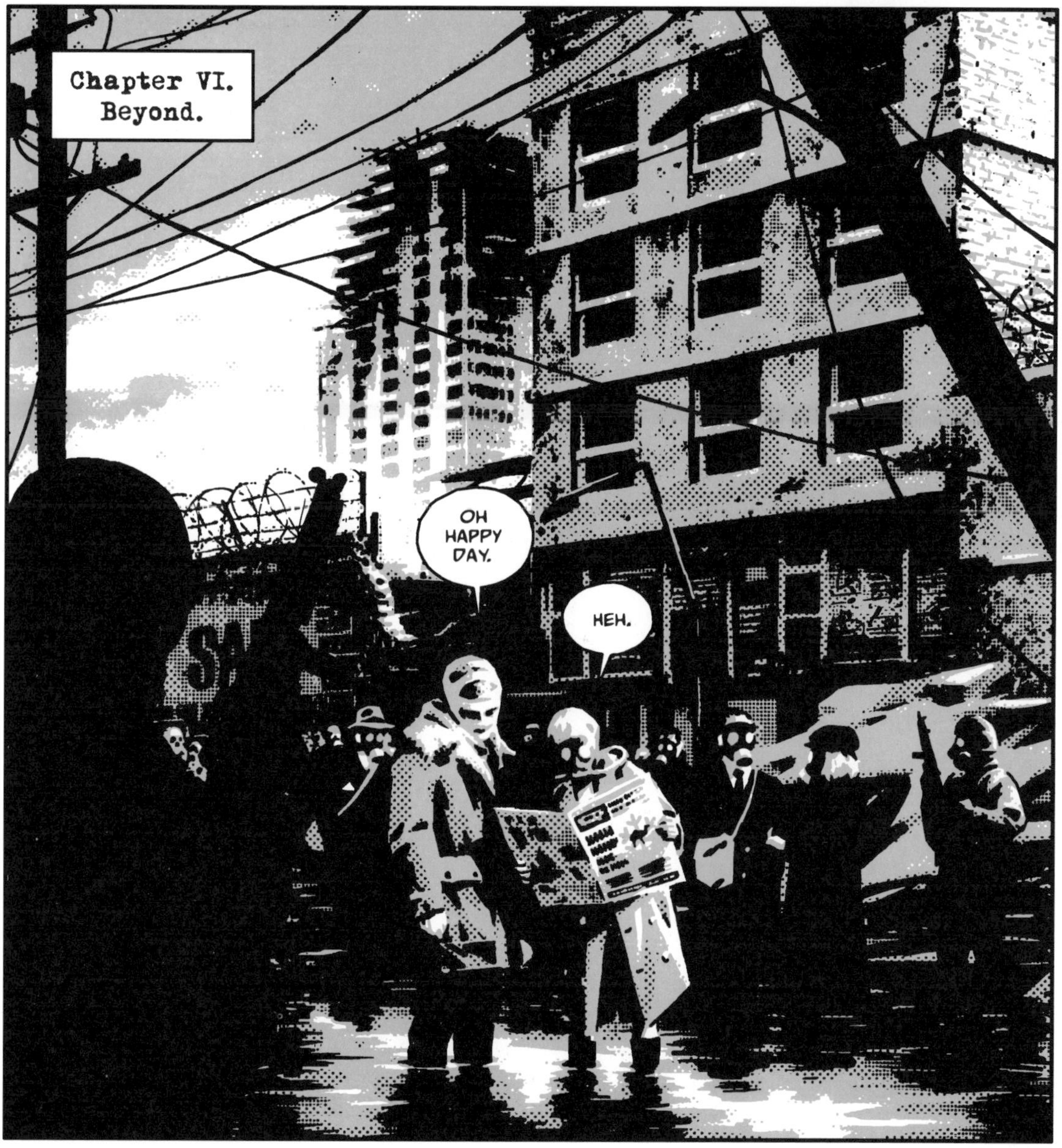
Chapter VI.
Beyond.
OH HAPPY DAY.
HEH.

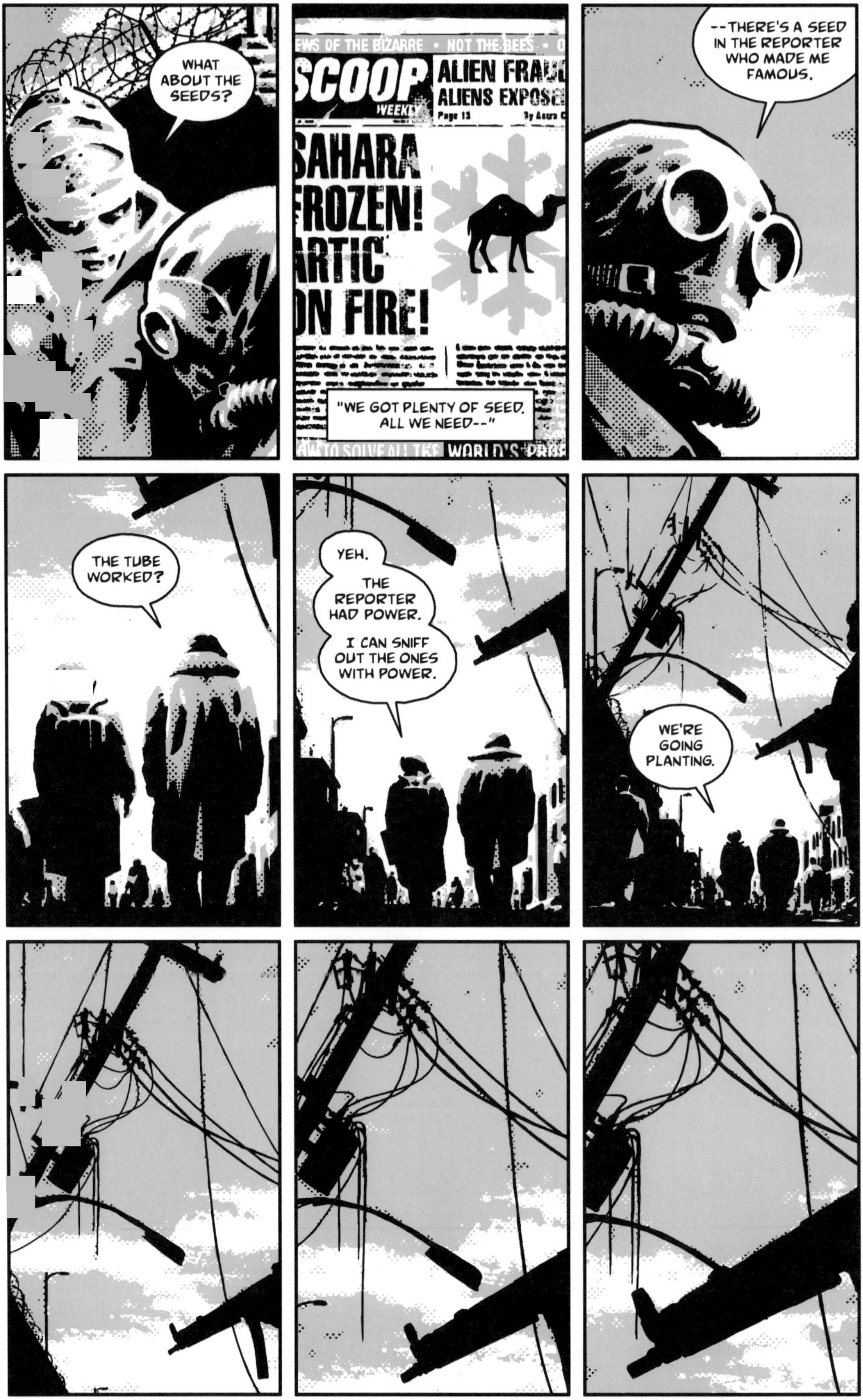
WHAT ABOUT THE SEEDS?
NOT THE BEES
SCOOP
WEEKLY
SAHARA FROZEN! ARTIC ON FIRE!
Page 13
"WE GOT PLENTY OF SEED. ALL WE NEED--"
WORLD'S
--THERE'S A SEED IN THE REPORTER WHO MADE ME FAMOUS.
THE TUBE WORKED?
YEH.
THE REPORTER HAD POWER.
I CAN SNIFF OUT THE ONES WITH POWER.
WE'RE GOING PLANTING.

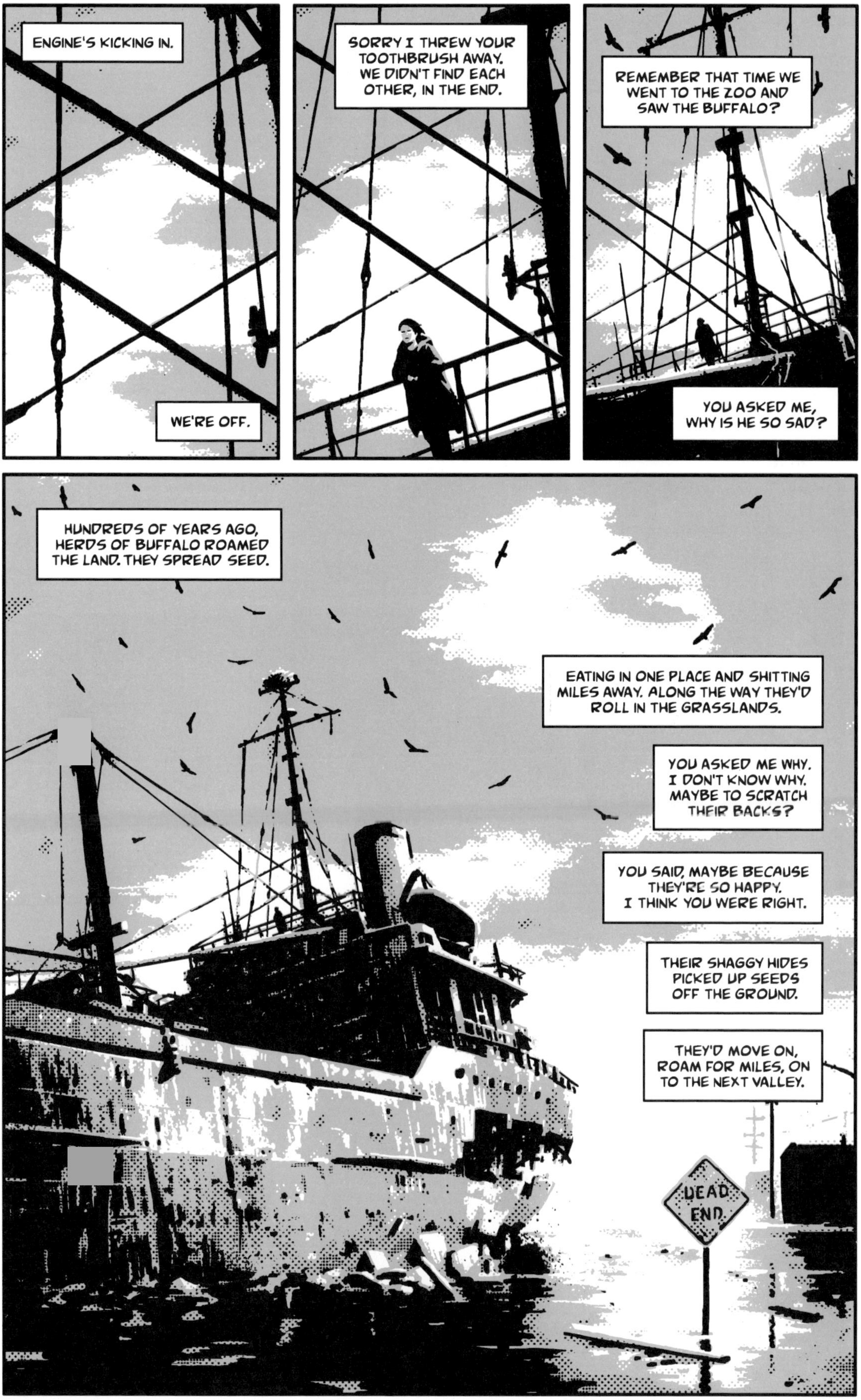
ENGINE'S KICKING IN.
WE'RE OFF.
SORRY I THREW YOUR TOOTHBRUSH AWAY. WE DIDN'T FIND EACH OTHER, IN THE END.
REMEMBER THAT TIME WE WENT TO THE ZOO AND SAW THE BUFFALO?
YOU ASKED ME, WHY IS HE SO SAD?
HUNDREDS OF YEARS AGO, HERDS OF BUFFALO ROAMED THE LAND. THEY SPREAD SEED.
EATING IN ONE PLACE AND SHITTING MILES AWAY. ALONG THE WAY THEY'D ROLL IN THE GRASSLANDS.
YOU ASKED ME WHY. I DON'T KNOW WHY. MAYBE TO SCRATCH THEIR BACKS?
YOU SAID, MAYBE BECAUSE THEY'RE SO HAPPY. I THINK YOU WERE RIGHT.
THEIR SHAGGY HIDES PICKED UP SEEDS OFF THE GROUND.
THEY'D MOVE ON, ROAM FOR MILES, ON TO THE NEXT VALLEY.
DEAD END

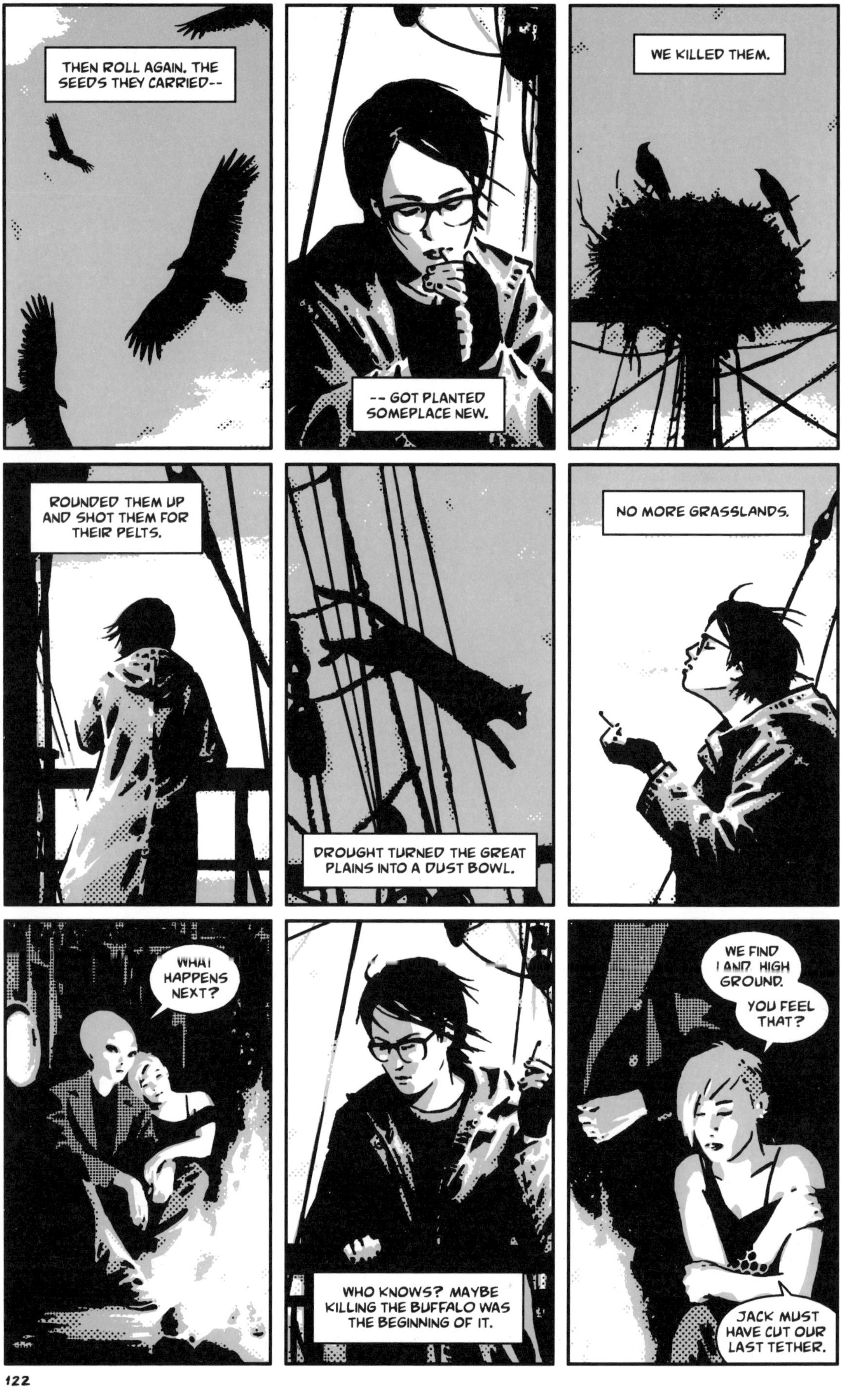
THEN ROLL AGAIN. THE SEEDS THEY CARRIED--
-- GOT PLANTED SOMEPLACE NEW.
WE KILLED THEM.
ROUNDED THEM UP AND SHOT THEM FOR THEIR PELTS.
DROUGHT TURNED THE GREAT PLAINS INTO A DUST BOWL.
NO MORE GRASSLANDS.
WHAT HAPPENS NEXT?
WHO KNOWS? MAYBE KILLING THE BUFFALO WAS THE BEGINNING OF IT.
WE FIND LAND. HIGH GROUND.
YOU FEEL THAT?
JACK MUST HAVE CUT OUR LAST TETHER.

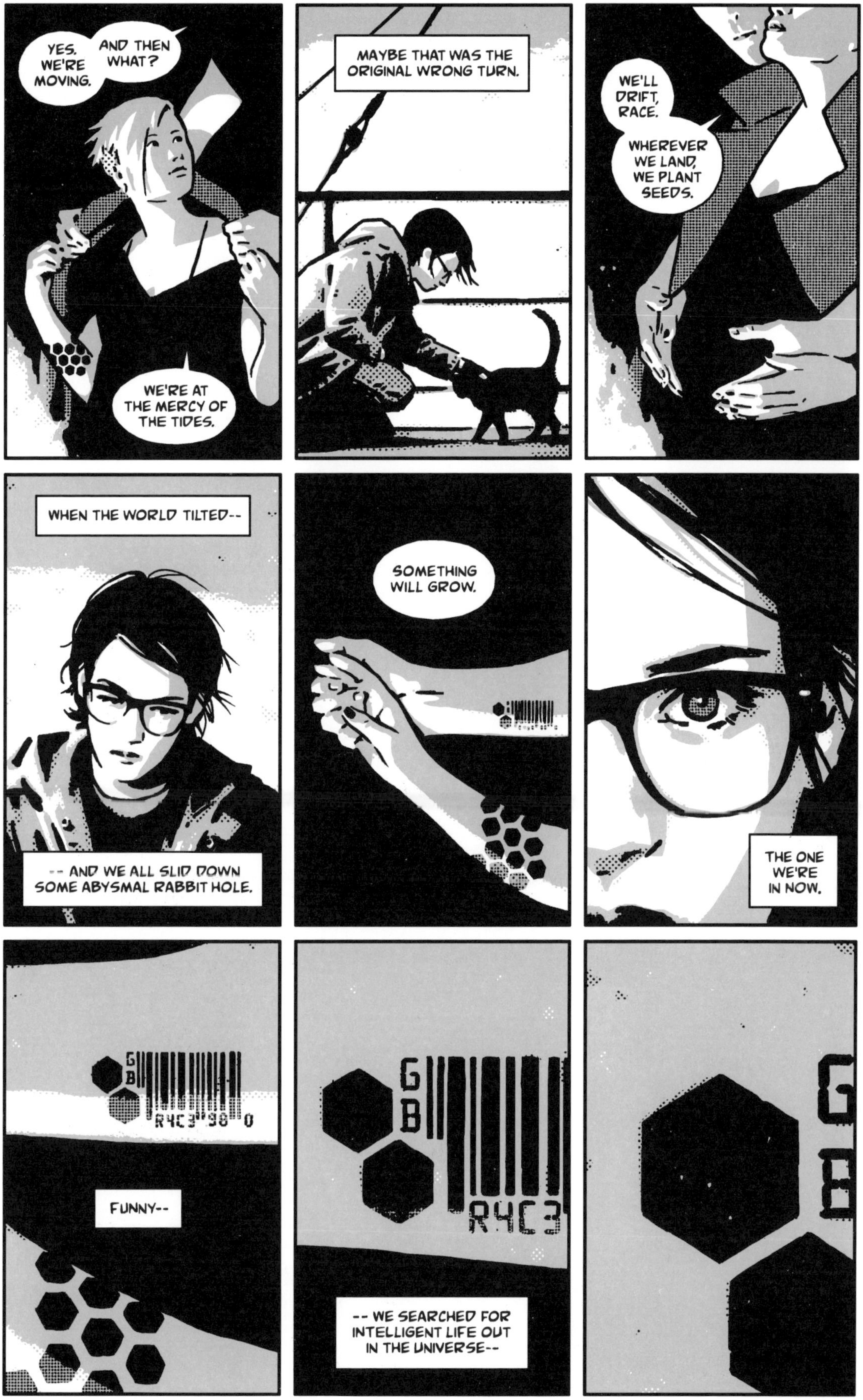
YES. WE'RE MOVING.
AND THEN WHAT?
WE'RE AT THE MERCY OF THE TIDES.
MAYBE THAT WAS THE ORIGINAL WRONG TURN.
WE'LL DRIFT, RACE.
WHEREVER WE LAND, WE PLANT SEEDS.
WHEN THE WORLD TILTED--
-- AND WE ALL SLID DOWN SOME ABYSMAL RABBIT HOLE.
SOMETHING WILL GROW.
THE ONE WE'RE IN NOW.
GB
R4C3 98 0
FUNNY--
GB
R4C3
-- WE SEARCHED FOR INTELLIGENT LIFE OUT IN THE UNIVERSE--
GB

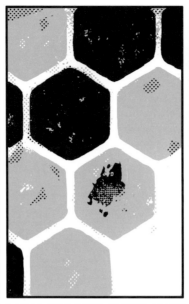

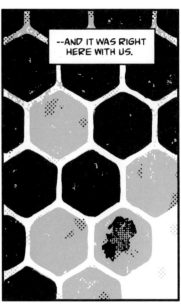
--AND IT WAS RIGHT HERE WITH US.

ALL AROUND US.

WE'LL GO WHEREVER IT TAKES US.

End.